GIANLUCA SPOSITO

GREAT SPEECHES
THE ART OF PUBLIC SPEAKING

intra

Rhetorically Series

ISBN 979-12-5991-444-6

CONTENTS

CONTENTS

TWO PRELIMINARY QUESTIONS

What is rhetoric?

Every one of us, every day, makes an unknown number of speeches, with different purposes: political speeches, email, closing argument in a trial, love declaration etc. And each of us wants to be convincing and achieve the goal.

What is less known is that - in all the cases listed above and in many more - there is an unconscious use of rhetoric. Rhetoric is everywhere, yet few know what it really is and where exactly it appears. The adjective 'rhetorical' nowadays identifies what is redundant, pretentious, useless: a 'rhetorical' speech would, therefore, be one that aims at effect and not substance, where the glitter of form seeks to embellish emptiness or, rather, to distract and lead away the reader or listener from that emptiness. A 'rhetorical' person is who has nothing particular to say but tries to say it with special effects.

So 'rhetorical' can end up labeling the even dishonest speaker, who of the use of that 'emptiness' has made a profession, seducing his neighbor.

The transition of rhetoric from science to 'meretriciousness' was the last mile traveled by what is and remains a noble art that we all use daily, unknowingly and without necessarily evil purposes.

Our written and spoken language is rich in rhetorical figures and patterns, carried out mostly unconsciously (but also often incorrectly). There's more: even when we think about what to say to someone, how to expound a concept, how to try to get a thesis of ours accepted, we use elements that rhetoric has long identified and proposed as reference points for the speaker of every context and time. Knowing and knowing how to use rhetoric enables one to know how to organize one's thinking into a reasoned and persuasive speech (a persuasion not by seduction but based on rational argumentation).

Therefore, rhetoric is and must remain the art of saying, that is, of speaking and writing effectively and persuasively, in use by the ancient Greeks and Romans and then transmitted to later cultures; an art that makes use of certain expressions and constructs, known as rhetorical figures. Rhetoric is historically the art intended to enable the speaker to communicate, to effectively reach the listener (or reader) and convince them to agree to one's thesis.

But rhetoric is not only about the use of words. Rhetoric can be used starting from the creation of a speech to the oratorical performance in front of an audience: it is a science that not only provides tools for the construction of a speech but also regulates nonverbal and paraverbal communication (posture, use of voice and body, etc. – the ancient Romans spoke of *actio*).

Today communication, to be effective, must be based on the mixture in balanced doses of primary elements such as rhetoric, psychology, nonverbal and paraverbal communication.

Can rhetoric make history?

Yes, rhetoric has made it possible to enhance some extraordinary moments in history, or even to make some moments memorable precisely because of the use of words. This selection includes 54 famous public speeches from the past 150 years, listed in alphabetical order according to their authors. They range from the political speeches of Abraham Lincoln to those of Churchill, Blair and Obama, as well as Roosevelt and Kennedy, and ending with Elizabeth II and Charles III. However, also great speeches on civic issues are mentioned: from Martin Luther King Jr. to Nelson Mandela, from Jose Mujica Cordano to Sidney Poitier and Greta Thunberg. Moreover, some Nobel Prize acceptance speeches: from Ernest Hemingway to William Faulkner and Gabriel García Márquez, from John Steinbeck to Elie Wiesel and Malala Yousafzai. There is also one of the most famous motivational speeches ever, that of Steve Jobs, and the speeches of figures who also ruled history through words, such as Hitler and Mussolini.

For each speech it would have been possible to write a book about it; therefore, I have chosen single introductory notes on the context and its author. I am convinced that these are essential readings for an essential approach to rhetoric and its great products, belonging to very different historical (and other) contexts. Rhetoric has taught and can still teach today how to construct a discourse and how to share it with one's audience in a collective multi-sensory sharing experience.

This is the goal of great oratory.

Nancy Astor, *Maiden Speech in the House of Commons*

[February 24, 1920, London]

NOTE Nancy Astor was Britain's first elected woman to take her seat in Parliament. In a political career that spanned over thirty years, Astor recognised her position as the first female in the House of Commons and aspired to be an MP for all women. On the 24th February 1920, Astor delivered her maiden speech, her first contribution to parliament, alone to an audience filled with men. Astor gave her first address to her new peers on a topic she passionately endorsed during her career: drink restrictions. As a contentious question - and one that she continuously described a 'vexatious' - her pursuit in encouraging sobriety was met with a wave hostility both in and out of Parliament.

I shall not begin by craving the indulgence of the House. I am only too conscious of the indulgence and the courtesy of the House. I know that it was very difficult for some hon. Members to receive the first lady M.P. into the House. [Hon. Members: "Not at all!"] It was almost as difficult for some of them as it was for the lady M.P. herself to come in. Hon. Members, however, should not be frightened of what Plymouth sends out into the world. After all, I suppose when Drake and Raleigh wanted to set out on their venturesome careers, some cautious person said, "Do not do it; it has never been tried before. You stay at home, my sons, cruising around in home waters." I have no doubt that the same thing occurred when the Pilgrim Fathers set out. I have no doubt that there were cautious Christian brethren who did not understand their going into the wide seas to worship God in their own way. But, on the whole, the world is all the better for those venturesome and courageous west country people, and I would like to say that I am quite certain that the women of the whole world will not forget that it was the fighting men of Devon who dared to send the first woman to represent women in the Mother of Parliaments. Now, as the west country people are a courageous lot, it is only right that one of their representatives should show some courage, and I am perfectly aware that it does take a bit of courage to address the House on that vexed question, Drink...

Do we want the welfare of the community, or do we want the prosperity of the Trade? Do we want national efficiency, or do we want national inefficiency? That is what it comes to. So I hope to be able to persuade the House. Are we really trying for a better world, or are we going to slip back to the same old world before 1914? I think that the hon. Member is not moving with the times...

He talks about the restrictions. I maintain that they brought a great deal of good to the community. There were two gains. First, there were the moral gains. I should like to tell you about them. The convictions of drunkenness among women during the War were reduced to one-fifth after these vexatious restrictions were brought in. I take women, because, as the hon. Member has said, most of the men were away fighting...

I do not think the country is really ripe for prohibition, but I am certain it is ripe for drastic drink reforms. [Hon. Members: "No!"] I know what I am talking about, and you must remember that women have got a vote now and we mean to use it, and use it wisely, not for the benefit of any section of society, but for the benefit of the whole. I want to see what the Government is going to do...

Tony Blair, *General Election Victory Speech*

[May 2, 1997, London]

NOTE Tony Blair (1953, Edinburgh, Scotland) is a British politician who served as Prime Minister of the United Kingdom from 1997 to 2007. He is the longest serving Labour Prime Minister (1997-2007), oversaw the Northern Irish peace process, public sector reform and the response to the 9/11 and 7/7 terrorist attacks.

I have just accepted Her Majesty the Queen's kind offer to form a new administration and government for the country. John Major's dignity and courage over the last few days and the manner of his leaving, is the mark of the man. I am pleased to pay tribute to him.

As I stand here before 10 Downing Street I know all too well the huge responsibility that is upon me and the great trust that the British people have placed in me.

I know well what this country has voted for today. It is a mandate for New Labour and I say to the people of this country – we ran for office as New Labour, we will govern as New Labour.

This is not a mandate for dogma or for doctrine, or for a return to the past, but it was a mandate to get those things done in our country that desperately need doing for the future. And this new Labour government will govern in the interests of all our people – the whole of this nation. That I can promise you. When I became leader of the Labour party some three years ago I set a series of objectives. By and large I believe we have achieved them. Today we have set objectives for new Labour Government – a world class education system. Education is not the privilege of the few but the right of the many.

A new Labour Government that remembers that it was a previous Labour Government that formed and fashioned the welfare state and the National Health Service. It was our proudest creation. It shall be our job and our duty now to modernize it for a modern world, and that we will also do.

We will work in partnership with business to create the dynamic economy, the competitive economy of the future. The one that can meet the challenges of an entirely new century and new age.

And it will be a government that seeks to restore trust in politics in this country. That cleans it up, that decentralizes it, that gives people hope once again that politics is and always should be about the service of the public. And it shall be a government, too, that gives this country strength and confidence in leadership both at home and abroad, particularly in respect of Europe.

It shall be a government rooted in strong values, the values of justice and progress and community, the values that have guided me all my political life. But a government ready with the courage to embrace the new ideas necessary to make those values live again for today's world – a government of practical measures in pursuit of noble causes. That is our objective for the people of Britain.

Above all, we have secured a mandate to bring this nation together, to unite us – one Britain, one nation in which our ambition for ourselves is matched by our sense of compassion and decency and duty towards other people. Simple values, but the right ones.

For 18 years – for 18 long years – my party has been in opposition. It could only say, it could not do. Today we are charged with the deep responsibility of government. Today, enough of talking – it is time now to do.

Tony Blair, *Leader's Speech*

[September 30, 1997, Brighton]

NOTE On 1 May, Labour had won a landslide victory over the Conservatives and formed a government for the first time in 18 years. This was Blair's first conference speech since becoming Prime Minister, and he outlined some of the election pledges Labour had already fulfilled.

After 18 long years of Opposition, of frustration and despair, I am proud, privileged, to stand before you as the new Labour Prime Minister of our country. I believe in Britain. I believe in the British people. One cross on the ballot paper. One nation was reborn.

Today I want to set an ambitious course for this country. To be nothing less than the model 21st century nation, a beacon to the world. It means drawing deep into the richness of the British character. Creative. Compassionate. Outward-looking. Old British values, but a new British confidence. We can never be the biggest. We may never again be the mightiest. But we can be the best. The best place to live. The best place to bring up children, the best place to lead a fulfilled life, the best place to grow old.

14 years ago our Party was written off as history. This year we made it. Let our first thanks be to the British people. You kept faith with us. And we will keep faith with you. Thank you to the Party organisation, the volunteers, the professionals who fashioned the finest political fighting machine anywhere in the world. And thanks to those that led before me. To Neil Kinnock: the mantle of Prime Minister was never his. But I know that without him, it would never have been mine. To John Smith: who left us a fine legacy,

and to whom we can now leave a fitting monument – a Scottish Parliament in the city where he lived, serving the country he loved and the people who loved him. To Jim Callaghan: who was attending Labour Party Conferences before I was born; and by the look of him, will be attending long after I've gone. My own debt of honour to Michael Foot: you led this Party when, frankly, it was incapable of being led and without ever losing a shred of your decency or your integrity. Thank you.

I should also say a final word of thanks to the Tory Party. Let's be honest, we'd never have done so well without them. So thanks to Michael Howard, to John Redwood, to Peter Lilley, to Brian Mawhinney. Of course, it's a fresh start now – with Michael Howard, John Redwood, Peter Lilley, Brian Mawhinney. Sorry – 'Sir' Brian Mawhinney – knighted for services to the Conservative Party. John Prescott wanted to give him a peerage – for services to the Labour Party.

As for Government, well, it beats the hell out of Opposition. They really do say 'Yes, Prime Minister.' You have to learn a whole new language. They're not in the habit of calling anything a good idea, which given the last 18 years is hardly surprising. When they describe a proposal as 'ambitious,' or, even worse, 'interesting,' what they really mean is they think it was a stupid idea, dreamed up at the last minute for the manifesto. When they describe it as 'challenging,' they mean there's not a hope in hell of making it work. And when they say of a policy 'that it really is quite a brave proposal Prime Minister,' it means they've got the doctor outside waiting to sign the certificates and they've just applied for a transfer to a senior job administering one of our few remaining dependent territories.

It's not the titles and the cars and the trappings that make government worthwhile. It's letters like this from 11 year old Emma O'Brien from Ellesmere Port. 'Summer School was a good idea. I have started to read more books. I have learned more spellings. We've had fun. All of us have made new friends. I think you and parliament have done the right thing. I have got a better education.' Or this one from Mrs Patricia Lewis, of South London. 'Each afternoon I collected him from school. By the fourth day the change was showing in Stephen. His enthusiasm grew, confidence gained, his ability to read, write, spell, speak, and question politely, was amazing.' That is why we are here. That is what made winning worth the fight.

Ours was not a victory of politicians but of people. The people took their trust, and gave it to us. I want them to say, this week as they watch us here in Brighton: we did the right thing. I want the British people to be as proud of having elected us as we are to serve them. We won because we are New Labour, because we had the courage to change ourselves, and the discipline to take hard decisions, whilst remaining united. The lessons we learned in Opposition we carry on applying in Government. The moment we stop that is the moment we will stop being in government. Even now, especially now, no complacency.

I know I'm obsessive about this. But I will admit now that I perhaps went over the top when I phoned Millbank Tower on election night to say people were behaving as though it was in the bag. 'Look,' I was told, 'We've got 150 seats. The Tories have got 6. It's hard to persuade the media this thing's on a knife edge.' But still, no complacency.

May 1st was the beginning, not the end. We have never won two full consecutive terms of office. Never. That is one more record I want to break. No cockiness about the Tories even now. They're not dead. Just sleeping. Let their fate serve as a warning to us. What the people give, the people can take away. We are the servants. They are the masters now. To govern Britain is a privilege not a right. Never forget it.

Last year we were talking about what we would do. This

year we're doing it. That ten point contract with the British people – we are honouring.

We said we would get more money into schools and hospitals. We have – 2.2 billion more than Tories planned to spend next year.

We said we'd sign the Social Chapter. We did.

We said we'd restore trade unions at GCHQ. On May 19, free and independent trade unions came back to GCHQ.

We said we'd set up a Low Pay Commission. We have, and the national minimum wage is on its way.

We said we'd legislate to release the money from selling council homes in order to house the homeless. We've done it.

We said we'd cut class sizes, by scrapping the Assisted Places Scheme. The law to do it has been passed.

We've given the people of Scotland and Wales the devolution referendums we promised, and they have voted: yes, yes, and yes again.

We said we'd reform the Lottery to address the people's priorities. We have, and today more proposals on how we'll reform it further and get more money to more local projects, the length and breadth of Britain, preparing for the millennium.

We said we'd cut VAT on fuel. We have.

We never said we'd cut corporation tax. But we did anyway, to the lowest level it's ever been. And we have brought Britain's top business brains right into the heart of Government.

And we said we'd force the water companies to give a better deal to their customers. A few hours of quiet diplomacy by Mr John Prescott did the necessary, and the companies did the business.

We owed a debt to the people of Dunblane. We said MPs would vote to ban handguns. MPs have had that vote.

The people have spoken. Parliament has spoken. Handguns are banned. We have honoured our debt.

We said we'd ban landmines. They're banned in Britain and we'll keep working until they are banned the world over.

Of all we have done, ask me what has taken the most time, the most effort, it's probably Northern Ireland. There is no tougher job in Government than Northern Ireland Secretary, and there is no better person to do it than Mo Mowlam. The effort has been worth it. The cease-fire has been renewed. Republicans and Unionists are talking for the first time since 1921. There is a long, long way to go. Every step is fragile. But in the name of humanity, I ask that ancient enmities be put aside. Talking is no treachery. Agreeing is no betrayal. The real betrayal would be to let violence take the place of democracy in Northern Ireland again.

But I want to do more than keep our promises. I sense the British people demand more of us, too. People ask me the highlight of the election. Mine was driving from home to Buckingham Palace, along streets we had driven hundreds of times, past soulless buildings and sullen faces on their way to work. This drive was so different. As we turned into Gower Street, people watching our journey on TV came pouring out of the doorways, waving and shouting and clapping, with an energy and excitement that went beyond anything I imagined would happen. They were liberated. Theirs were the smiles of tolerant, broad-minded, outward-looking, compassionate people and suddenly they learned that they were in the majority after all. As one woman put it to me: 'We've got our Government back.' And with them I could sense confidence returning to the British people, compassion to the British soul, unity to the British nation, and that all three would give us new-found strength. The people were yearning for change in their country, at a time when they could see we had had the guts to modernise our party. The two came together. The result is a quiet revolution now taking place. Led by the real modernisers – the British people.

The size of our victory imposes a very special responsibility on us. To be a government of high ideals and hard choices. Not popular for one time but remembered for all time. Not just a better government than the Tories but one of the great, radical, reforming Governments of our history. To modernise Britain as we modernised the Labour Party. To build a Britain, not for a few, but for all the people. And it will require change. Hard choices. I know this country can make them if we show how and why.

The British don't fear change. We are one of the great innovative peoples. From the Magna Carta to the first Parliament to the industrial revolution to an empire that covered the world; most of the great inventions of modern times with Britain stamped on them: the telephone; the television; the computer; penicillin; the hovercraft; radar. Change is in the blood and bones of the British we are by our nature and tradition innovators, adventurers, pioneers. As our great poet of renewal and recovery, John Milton, put it, we are 'A nation not slow or dull, but of quick, ingenious and piercing spirit, acute to invent, subtle and sinewy to discourse, not beneath the reach of any point that human capacity can soar to.'

Even today, we lead the world, in design, pharmaceuticals, financial services, telecommunications. We have the world's first language. Britain today is an exciting, inspiring place to be. And it can be much more. If we face the challenge of a world with its finger on the fast forward button; where every part of the picture of our life is changing. Today I say to the British people: the chains of mediocrity have broken, the tired days are behind us, we are free to excel once more. We are free to build that model 21st Century nation, to become that beacon to the world.

Creative. Compassionate. Confident of our place in the

world.

And when people say sorry, that's too ambitious, it can't be done, I say: this is not a sorry country, we are not a sorry people. It can be done. We know what makes a successful creative economy. Educate the people. Manage the country's finances well. Encourage business and enterprise. But each bit requires us to modernise and take the hard choices to do it. We have been a mercantile power. An industrial power. Now we must be the new power of the information age. Our goal: to make Britain the best educated and skilled country in the world; a nation, not of a few talents, but of all the talents. And every single part of our schools system must be modernised to achieve it.

Nearly 40 per cent of 11 year olds can't read, write or add up properly. 42nd in the world education league. This is the scandalous legacy not just of 18 years of Tory Government but of a country too often content to educate the elite and ignore education for all. Education, education, education. Remember? In just 5 months, we made a remarkable beginning, under the brilliant leadership of David Blunkett. But we will do more.

We are publishing today details of agreements involving Government and the private sector, for the biggest public/private partnership in any education system, anywhere in the world, which will mean:

By 2002 every one of the 32,000 schools in Britain will have modern computers, the educational programmes to go on them, the teachers skilled to teach on them, the pupils skilled to use them, connected to the superhighway for free and with phone bills slashed to as low as £1 per pupil per year.

We are setting a new target of £2 billion for this parliament for our school repairs and equipment programme. A list of the first 2,300 schools to benefit is being published today. The money is being allocated today. One of the headteachers is here with us. By 2002 up to 10,000 schools will have benefited.

We are launching the biggest assault on poor literacy and numeracy standards this country has seen. We are setting a target of 80% up to the standard in literacy, 75% for numeracy by the year 2002, and we'll keep on until every 11 year old in every school in every part of Britain gets the start in life that they deserve. And I repeat the promise I made at the election, that over the lifetime of this parliament, we will reverse the Tory policy of cutting spending on education as a proportion of our national income and raise it once again, beginning with £1 billion extra next year.

Nursery vouchers have gone and instead we'll get nursery places for all four year olds and we're on the way to places for all three year olds too. The money will be there, but in return hard choices and modernisation. No failure. No muddling through. No second best. High standards. The pursuit of excellence. Discipline and leadership. Support from home. Not for some children in some schools. But for all children in all schools. Each school that needs it, and every LEA, will be set targets for improvement. Failing schools and LEAs will be taken over. Teacher training will be reformed. Head teachers will have a proper qualification. Poor teachers will go.

People say my job's pressurised. So is teaching. And don't let anybody think that we are tough on bad teaching because we don't value teachers. We are tough on bad teachers precisely because we DO value good teachers who need high quality teachers working alongside them. And parents have to play their part. There will be home school contracts for all pupils. Sign them. There will be new measures to tackle truancy and disruptive children, new homework requirements. Support them. When a school disciplines a child, back the teacher. The high ideal of the best schools in the world. Reached through hard choices.

Universities in Britain had their funding cut by 40% per student under the Tories. The science and research base – once the envy of the world – under threat. The Tories put a cap on student numbers. Only 30% of youngsters in Britain admitted to go to university. Fewer not just than France or the USA, but fewer than South Korea. The hard choice: stay as we are and decline. Or modernise and win. Under our proposals, no parent will have to pay more. Low income families will be entirely exempt from tuition fees. All students will repay only as they can afford to. And if we reform, I am going to pledge to you, that by the end of this parliament, we will put resources saved through reform into frontline provision in universities and further education; and the first 165 million pounds is already in next year's budgets. We will lift the cap on student numbers and set a target for an extra 500,000 people into higher and further education by 2002. Our education system – a beacon to the world.

Within days of taking office, we took one of the hardest choices of all: we gave the Bank of England the right to decide interest rates and take the politics out of mortgages. And in the short term it's tough. Interest rates have gone up. But I say to people, better to go up now, still only by 1%, than to go back to the days of the last Tory government when mortgages were at 15% for a year, 1 million homes in negative equity, a whole swathe of industry wiped out. We are cutting the Tory deficit too. We are sorting out the public finances. Borrow only for investment. Hold debt down. Earn before you spend. Don't live on tick. I want this to be the New Labour Government that ended Tory boom and bust for ever.

Twenty years ago, the IMF came to bury us. Now they come to praise us. Yes, new Labour's got new friends everywhere. I want Britain to be a country of enterprise and ambition where small businesses grow, manufacturing and engineering revive, where we learn the lessons of British industrial relations over the past 100 years. Fairness at work yes. But flexibility will remain. For business, this will be a Government on your side not in your way. And I say to both sides of industry, there is no place for militant trade unionism or uncaring management today. Partnership is the key. That is the only language this New Labour Government will respect.

It's pretty simple the type of country I want. It's a country where our children are proud and happy to grow up in, feeling good not just about themselves, but about the community around them. I don't want them living in a country where some of them go to school, hungry, unable to learn because their parents can't afford to feed them; where they can see drugs being traded at school gates; where gangs of teenagers hang around street corners, nothing to do, but spit and swear and abuse passers-by; I don't want them brought up in a country where the only way pensioners can get long-term care is by selling their home, where people who fought to keep that country free are now faced every winter with the struggle for survival, skimping and saving, cold and alone, waiting for death to take them. And I will not rest until that country is gone and all our children live in a Britain where no child goes hungry, the young are employed, and the old are cherished and valued to the end of their days.

But let me spell out some facts. After eighteen years of Tory Government, of cuts and closures, of declining public services, the country was taxed more than under the last Labour Government. This country, any country, will not just carry on paying out more in taxes and getting less. Our new society will have the same values as it ever did. Fighting poverty and unemployment. Securing justice and opportunity. It should be a compassionate society. But it is compassion with a hard edge. A strong society cannot be built on soft choices. It means fundamental reform of our welfare state, of the deal between citizen and society. It means getting money out of social breakdown and into schools and hospitals where we want to see it.

The new welfare state must encourage work, not dependency. We are giving young people and the long-term unemployed the opportunity. A £3.5 billion investment. We are adding today the option of self employment as part of the new deal. But they have to take one of the options on offer. We want single mothers with school age children at least to visit a job centre, not just stay at home waiting for the benefit cheque every week until the children are sixteen. Modern welfare means a better balance between public and private money. We need to invest more as a country in savings and pensions. But government's role is going to be to organise provision – like new stakeholder pensions not fund it all through ever-higher taxes. And our number one duty is to get help to the poorest pensioners first.

Housing benefit, in some areas, is virtually designed for fraud. It has to change. We will not be that beacon to the world in the year 2005 with a welfare state built for the very different world of 1945. Our tax system should reward hard work. In the 80s the Tories took down high marginal tax rates for high earners. It is time we did the same for Britain's working poor.

And the same drive for reform applies to the NHS. I'm tired of hearing the NHS described as if it were a relic. It isn't. It was the greatest act of modernisation any Labour Government ever did. My vision is not just to save the NHS but make it better. The money will be there. I promise you that. This year. Every year. Millions saved from red tape, millions more into breast cancer treatment already. The values will remain. From next April, the two-tier NHS of the Tories will go. And I tell you. I will never countenance an NHS that departs from its fundamental principle of health care based on need not wealth. The hospitals will be built. 14 of them, the biggest hospital building programme in the history of the NHS. It will mean an extra £1.3 billion in 14 towns and cities serving 5 million people. And as of today, it is 15.

But money is not the only problem with healthcare in Britain. The NHS itself needs modernisation and hard choices. We appointed the first Minister for Public Health because the NHS should not lose millions every year because of avoidable illnesses like those from smoking. Barriers between GPs, social services and hospitals must be broken down. Hospitals cannot stand still. Increasingly, general hospitals will provide routine care, supported by specialist centres of excellence in treatment, research and education. GPs and nurses will do more of what hospitals used to do, often working on the same site in partnership with chemists, dentists, opticians and physiotherapists.

New technology offers huge opportunities in healthcare but we haven't yet begun to seize them properly. We will get the money in. But in return, I want reform. From next April, there will be up to ten specially-funded Health Action Zones set up in Britain. Their remit: to experiment with new ideas in the way healthcare is delivered, so that patients get a better deal from their health service for the 21st century. The NHS was a beacon to the world in 1948. I want it to be so again. It will always be safe with us. But I want it to be better with us.

I say to the country in all honesty. You can have the education revolution, the health revolution, the welfare revolution. But it means hard choices. It means us all getting involved. And it means modernisation. And we need to bring a change to the way we treat each other. I tell you: a decent society is not based on rights. It is based on duty. Our duty to each other. To all should be given opportunity, from all responsibility demanded. The duty to show respect and tolerance to others. I make no apology. I back zero tolerance on crime. I back powers to tackle anti-social neighbours; to make parents responsible for their children; to overhaul the youth justice system so that youngsters stop thinking they can commit a crime, get a caution and carry on being a criminal. At every level of the fight against crime – today acting on serious organised crime – this New Labour Government is taking it on. It will take time. And it will be tough. But to those who say it's all a threat to our civil liberties, I say the threat to civil liberties is of women afraid to go out, and pensioners afraid to stay at home, because of crime and the fear of crime, and we're going to help them.

And we cannot say we want a strong and secure society when we ignore its very foundation: family life. This is not about preaching to individuals about their private lives. It is addressing a huge social problem. Attitudes have changed. The world has changed. But I am a modern man leading a modern country and this is a modern crisis. Nearly 100,000 teenage pregnancies every year. Elderly parents with whom families cannot cope. Children growing up without role models they can respect and learn from. More and deeper poverty. More crime. More truancy. More neglect of educational opportunities. And above all more unhappiness. I give you this pledge. Every area of this Government's policy will be scrutinised to see how it affects family life. Every policy examined, every initiative tested, every avenue explored to see how we strengthen our families and there will be a Ministerial group to drive it through.

Don't think we're asking everyone to change but not Government itself. We will publish a White Paper in the new year for what we call Simple Government, to cut the bureaucracy of Government and improve its service. We are setting a target that within five years, one quarter of dealings with Government can be done by a member of the public electronically through their television, telephone or computer. Our politics are being reformed. We will deliver the Scottish Parliament and the Welsh Assembly after one hundred years of trying, and I say to the House of Lords, before it is reformed, don't try to wreck this legislation: we have the votes of the people, you've got the votes of nobody.

We will have a strategic authority and elected Mayor for London if the people vote for it. I can announce to you we are going to bring forward a Bill to ban foreign donations to political parties and to compel all parties to make contributions above £5,000 public. And we will ask the Nolan Committee to look at the wider question of Party funding. At the next election all political parties will at last compete on a level playing field. And I know some of you are a bit nervous about what I am doing with the Liberal Democrats. Though not half as nervous as they are. Since this is a day for honesty, I'll tell you: my heroes aren't just Ernie Bevin, Nye Bevan and Attlee. They are also Keynes, Beveridge, Lloyd George. Division among radicals almost one hundred years ago resulted in a 20th century dominated by Conservatives. I want the 21st century to be the century of the radicals.

We cannot be a beacon to the world unless the talents of all the people shine through. Not one black High Court Judge; not one black Chief Constable or Permanent Secretary. Not one black Army officer above the rank of Colonel. Not one Asian either. Not a record of pride for the British establishment. And not a record of pride for the British Parliament that there are so few black and Asian MPs. I am against positive discrimination. But there is no harm in reminding ourselves just how much negative discrimination there is.

On taking office, we discovered that the last Government planned to cut from £83m to £43m the Home Office section 11 budget and make redundant 7,000 teachers and classroom assistants who help children for whom English is a second language. Today I announce; that Tory cut will not stand. I'll tell you why. That money is not a cost, it is an investment. And it's one a civilised nation should make. A nation tolerant and open. Free from prejudice but not from rules. A beacon for good at home and abroad. There is huge interest in Britain now. Because people know that this is a country changing for the better. A go-ahead place. The gates of xenophobia falling down. This Government can be the Government of enlightened patriotism.

Again my vision for post-Empire Britain is clear. It is to make this country pivotal, a leader in the world. To use the strengths of our history to build our future. With the US our friend and ally. Within the Commonwealth. In the United Nations. In NATO. To use the superb reputation of our Armed Forces, not just for defence, but as an instrument of influence in a world of collective security and cooperation. And to lead in Europe again. Not so that we 'don't get left behind.' That is a weak reason. It is because for four centuries or more, we have been a leading power in Europe. And we have at times been absolutely critical to the survival of not just Europe but the world. It is our destiny.

And Europe needs us. For we have a vision of Europe. We want a people's Europe: free trade, industrial strength, high levels of employment and social justice, democratic. Against that vision is the bureaucrat's Europe: the Europe of thwarting open trade, unnecessary rules and regulations, the Europe of the C.A.P. and the endless committees leading nowhere. But we cannot shape Europe unless we matter in Europe. I know there will be a hard choice to come over a single currency. And our policy, based on the British national interest, remains unchanged. But in or out, we will be affected by it and must remain able to influence the way it works. Next year Britain now takes on the Presidency of the EU and it will do so as, once again, a respected leading European nation. That is an achievement of the new Labour government of which I am proud.

And elsewhere too, new respect and influence. In tackling Third World debt. On the environment. Today in

London the Government's Chief Scientific Adviser is issuing a report on global warming which I commissioned on coming into government. Read it and you will see why I am so passionate in my commitment to action not just in Britain but throughout the world, which is why we will take that action and get the rest of the world to take that action too. So much to do. So much to change. So hard to do it. But the vision is as old as humanity.

Modernisation is not an end in itself. It is for a purpose.

Modernisation is not the enemy of justice, but its ally.

Progress and justice are the two rocks upon which the New Britain is raised to the heights. Lose either one and we come crashing down until we are just another average nation, scrabbling around for salvation in the ebbing tide of the 20th Century.

That is why we changed the Labour Party. To make New Britain. It is why we will carry on changing. It is why it was right yesterday to take another historic step on the road to reform of our Party so that never again will a Labour government be torn about by divisions between leadership in Parliament and Party in the country. Yes, we are New Labour. Yes, our policies and attitudes have changed. But there are no Old Labour or New Labour values. There are Labour values. They are what make us the Party of compassion; of social justice; of the struggle against poverty and inequality; of liberty; of basic human solidarity; and the day we cease to be those things is the day we keep the name of the Labour Party but lose the reason for its existence. And these are indeed the best of British values too. The point of modern Britain is not to dishonour the past. But to honour it by improving it, by taking the best of it and adding to it. Ours is a simple enough vision. But it will require a supreme national effort. It is a task for a whole people, not just a government.

But great rewards for all of us if we rise to them as we

can. As one nation. Held together by our values and by the strength of our character. We are a giving people. In the face of crisis or challenge we pull together, strengthened by unity. It says nothing about our politics. It speaks volumes about our character. You remember how your parents, like mine, used to say to you: Just do your best. Well let's do our best.

On May 1, the people entrusted me with the task of leading their country into a new century. That was your challenge to me. Proudly, humbly, I accepted it. Today, I issue a challenge to you. Help us make Britain that beacon shining throughout the world. Unite behind our mission to modernise our country. There is a place for all the people in New Britain, and there is a role for all the people in its creation. Believe in us as much as we believe in you. Give just as much to our country as we intend to give. Give your all. Make this the giving age. 'By the strength of our common endeavour we achieve more together than we can alone.'

On 1st May 1997, it wasn't just the Tories who were defeated. Cynicism was defeated. Fear of change was defeated. Fear itself was defeated. Did I not say it would be a battle of hope against fear? On 1st May 1997, fear lost. Hope won. The Giving Age began.

Now make the good that is in the heart of each of us, serve the good of all of us. Give to our country the gift of our energy, our ideas, our hopes, our talents. Use them to build a country each of whose people will say that 'I care about Britain because I know that Britain cares about me.' Britain, head and heart, can be unbeatable. That is the Britain I offer you. That is the Britain that together can be ours.

Tony Blair, *Speech at the Ditchley Annual Lecture*

[July 16, 2022, Chipping Norton]

NOTE Delivering the annual Ditchley lecture, the former prime minister called for a policy towards Beijing of "strength plus engagement" as he warned the era of Western political and economic dominance was coming to an end.

Like 1945 or 1980, the West is at an inflection point. In 1945, the West had to create new institutions of international governance, of defence, and of European cooperation in place of not one but two world wars caused by conflict between European nations.

In 1980, after years of nuclear proliferation, we sought the final collapse of the Soviet Union and the triumph of liberal democratic values.

In each case, the objective of Western foreign policy was accompanied by an objective of domestic policy.

In 1945, in Europe, in the UK under the Attlee government and in the USA, it was the building of a welfare state, modern infrastructure, health and education services to make available to the broad mass of the people what had hitherto been restricted to a privileged few.

In 1980, it was the Reagan/Thatcher revolution in favour of markets and private enterprise and in reaction against a burgeoning state power which seemed to hold back the enterprise of the people, not nurture it.

Agreeing or disagreeing with either inflection point is not what is material. What matters is that there was a governing project, a plan, a way of looking at the world which sought to make sense of it and provide for the advancement of the people.

In both cases, in their own terms at least, the project succeeded. Europe became at peace. The Soviet Union collapsed. Up until the early part of this century, the people saw rises in living standards and real wages. Things got better. The West was strong.

In 2022, we can reasonably say the following. For a large part of the Western population, living standards are stagnating, millions are struggling with basic necessities, and inflation is set to cause real wages to fall. If we take Britain, we will soon be taxed more than at any time since the 1940s, spending more than ever and yet our public services are creaking at the joints. The NHS, despite now accounting for 44 per cent of day-to-day public-service spending, is pretty much on its knees.

To varying degrees, we could go round the Western world and see the same pattern.

Covid has taken its toll. And now the Ukraine conflict.

Following the financial crisis, we staved off a depression through unconventional monetary policy and bank recapitalisation. There was no realistic alternative, but the policy distorted our economies, rewarding those with assets, penalising those without and was combined with austerity, cutting services upon which the poorest in society depended.

The political consequence over the past 15 years has been rampant populism. Traditional parties have seen a new generation of activists take them over, roiling conventional politics and laying blame for the condition of the people at the door of "elites". The right has gone nationalist, placing as much emphasis on cultural as economic issues; the left to a mix of old-style state power as the answer to inequality and identity politics as the new radicalism. But there have also sprung up new parties, some green, some centrist, some to the far extremes of left and right.

Western politics is in turmoil – more partisan, ugly,

unproductive; and fuelled by social media.

This has had its foreign-policy consequence. Recently a leader described to me their despair at trying to work out any consistency to American engagement in the world. Characterising the Bush, Obama, Trump and now Biden administrations, he said: "too much; too little; too weird; too weak". I pushed back. I think the characterisation genuinely unfair. In the case of each president, there were significant achievements, most recently in President Biden's rallying of support for Ukraine. But what he really meant, I think, is that those dealing with America today feel American internal politics dominate external policy in a way destructive of policy coherence, an analysis unfortunately shared by those who are not our friends.

The effect of all this is that, to our own people, domestic politics appear dysfunctional; and to the outside world, foreign policy looks unpredictable. Neither helps the cause of Western democracy.

After ten years of being British PM, and now 15 years of experience working with governments around the world, I have learnt one thing. It's all about delivery. Whether in a democracy or not. That is what sustains leaders and systems or undermines them.

The challenge of democracy is efficacy. The political discourse often makes it all about transparency, honesty, authenticity. These things are important. But they don't beat delivery. In the end, the reason Boris Johnson fell was not simply the outrage around "partygate" but the absence of a plan for Britain's future. When the authenticity crumbled, there was nothing of substance left to fight for.

Today, Western democracy needs a new project. Something which gives direction, inspires hope, is a credible explanation of the way the world is changing and how we succeed within it.

In domestic policy, my view is that it is all about harnessing the technology revolution. That is the single biggest real-world change which is happening. It will disrupt everything. It should disrupt the way government works. It is the 21st-century equivalent of the 19th-century industrial revolution. It is the only solution I see to poor growth and productivity and therefore to raising living standards; the only way to improve services whilst reducing costs, for example in health care; the only answer to climate change if we want to maintain development at the same time as cutting emissions.

The problem is 20th-century politics of right and left don't really fit with it; and politicians, now habitually more familiar with the politics of grievance, find it too "technocratic" and in any event too hard to understand.

But if we're searching for the overarching project for modern domestic governance, I believe understanding the technology revolution, accessing its vast opportunities and mitigating its undoubted risks, is it.

Fortunately, in technology, Britain is well placed. But it requires politics to put it centre stage. And the current Conservative leadership debate revolving around "tax cuts", presumably to be set against Labour as the "tax and spend" party, has a depressingly 1980's feel to it.

For foreign policy, Ukraine should become a pivot point reviving our sense of mission.

Not only because of Russia but because of what it means in respect of China.

The conflict in Ukraine, where a peaceful democratic European nation has been subject to a brutal and unjustified act of aggression, with the explicit purpose of suppressing its freedom to choose its own path, on the absurd pretext that it somehow threatened the aggressor, whose leader believes in an eccentric interpretation of Russian history delegitimising Ukrainian nationhood has, for the Western foreign-policy cognoscenti, been like a very cold bucket of water thrown over the head of someone sitting in a café quietly reading their newspaper.

The first reaction to the Ukraine invasion is shock: at the horrible, unnecessary death and destruction.

But after the shock comes the realisation: this is the up-ending of our belief in big-nation rationality. Yes, terrorists behave like this. Occasionally far-off nations in far-off places fight each other. But this is a permanent member of the United Nations Security Council. The nation with the largest land mass in the world. Whose leader mixes with the other leaders of major countries on roughly equal terms.

We can point to Crimea in 2014 or Georgia in 2008 and say we were warned. But the truth is that this – a full scale war waged to subjugate an entire democratic European nation – was unexpected because it is of a nature that we thought inconceivable.

Six months ago, the idea that Putin could invade the Baltic states or Sweden or Finland would have been dismissed as fantastical. Now, for good reason, the leaders of those countries know they need NATO.

At the beginning of the conflict, I argued for a dual strategy for Ukraine: as much military support as we could give short of joining the fight directly plus the toughest sanctions; but so that the military strategy could create the leverage for a negotiated solution, of course on terms acceptable to Ukraine and its people. I still advocate that approach.

The question is what Ukraine means for wider Western foreign policy. A few years back, many people in the West even queried the need for something called "Western policy". It sounded to some provocative, even aggressive, especially after the fall of the Berlin Wall and post 9/11. Ukraine largely removed that query.

However, the biggest geopolitical change of this century will come from China not Russia. We are coming to the end of Western political and economic dominance. The world is going to be at least bi-polar and possibly multi-polar.

China is already the world's second superpower. Russia has significant military might though, as Ukraine has exposed, also some military weakness. But its economy is 70 per cent the size of Italy's.

The power of China is on a wholly different level. It has over 1.3 billion people: many more than the combined population of Europe and North America. Its economy is close to parity with that of the USA. Over the past two decades, it has pursued an active and successful engagement with the world, building connections in respect of which, as I can witness, there is deep reluctance, even on the part of traditional American allies, to yield up.

It has an ancient civilisation, one of the pre-eminent cultures, and a people increasingly well-educated and prosperous.

So, China's place as a superpower is natural and justified. It is not the Soviet Union.

However, in recent times, President Xi has re-established the supreme power of the Communist party, has made no secret of his disdain for Western "decadence", or his personal admiration for President Putin and his genre of leadership. He intends to remain in power for at least another decade and his clear, unconcealed ambition is to return Taiwan to Beijing control. Hong Kong is proof of what that means. It is therefore virtually impossible to think Taiwan will return voluntarily, hence the fear that China will use force rather than persuasion.

Plus, China has now caught up America in many fields of technology and could surpass it in others.

This new inflection point is qualitatively different from 1945 or 1980. It is the first time in modern history that the East can be on equal terms with the West. And at both other inflection points, Western democracy was essentially in the ascendant.

That is not true of 2022. Or at least not clear.

The importance of Ukraine is that it clarifies. As a result of the actions of Putin, we cannot rely on the Chinese leadership to behave in the way we would consider rational.

Don't misunderstand me. I am not saying in the near term that China would attempt to take Taiwan by force.

But we can't base our policy on the certainty that it wouldn't. And even leaving to the side Taiwan, the reality is China under Xi's leadership is competing for influence and doing so aggressively.

China will not be alone. It will have allies. Russia now for sure. Possibly Iran. But the world over, it will pull nations towards it as the divisions evidenced in the G20 over Ukraine should instruct us. Sometimes out of interests. Sometimes out of dislike of the West. Sometimes because leaders share the propensity for the undemocratic model. Sometimes the nations will be pulled only part of the way. But China will compete not just for power but against our system, our way of governing and living.

At least for now. And that is a crucial qualification.

I favour a policy towards China which is what I call "strength plus engagement". We should be strong enough to deal with whatever China's future disposition brings us, so that we maintain our system and its values. But we should not seek comprehensive "decoupling" or shut down lines of interaction or cooperation. We are clear-eyed but not hostile.

We should show that with different Chinese attitudes to us, come different attitudes from us; that we accept China's status as a world power; that we respect Chinese culture and its people.

China should always be given plenty to reflect upon. It does not have a monolithic political system in the same way as Russia. Xi will get his renewed mandate. But he is not invincible. And as his Covid policy has shown, strongman leadership carries inherent weakness when people fear to challenge what should be challenged.

We need to be open to the possibility China changes. But strong enough to withstand it if it doesn't.

For this, the West needs strategy. No project succeeds without it. Pursued with coordination, commitment and competence.

The transatlantic partnership between Europe and America is at the crux. But it needs content and vigour. With our key allies amongst developed nations like Japan, Canada and Australia, and those in the developing world, particularly in the Middle and Far East, we need to agree our objectives. And stick to them. The USA will lead but must involve allies in the formulation and execution of policy.

We need political leaders prepared to stand up to domestic political pressures.

Frequently there is a crude delineation made between "realpolitik" foreign policy – basically unprincipled, and "values-driven" foreign policy – that pursued by the decent people.

But values can't be protected unless we are strong enough to overcome those who oppose them. Strength doesn't come from wishful thinking but from hard-headed appreciation of reality.

Governments aren't NGOs. Leaders aren't writing commentaries; they're making policy.

What does this mean in practical terms?

We should increase defence spending and maintain military superiority. The USA has still far and away the world's largest and best-equipped military. But it, and we, should be superior enough to cater for any eventuality or type of conflict and in all areas. The Americans are catching up fast in hypersonic-missile capability; but the fact that they need to should teach us a lesson.

Cybersecurity is the new defence frontier. It demands a globally coordinated response.

Second, the West has been lamentable in the "soft power" space in these last years, though thankfully, there are indications that the Biden administration is correcting course. I see this continually with my Institute working all over Africa and in South-East Asia. Not only China but Russia, Turkey, even Iran have been pouring resources into the developing world and putting down thick roots in the defence and political spheres. Meanwhile the West and the international institutions it controls have been bureaucratic, unimaginative and often politically intrusive without being politically effective.

Yet we have a great opportunity. Developing countries prefer Western business. They're much more sceptical now of Chinese contracting than a decade ago. They admire the Western system more than we realise.

But we need to make our institutions and governments more agile, more responsive to countries' real needs, and co-ordinate together. Just one example: in the SAHEL region, there awaits the next explosion of immigration and extremism. We should be gearing up now to prevent it.

Africa's population will double in the next 30 years as China's declines. We should be helping the new generation of African leaders to grow sustainably, to reform agriculture so that countries with masses of arable land aren't food insecure, to process and add value to the commodities they possess in abundance.

The G7 announcement of a $600 billion "Partnership for Global Infrastructure and Investment" is a welcome but overdue response to China's OBOR.

Covid-19 has spurred huge advances in medical science. There will shortly be launched the "One Shot" campaign to ensure that the new generation of vaccines and injectables for diseases like malaria, TB, dengue and even HIV/AIDS be made available to the developing world and elsewhere. Millions of lives could be saved. The West should lead it.

We must not relinquish leadership in the Middle East. This has nothing to do with oil. Or even security in the narrow sense of working with allies to thwart planned acts of terror. The modernisation movement sweeping the region – whose broad regional support is amply demonstrated by my Institute's poll published earlier in the week – is massively important for our long-term security. The Abraham Accords with which I was involved, are proof the Middle East is changing. It is literally the last moment to give up on it.

The West has some great institutions of cultural soft power, like the British Council and the BBC. We should support them.

We should continue to lead in the climate debate.

And, as you would expect me to say, we must be leaders in technology. The US-EU Trade and Technology Council could be made into an effective piece of collective policy-making machinery.

We should ensure that legitimate concerns around data privacy and technology abuses do not shackle innovation or lose us competitive advantage. A common approach to regulation would help.

There are good policy reasons for countries near shoring, reshoring and even friend shoring, for security of supply chains. But if we let this turn into a general thrust against globalisation, in favour of protectionism, it will do us harm.

We must show staying power – commitment – even when it is tough. Even when it is not popular. This is one lesson of the Afghanistan withdrawal and, to a degree, also reduced engagement with Iraq and Libya.

This commitment must embrace our allies. If we have disagreements over human rights we should say so, but that shouldn't prevent us supporting them when they're faced with threats common to all of us.

India – which could and should achieve superpower status and is the world's largest democracy – must be kept onside and inside our prioritisation and thinking. Building strong relations with emerging nations such as Indonesia is critical.

People round the world need to see we know what we're doing. That we have a strategy. That we operate according to a plan fashioned not by the latest Twitter feed, but by deep policy grip.

Even if led by America, we all have our part to play. I won't induce agony by talking about Brexit, but it is urgent the UK rebuild a sensible relationship with Europe, which allows us to work together in our mutual interest with the other nations of the continent to which we belong and in harmony with American leadership.

This is the foreign-policy project of Western democracy in the third decade of the 21st century: to protect our values and way of life in the era of China not rising but risen.

Like 1945 or 1980, we can succeed. One of the lessons from my time spent out in the world since leaving office, is that in the end the human spirit wants to be free – and that spirit is uncrushable.

After all, that is what is motivating the brave people of Ukraine to suffer such heartbreak. They do it because they know freedom is worth fighting for. Their peril should awaken us to ours. The old assumptions have disintegrated. The world is moving at its own pace and it won't wait for us.

This inflection point is, in some respects, more grave than those of 1945 or 1980. We require organisation, intellectual heft, sustained focus, a sense of common purpose and a shared strategy to achieve it.

My final point: this won't happen unless we heal our own politics. How did Britain ever reach a point where Nigel Farage and Jeremy Corbyn came for a short but consequential time to shape our politics? Or America to a place where whether you got vaccinated denoted political allegiance?

The craziness in our own politics has to stop. We can't afford the luxury of indulging fantasy. We need to put reason and strategy back in the saddle. And we need to do so with urgency.

George W. Bush, *9/11 Address to the Nation*

[September 11, 2001, Washington]

NOTE George W. Bush (1946), America's 43rd President (2001-2009), was transformed into a wartime President in the aftermath of the airborne terrorist attacks on September 11, 2001, facing the "greatest challenge of any President since Abraham Lincoln."

Today, our fellow citizens, our way of life, our very freedom came under attack in a series of deliberate and deadly terrorist acts. The victims were in airplanes or in their offices: secretaries, business men and women, military and federal workers, moms and dads, friends and neighbors. Thousands of lives were suddenly ended by evil, despicable acts of terror. The pictures of airplanes flying into buildings, fires burning, huge – huge structures collapsing have filled us with disbelief, terrible sadness, and a quiet, unyielding anger. These acts of mass murder were intended to frighten our nation into chaos and retreat. But they have failed. Our country is strong.

A great people has been moved to defend a great nation. Terrorist attacks can shake the foundations of our biggest buildings, but they cannot touch the foundation of America. These acts shatter steel, but they cannot dent the steel of American resolve. America was targeted for attack because we're the brightest beacon for freedom and opportunity in the world. And no one will keep that light from shining. Today, our nation saw evil – the very worst of human nature – and we responded with the best of America. With the daring of our rescue workers, with the caring for strangers and neighbors who came to give blood and help in any way they could.

Immediately following the first attack, I implemented our government's emergency response plans. Our military is powerful, and it's prepared. Our emergency teams are working in New York City and Washington D.C. to help with local rescue efforts. Our first priority is to get help to those who have been injured, and to take every precaution to protect our citizens at home and around the world from further attacks. The functions of our government continue without interruption. Federal agencies in Washington which had to be evacuated today are reopening for essential personnel tonight and will be open for business tomorrow. Our financial institutions remain strong, and the American economy will be open for business as well.

The search is underway for those who were behind these evil acts. I have directed the full resources of our intelligence and law enforcement communities to find those responsible and to bring them to justice. We will make no distinction between the terrorists who committed these acts and those who harbor them.

I appreciate so very much the members of Congress who have joined me in strongly condemning these attacks. And on behalf of the American people, I thank the many world leaders who have called to offer their condolences and assistance. America and our friends and allies join with all those who want peace and security in the world, and we stand together to win the war against terrorism.

Tonight, I ask for your prayers for all those who grieve, for the children whose worlds have been shattered, for all whose sense of safety and security has been threatened. And I pray they will be comforted by a Power greater than any of us, spoken through the ages in Psalm 23:

> Even though I walk through the valley of the shadow of death, I fear no evil for you are with me.

This is a day when all Americans from every walk of life unite in our resolve for justice and peace. America has stood down enemies before, and we will do so this time. None of us will ever forget this day, yet we go forward to defend freedom and all that is good and just in our world.

Thank you. Good night. And God bless America.

George W. Bush, *The Space Shuttle "Columbia" Tragedy Speech to the Nation*

[February 1, 2003, Washington]

NOTE On February 1, 2003, the Space Shuttle Columbia, a partially-reusable spacecraft, disintegrated as it reentered the atmosphere, killing all seven crew members. The disaster was the second of two fatal accidents in the Space Shuttle program, after the 1986 breakup of Challenger soon after liftoff.

My fellow Americans, this day has brought terrible news and great sadness to our country. At nine o'clock this morning, Mission Control in Houston lost contact with our Space Shuttle Columbia. A short time later, debris was seen falling from the skies above Texas. The Columbia is lost; there are no survivors.

On board was a crew of seven: Colonel Rick Husband; Lt. Colonel Michael Anderson; Commander Laurel Clark; Captain David Brown; Commander William McCool; Dr. Kalpana Chawla; and Ilan Ramon, a Colonel in the Israeli Air Force. These men and women assumed great risk in the service to all humanity.

In an age when space flight has come to seem almost routine, it is easy to overlook the dangers of travel by rocket, and the difficulties of navigating the fierce outer atmosphere of the Earth. These astronauts knew the dangers, and they faced them willingly, knowing they had a high and noble purpose in life. Because of their courage, and daring, and idealism, we will miss them all the more.

All Americans today are thinking, as well, of the families of these men and women who have been given this sudden shock and grief. You're not alone. Our entire nation grieves with you. And those you loved will always have the respect and gratitude of this country. The cause in which they died will continue. Mankind is led into the darkness beyond our world by the inspiration of discovery and the longing to understand.

Our journey into space will go on.

In the skies today we saw destruction and tragedy. Yet farther than we can see, there is comfort and hope. In the words of the prophet Isaiah, "Lift your eyes and look to the heavens. Who created all these? He who brings out the starry hosts one by one and calls them each by name. Because of His great power, and mighty strength, not one of them is missing."

The same Creator who names the stars also knows the names of the seven souls we mourn today. The crew of the shuttle Columbia did not return safely to Earth; yet we can pray that all are safely home.

May God bless the grieving families. And may – may God continue to bless America.

Charles III, *First Address to the Nation*

[September 8, 2022, London]

NOTE King Charles III addressed the United Kingdom for the first time today following the death of his mother, Queen Elizabeth, on September 8, 2022.

I speak to you today with feelings of profound sorrow. Throughout her life, Her Majesty The Queen – my beloved mother – was an inspiration and example to me and to all my family, and we owe her the most heartfelt debt any family can owe to their mother; for her love, affection, guidance, understanding and example.

Queen Elizabeth's was a life well-lived, a promise with destiny kept, and she is mourned most deeply in her passing. That promise of lifelong service I renew to you all today.

Alongside the personal grief that all my family are feeling, we also share with so many of you in the United Kingdom, in all the countries where the Queen was head of state, in the Commonwealth and across the world, a deep sense of gratitude for the more than 70 years in which my mother, as Queen, served the people of so many nations.

In 1947, on her 21st birthday, she pledged in a broadcast from Cape Town to the Commonwealth to devote her life, whether it be short or long, to the service of her peoples.

That was more than a promise: it was a profound personal commitment which defined her whole life. She made sacrifices for duty.

Her dedication and devotion as sovereign never wavered, through times of change and progress, through times of joy and celebration, and through times of sadness and loss.

In her life of service we saw that abiding love of tradition, together with that fearless embrace of progress, which make us great as nations. The affection, admiration and respect she inspired became the hallmark of her reign.

And, as every member of my family can testify, she combined these qualities with warmth, humour and an unerring ability always to see the best in people.

I pay tribute to my mother's memory and I honour her life of service. I know that her death brings great sadness to so many of you and I share that sense of loss, beyond measure, with you all.

When the Queen came to the throne, Britain and the world were still coping with the privations and aftermath of the second world war, and still living by the conventions of earlier times.

In the course of the last 70 years we have seen our society become one of many cultures and many faiths.

The institutions of the state have changed in turn. But, through all changes and challenges, our nation and the wider family of realms – of whose talents, traditions and achievements I am so inexpressibly proud – have prospered and flourished. Our values have remained, and must remain, constant.

The role and the duties of monarchy also remain, as does the sovereign's particular relationship and responsibility towards the Church of England – the church in which my own faith is so deeply rooted.

In that faith, and the values it inspires, I have been brought up to cherish a sense of duty to others, and to hold in the greatest respect the precious traditions, freedoms and responsibilities of our unique history and our system of parliamentary government.

As the Queen herself did with such unswerving devotion, I too now solemnly pledge myself, throughout the remaining time God grants me, to uphold the constitutional principles at the heart of our nation.

And wherever you may live in the United Kingdom, or in the realms and territories across the world, and whatever may be your background or beliefs, I shall endeavour to serve you with loyalty, respect and love, as I have throughout my life.

My life will of course change as I take up my new responsibilities.

It will no longer be possible for me to give so much of my time and energies to the charities and issues for which I care so deeply. But I know this important work will go on in the trusted hands of others.

This is also a time of change for my family. I count on the loving help of my darling wife, Camilla.

In recognition of her own loyal public service since our marriage 17 years ago, she becomes my Queen Consort.

I know she will bring to the demands of her new role the steadfast devotion to duty on which I have come to rely so much.

As my heir, William now assumes the Scottish titles which have meant so much to me.

He succeeds me as Duke of Cornwall and takes on the responsibilities for the Duchy of Cornwall which I have undertaken for more than five decades.

Today, I am proud to create him Prince of Wales, Tywysog Cymru, the country whose title I have been so greatly privileged to bear during so much of my life and duty.

With Catherine beside him, our new Prince and Princess of Wales will, I know, continue to inspire and lead our national conversations, helping to bring the marginal to the centre ground where vital help can be given.

I want also to express my love for Harry and Meghan as they continue to build their lives overseas.

In a little over a week's time we will come together as a

nation, as a Commonwealth and indeed a global community, to lay my beloved mother to rest.

In our sorrow, let us remember and draw strength from the light of her example.

On behalf of all my family, I can only offer the most sincere and heartfelt thanks for your condolences and support.

They mean more to me than I can ever possibly express.

And to my darling Mama, as you begin your last great journey to join my dear late Papa, I want simply to say this: thank you.

Thank you for your love and devotion to our family and to the family of nations you have served so diligently all these years.

May 'flights of Angels sing thee to thy rest'.

Winston Churchill, *Blood, Sweat and Tears*

[May 13, 1940, London]

NOTE Winston Churchill (1874-1965) was an inspirational statesman, writer, orator and leader who led Britain to victory in the Second World War. He served as Conservative Prime Minister twice – from 1940 to 1945 (before being defeated in the 1945 general election by the Labour leader Clement Attlee) and from 1951 to 1955. He delivered many superlative speeches in his life.
This was the first of three major speeches given around the period of the Battle of France; the others are the "We Shall Fight on the Beaches" speech of June 9, 1940, and the "This was their finest hour" speech of June 18, 1940. Events developed dramatically over the five-week period, and although broadly similar in themes, each speech addressed a different military and diplomatic context.

On Friday evening last I received His Majesty's commission to form a new Administration. It was the evident wish and will of Parliament and the nation that this should be conceived on the broadest possible basis and that it should include all parties, both those who supported the late Government and also the parties of the Opposition.

I have completed the most important part of this task. A War Cabinet has been formed of five Members, representing, with the Liberal Opposition, the unity of the nation. The three party Leaders have agreed to serve, either in the War Cabinet or in high executive office. The three Fighting Services have been filled. It was necessary that this should be done in one single day, on account of the extreme urgency and rigour of events. A number of other key positions were filled yesterday, and I am submitting a further list to His Majesty tonight. I hope to complete the appointment of the principal Ministers during tomorrow. The appointment of the other Ministers usually takes a little longer, but I trust that, when Parliament meets again, this part of my task will be completed, and that the Administration will be complete in all respects.

Sir, I considered it in the public interest to suggest that the House should be summoned to meet today. Mr. Speaker agreed and took the necessary steps, in accordance with the powers conferred upon him by the Resolution of the House. At the end of the proceedings today, the Adjournment of the House will be proposed until Tuesday, the 21st May, with, of course, provision for earlier meeting, if need be. The business to be considered during that week will be notified to Members at the earliest opportunity. I now invite the House, by the Resolution which stands in my name, to record its approval of the steps taken and to declare its confidence in the new Government.

Sir, to form an Administration of this scale and complexity is a serious undertaking in itself, but it must be remembered that we are in the preliminary stage of one of the greatest battles in history, that we are in action at many points in Norway and in Holland, that we have to be prepared in the Mediterranean, that the air battle is continuous and that many preparations have to be made here at home. In this crisis I hope I may be pardoned if I do not address the House at any length today. I hope that any of my friends and colleagues, or former colleagues, who are affected by the political reconstruction, will make all allowances for any lack of ceremony with which it has been necessary to act. I would say to the House, as I said to those who've joined this government: "I have nothing to offer but blood, toil, tears and sweat."

We have before us an ordeal of the most grievous kind. We have before us many, many long months of struggle and of suffering. You ask, what is our policy? I will say: It is to wage war, by sea, land and air, with all our might and with all the strength that God can give us; to wage war against a monstrous tyranny, never surpassed in the dark and lamentable catalogue of human crime. That is our policy. You ask, what is our aim? I can answer in one word: victory. Victory at all costs, victory in spite of all terror, victory, however long and hard the road may be; for without victory, there is no survival. Let that be realised; no survival for the British Empire, no survival for all that the British Empire has stood for, no survival for the urge and impulse of the ages, that mankind will move forward towards its goal.

But I take up my task with buoyancy and hope. I feel sure that our cause will not be suffered to fail among men. At this time I feel entitled to claim the aid of all, and I say, "Come then, let us go forward together with our united strength."

Winston Churchill, *We Shall Fight on the Beaches*

[June 4, 1940, London]

NOTE This was the second of three major speeches given around the period of the Battle of France; the others are the "Blood, Sweat and Tears" speech of May 13, 1940, and the "This was their finest hour" speech of June 18, 1940. Events developed dramatically over the five-week period, and although broadly similar in themes, each speech addressed a different military and diplomatic context.
In this speech, Churchill had to describe a great military disaster, and warn of a possible invasion attempt by Nazi Germany, without casting doubt on eventual victory.

From the moment that the French defenses at Sedan and on the Meuse were broken at the end of the second week of May, only a rapid retreat to Amiens and the south could have saved the British and French Armies who had entered Belgium at the appeal of the Belgian King; but this strategic fact was not immediately realized. The French High Command hoped they would be able to close the gap, and the Armies of the north were under their orders. Moreover, a retirement of this kind would have involved almost certainly the destruction of the fine Belgian Army of over 20 divisions and the abandonment of the whole of Belgium. Therefore, when the force and scope of the German penetration were realized and when a new French Generalissimo, General Weygand, assumed command in place of General Gamelin, an effort was made by the French and British Armies in Belgium to keep on holding the right hand of the Belgians and to give their own right hand to a newly created French Army which was to have advanced across the Somme in great strength to grasp it.

However, the German eruption swept like a sharp scythe around the right and rear of the Armies of the north. Eight or nine armored divisions, each of about four hundred armored vehicles of different kinds, but carefully assorted to be complementary and divisible into small self-contained units, cut off all communications between us and the main French Armies. It severed our own communications for food and ammunition, which ran first to Amiens and afterwards through Abbeville, and it shore its way up the coast to Boulogne and Calais, and almost to Dunkirk. Behind this armored and mechanized onslaught came a number of German divisions in lorries, and behind them again there plodded comparatively slowly the dull brute mass of the ordinary German Army and German people, always so ready to be led to the trampling down in other lands of liberties and comforts which they have never known in their own.

I have said this armored scythe-stroke almost reached Dunkirk-almost but not quite. Boulogne and Calais were the scenes of desperate fighting. The Guards defended Boulogne for a while and were then withdrawn by orders from this country. The Rifle Brigade, the 60th Rifles, and the Queen Victoria's Rifles, with a battalion of British tanks and 1,000 Frenchmen, in all about four thousand strong, defended Calais to the last. The British Brigadier was given an hour to surrender. He spurned the offer, and four days of intense street fighting passed before silence reigned over Calais, which marked the end of a memorable resistance. Only 30 unwounded survivors were brought off by the Navy, and we do not know the fate of their comrades. Their sacrifice, however, was not in vain. At least two armored divisions, which otherwise would have been turned against the British Expeditionary Force, had to be sent to overcome them. They have added another page to the glories of the light divisions, and the time gained enabled the Graveline water lines to be flooded and to be held by the French troops.

Thus it was that the port of Dunkirk was kept open. When it was found impossible for the Armies of the north to reopen their communications to Amiens with the main French Armies, only one choice remained. It seemed, indeed, forlorn. The Belgian, British and French Armies were almost surrounded. Their sole line of retreat was to a single port and to its neighboring beaches. They were pressed on every side by heavy attacks and far outnumbered in the air.

When, a week ago today, I asked the House to fix this afternoon as the occasion for a statement, I feared it would be my hard lot to announce the greatest military disaster in our long history. I thought-and some good judges agreed with me-that perhaps 20,000 or 30,000 men might be re-embarked. But it certainly seemed that the whole of the French First Army and the whole of the British Expeditionary Force north of the Amiens-Abbeville gap would be broken up in the open field or else would have to capitulate for lack of food and ammunition. These were the hard and heavy tidings for which I called upon the House and the nation to prepare themselves a week ago. The whole root and core and brain of the British Army, on which and around which we were to build, and are to build, the great British Armies in the later years of the war, seemed about to perish upon the field or to be led into an ignominious and starving captivity.

That was the prospect a week ago. But another blow which might well have proved final was yet to fall upon us. The King of the Belgians had called upon us to come to his aid. Had not this Ruler and his Government severed themselves from the Allies, who rescued their country from extinction in the late war, and had they not sought refuge in what was proved to be a fatal neutrality, the French and British Armies might well at the outset have saved not only Belgium but perhaps even Poland. Yet at the last moment, when Belgium was already invaded, King Leopold called upon us to come to his aid, and even at the last moment we came. He and his brave, efficient Army, nearly half a million strong, guarded our left flank and thus kept open our only line of retreat to the sea. Suddenly, without prior consultation, with the least possible notice, without the advice of his Ministers and upon his own personal act, he sent a plenipotentiary to the German Command, surrendered his Army, and exposed our whole flank and means of retreat.

I asked the House a week ago to suspend its judgment because the facts were not clear, but I do not feel that any reason now exists why we should not form our own opinions upon this pitiful episode. The surrender of the Belgian Army compelled the British at the shortest notice to cover a flank to the sea more than 30 miles in length. Otherwise all would have been cut off, and all would have shared the fate to which King Leopold had condemned the finest Army his country had ever formed. So in doing this and in exposing this flank, as anyone who followed the operations on the map will see, contact was lost between the British and two out of the three corps forming the First French Army, who were still farther from the coast than we were, and it seemed impossible that any large number of Allied troops could reach the coast.

The enemy attacked on all sides with great strength and fierceness, and their main power, the power of their far more numerous Air Force, was thrown into the battle or else concentrated upon Dunkirk and the beaches. Pressing in upon the narrow exit, both from the east and from the west, the enemy began to fire with cannon upon the beaches by which alone the shipping could approach or depart. They sowed magnetic mines in the channels and seas; they sent repeated waves of hostile aircraft, sometimes more than a hundred strong in one formation, to cast their bombs upon the single pier that remained, and upon the sand dunes upon which the troops had their eyes for shelter. Their U-boats, one of which was sunk, and their motor launches took their toll of the vast traffic which now began. For four or five days an intense struggle reigned. All their armored divisions-or what Was left of them-together with great masses of infantry and artillery, hurled themselves in vain upon the ever-narrowing, ever-contracting appendix within which the British and French Armies fought.

Meanwhile, the Royal Navy, with the willing help of countless merchant seamen, strained every nerve to embark the British and Allied troops; 220 light warships and 650 other vessels were engaged. They had to operate upon the difficult coast, often in adverse weather, under an almost ceaseless hail of bombs and an increasing concentration of artillery fire. Nor were the seas, as I have said, themselves free from mines and torpedoes. It was in conditions such as these that our men carried on, with little or no rest, for days and nights on end, making trip after trip across the danger-ous waters, bringing with them always men whom they had rescued. The numbers they have brought back are the meas-ure of their devotion and their courage. The hospital ships, which brought off many thousands of British and French wounded, being so plainly marked were a special target for Nazi bombs; but the men and women on board them never faltered in their duty.

Meanwhile, the Royal Air Force, which had already been intervening in the battle, so far as its range would allow, from home bases, now used part of its main metropolitan fighter strength, and struck at the German bombers and at the fighters which in large numbers protected them. This struggle was protracted and fierce. Suddenly the scene has cleared, the crash and thunder has for the moment-but only for the moment-died away. A miracle of deliverance, achieved by valor, by perseverance, by perfect discipline, by faultless service, by resource, by skill, by unconquerable fi-delity, is manifest to us all. The enemy was hurled back by the retreating British and French troops. He was so roughly handled that he did not hurry their departure seriously. The Royal Air Force engaged the main strength of the German Air Force, and inflicted upon them losses of at least four to one; and the Navy, using nearly 1,000 ships of all kinds, carried over 335,000 men, French and British, out of the jaws of death and shame, to their native land and to the tasks which lie immediately ahead. We must be very careful not to assign to this deliverance the attributes of a victory. Wars are not won by evacuations. But there was a victory inside this deliverance, which should be noted. It was gained by the Air Force. Many of our soldiers coming back have not seen the Air Force at work; they saw only the bombers which escaped its protective attack. They underrate its achievements. I have heard much talk of this; that is why I go out of my way to say this. I will tell you about it.

This was a great trial of strength between the British and German Air Forces. Can you conceive a greater objective for the Germans in the air than to make evacuation from these beaches impossible, and to sink all these ships which were displayed, almost to the extent of thousands? Could there have been an objective of greater military importance and significance for the whole purpose of the war than this? They tried hard, and they were beaten back; they were frustrated in their task. We got the Army away; and they have paid fourfold for any losses which they have inflicted. Very large formations of German aeroplanes-and we know that they are a very brave race-have turned on several occasions from the attack of one-quarter of their number of the Royal Air Force, and have dispersed in different directions. Twelve aeroplanes have been hunted by two. One aeroplane was driven into the water and cast away by the mere charge of a British aeroplane, which had no more ammunition. All of our types-the Hurricane, the Spitfire and the new Defiant-and all our pilots have been vindicated as superior to what they have at present to face.

When we consider how much greater would be our advantage in defending the air above this Island against an overseas attack, I must say that I find in these facts a sure basis upon which practical and reassuring thoughts may rest. I will pay my tribute to these young airmen. The great French Army was very largely, for the time being, cast back and disturbed by the onrush of a few thousands of armored vehicles. May it not also be that the cause of civilization itself will be defended by the skill and devotion of a few thousand airmen? There never has been, I suppose, in all the world, in all the history of war, such an opportunity for youth. The Knights of the Round Table, the Crusaders, all fall back into the past-not only distant but prosaic; these young men, going forth every morn to guard their native land and all that we stand for, holding in their hands these instruments of colossal and shattering power, of whom it may be said that:

> Every morn brought forth a noble chance
> And every chance brought forth a noble knight,

deserve our gratitude, as do all the brave men who, in so many ways and on so many occasions, are ready, and continue ready to give life and all for their native land.

I return to the Army. In the long series of very fierce battles, now on this front, now on that, fighting on three fronts at once, battles fought by two or three divisions against an equal or somewhat larger number of the enemy, and fought fiercely on some of the old grounds that so many of us knew so well-in these battles our losses in men have exceeded 30,000 killed, wounded and missing. I take occasion to express the sympathy of the House to all who have suffered bereavement or who are still anxious. The President of the Board of Trade [Sir Andrew Duncan] is not here today. His son has been killed, and many in the House have felt the pangs of affliction in the sharpest form. But I will say this about the missing: We have had a large number of wounded come home safely to this country, but I would say about the missing that there may be very many reported missing who will come back home, some day, in one way or another. In the confusion of this fight it is inevitable that many have been left in positions where honor required no further resistance from them.

Against this loss of over 30,000 men, we can set a far heavier loss certainly inflicted upon the enemy. But our losses in material are enormous. We have perhaps lost one-third of the men we lost in the opening days of the battle of 21st March, 1918, but we have lost nearly as many guns — nearly one thousand-and all our transport, all the armored vehicles that were with the Army in the north. This loss will impose a further delay on the expansion of our military strength. That expansion had not been proceeding as far as we had hoped. The best of all we had to give had gone to the British Expeditionary Force, and although they had not the numbers of tanks and some articles of equipment which were desirable, they were a very well and finely equipped Army. They had the first-fruits of all that our industry had to give, and that is gone. And now here is this further delay. How long it will be, how long it will last, depends upon the exertions which we make in this Island. An effort the like of which has never been seen in our records is now being made. Work is proceeding everywhere, night and day, Sundays and week days. Capital and Labor have cast aside their interests, rights, and customs and put them into the common stock. Already the flow of munitions has leaped forward. There is no reason why we should not in a few months overtake the sudden and serious loss that has come upon us, without retarding the development of our general program.

Nevertheless, our thankfulness at the escape of our Army and so many men, whose loved ones have passed through an agonizing week, must not blind us to the fact that what has happened in France and Belgium is a colossal military disaster. The French Army has been weakened, the Belgian Army has been lost, a large part of those fortified lines upon which so much faith had been reposed is gone, many valuable mining districts and factories have passed into the enemy's possession, the whole of the Channel ports are in his hands, with all the tragic consequences that follow from that, and we must expect another blow to be struck almost immediately at us or at France. We are told that Herr Hitler has a plan for invading the British Isles. This has often been thought of before. When Napoleon lay at Boulogne for a year with his flat-bottomed boats and his Grand Army, he was told by someone. "There are bitter weeds in England." There are certainly a great many more of them since the British Expeditionary Force returned.

The whole question of home defense against invasion is, of course, powerfully affected by the fact that we have for the time being in this Island incomparably more powerful military forces than we have ever had at any moment in this war or the last. But this will not continue. We shall not be content with a defensive war. We have our duty to our Ally. We have to reconstitute and build up the British Expeditionary Force once again, under its gallant Commander-in-Chief, Lord Gort. All this is in train; but in the interval we must put our defenses in this Island into such a high state of organization that the fewest possible numbers will be required to give effective security and that the largest possible potential of offensive effort may be realized. On this we are now engaged. It will be very convenient, if it be the desire of the House, to enter upon this subject in a secret Session. Not that the government would necessarily be able to reveal in very great detail military secrets, but we like to have our discussions free, without the restraint imposed by the fact that they will be read the next day by the enemy; and the

Government would benefit by views freely expressed in all parts of the House by Members with their knowledge of so many different parts of the country. I understand that some request is to be made upon this subject, which will be readily acceded to by His Majesty's Government.

We have found it necessary to take measures of increasing stringency, not only against enemy aliens and suspicious characters of other nationalities, but also against British subjects who may become a danger or a nuisance should the war be transported to the United Kingdom. I know there are a great many people affected by the orders which we have made who are the passionate enemies of Nazi Germany. I am very sorry for them, but we cannot, at the present time and under the present stress, draw all the distinctions which we should like to do. If parachute landings were attempted and fierce fighting attendant upon them followed, these unfortunate people would be far better out of the way, for their own sakes as well as for ours. There is, however, another class, for which I feel not the slightest sympathy. Parliament has given us the powers to put down Fifth Column activities with a strong hand, and we shall use those powers subject to the supervision and correction of the House, without the slightest hesitation until we are satisfied, and more than satisfied, that this malignancy in our midst has been effectively stamped out.

Turning once again, and this time more generally, to the question of invasion, I would observe that there has never been a period in all these long centuries of which we boast when an absolute guarantee against invasion, still less against serious raids, could have been given to our people. In the days of Napoleon the same wind which would have carried his transports across the Channel might have driven away the blockading fleet. There was always the chance, and it is that chance which has excited and befooled the imaginations of many Continental tyrants. Many are the tales that are told. We are assured that novel methods will be adopted, and when we see the originality of malice, the ingenuity of aggression, which our enemy displays, we may certainly prepare ourselves for every kind of novel stratagem and every kind of brutal and treacherous maneuver. I think that no idea is so outlandish that it should not be considered and viewed with a searching, but at the same time, I hope, with a steady eye. We must never forget the solid assurances of sea power and those which belong to air power if it can be locally exercised.

I have, myself, full confidence that if all do their duty, if nothing is neglected, and if the best arrangements are made, as they are being made, we shall prove ourselves once again able to defend our Island home, to ride out the storm of war, and to outlive the menace of tyranny, if necessary for years, if necessary alone. At any rate, that is what we are going to try to do. That is the resolve of His Majesty's Government-every man of them. That is the will of Parliament and the nation.

The British Empire and the French Republic, linked together in their cause and in their need, will defend to the death their native soil, aiding each other like good comrades to the utmost of their strength. Even though large tracts of Europe and many old and famous States have fallen or may fall into the grip of the Gestapo and all the odious apparatus of Nazi rule, we shall not flag or fail.

We shall go on to the end, we shall fight in France, we shall fight on the seas and oceans, we shall fight with growing confidence and growing strength in the air, we shall defend our Island, whatever the cost may be, we shall fight on the beaches, we shall fight on the landing grounds, we shall fight in the fields and in the streets, we shall fight in the hills; we shall never surrender, and even if, which I do not for a moment believe, this Island or a large part of it were subjugated and starving, then our Empire beyond the seas, armed and guarded by the British Fleet, would carry on the struggle, until, in God's good time, the New World, with all its power and might, steps forth to the rescue and the liberation of the old.

67

Winston Churchill, *Their Finest House*

[June 18, 1940, London]

NOTE It was the third of three speeches which he gave during the period of the Battle of France, after the "Blood, toil, tears and sweat" speech of 13 May and the "We shall fight on the beaches" speech of 4 June. "This was their finest hour" was made after France had sought an armistice on the evening of 16 June.

I spoke the other day of the colossal military disaster which occurred when the French High Command failed to withdraw the northern Armies from Belgium at the moment when they knew that the French front was decisively broken at Sedan and on the Meuse. This delay entailed the loss of fifteen or sixteen French divisions and threw out of action for the critical period the whole of the British Expeditionary Force. Our Army and 120,000 French troops were indeed rescued by the British Navy from Dunkirk but only with the loss of their cannon, vehicles and modern equipment. This loss inevitably took some weeks to repair, and in the first two of those weeks the battle in France has been lost. When we consider the heroic resistance made by the French Army against heavy odds in this battle, the enormous losses inflicted upon the enemy and the evident exhaustion of the enemy, it may well be the thought that these 25 divisions of the best-trained and best-equipped troops might have turned the scale. However, General Weygand had to fight without them. Only three British divisions or their equivalent were able to stand in the line with their French comrades. They have suffered severely, but they have fought well. We sent every man we could to France as fast as we could re-equip and transport their formations.

I am not reciting these facts for the purpose of recrimination. That I judge to be utterly futile and even harmful. We cannot afford it. I recite them in order to explain why it was we did not have, as we could have had, between twelve and fourteen British divisions fighting in the line in this great battle instead of only three. Now I put all this aside. I put it on the shelf, from which the historians, when they have time, will select their documents to tell their stories. We have to think of the future and not of the past. This also applies in a small way to our own affairs at home. There are many who would hold an inquest in the House of Commons on the conduct of the Governments-and of Parliaments, for they are in it, too-during the years which led up to this catastrophe. They seek to indict those who were responsible for the guidance of our affairs. This also would be a foolish and pernicious process. There are too many in it. Let each man search his conscience and search his speeches. I frequently search mine.

Of this I am quite sure, that if we open a quarrel between the past and the present, we shall find that we have lost the future. Therefore, I cannot accept the drawing of any distinctions between Members of the present Government. It was formed at a moment of crisis in order to unite all the Parties and all sections of opinion. It has received the almost unanimous support of both Houses of Parliament. Its Members are going to stand together, and, subject to the authority of the House of Commons, we are going to govern the country and fight the war. It is absolutely necessary at a time like this that every Minister who tries each day to do his duty shall be respected; and their subordinates must know that their chiefs are not threatened men, men who are here today and gone tomorrow, but that their directions must be punctually and faithfully obeyed. Without this concentrated power we cannot face what lies before us. I should not think it would be very advantageous for the House to prolong this Debate this afternoon under conditions of public stress. Many facts are not clear that will be clear in a short time. We are to have a secret Session on Thursday, and I should think that would be a better opportunity for the many earnest expressions of opinion which Members will desire to make and for the House to discuss vital matters without having everything read the next morning by our dangerous foes.

The disastrous military events which have happened during the past fortnight have not come to me with any sense of surprise. Indeed, I indicated a fortnight ago as clearly as I could to the House that the worst possibilities were open; and I made it perfectly clear then that whatever happened in France would make no difference to the resolve of Britain and the British Empire to fight on, 'if necessary for years, if necessary alone." During the last few days we have successfully brought off the great majority of the troops we had on the line of communication in France; and seven-eighths of the troops we have sent to France since the beginning of the war-that is to say, about 350,000 out of 400,000 men-are safely back in this country. Others are still fighting with the French, and fighting with considerable success in their local encounters against the enemy. We have also brought back a great mass of stores, rifles and munitions of all kinds which had been accumulated in France during the last nine months.

We have, therefore, in this Island today a very large and powerful military force. This force comprises all our best-trained and our finest troops, including scores of thousands of those who have already measured their quality against the Germans and found themselves at no disadvantage. We have under arms at the present time in this Island over a million and a quarter men. Behind these we have the Local Defence Volunteers, numbering half a million, only a portion of whom, however, are yet armed with rifles or other firearms.

We have incorporated into our Defence Forces every man for whom we have a weapon. We expect very large additions to our weapons in the near future, and in preparation for this we intend forthwith to call up, drill and train further large numbers. Those who are not called up, or else are employed during the vast business of munitions production in all its branches-and their ramifications are innumerable-will serve their country best by remaining at their ordinary work until they receive their summons. We have also over here Dominions armies. The Canadians had actually landed in France, but have now been safely withdrawn, much disappointed, but in perfect order, with all their artillery and equipment. And these very high-class forces from the Dominions will now take part in the defence of the Mother Country.

Lest the account which I have given of these large forces should raise the question: Why did they not take part in the great battle in France? I must make it clear that, apart from the divisions training and organizing at home, only 12 divisions were equipped to fight upon a scale which justified their being sent abroad. And this was fully up to the number which the French had been led to expect would be available in France at the ninth month of the war. The rest of our forces at home have a fighting value for home defence which will, of course, steadily increase every week that passes. Thus, the invasion of Great Britain would at this time require the transportation across the sea of hostile armies on a very large scale, and after they had been so transported they would have to be continually maintained with all the masses of munitions and supplies which are required for continuous battle-as continuous battle it will surely be.

Here is where we come to the Navy-and after all, we have a Navy. Some people seem to forget that we have a Navy. We must remind them. For the last thirty years I have been concerned in discussions about the possibilities of oversea invasion, and I took the responsibility on behalf of the Admiralty, at the beginning of the last war, of allowing all regular troops to be sent out of the country. That was a very serious step to take, because our Territorials had only just been called up and were quite untrained. Therefore, this Island was for several months particularly denuded of fighting troops. The Admiralty had confidence at that time in their ability to prevent a mass invasion even though at that time the Germans had a magnificent battle fleet in the proportion of 10 to 16, even though they were capable of fighting a general engagement every day and any day, whereas now they have only a couple of heavy ships worth speaking of-the Scharnhorst and the Gneisenau. We are also told that the Italian Navy is to come out and gain sea superiority in these waters. If they seriously intend it, I shall only say that we shall be delighted to offer Signor Mussolini a free and safeguarded passage through the Strait of Gibraltar in order that he may play the part to which he aspires. There is a general curiosity in the British Fleet to find out whether the Italians are up to the level they were at in the last war or whether they have fallen off at all.

Therefore, it seems to me that as far as sea-borne invasion on a great scale is concerned, we are far more capable of meeting it today than we were at many periods in the last war and during the early months of this war, before our other troops were trained, and while the B.E.F. had proceeded abroad. Now, the Navy have never pretended to be able to prevent raids by bodies of 5,000 or 10,000 men flung suddenly across and thrown ashore at several points on the coast some dark night or foggy morning. The efficacy of sea power, especially under modern conditions, depends upon the invading force being of large size; It has to be of large size, in view of our military strength, to be of any use. If it is of large size, then the Navy have something they can find and meet and, as it were, bite on. Now, we must remember that even five divisions, however lightly equipped, would require 200 to 250 ships, and with modern air reconnaissance and photography it would not be easy to collect such an armada, marshal it, and conduct it across the sea without any powerful naval forces to escort it; and there would be very great possibilities, to put it mildly, that this armada would be intercepted long before it reached the coast, and all the men drowned in the sea or, at the worst blown to pieces with their equipment while they were trying to land. We also have a great system of minefields, recently strongly reinforced, through which we alone know the channels. If the enemy tries to sweep passages through these minefields, it will be the task of the Navy to destroy the mine-sweepers and any other forces employed to protect them. There should be no difficulty in this, owing to our great superiority at sea.

Those are the regular, well-tested, well-proved arguments on which we have relied during many years in peace and war. But the question is whether there are any new methods by which those solid assurances can be circumvented. Odd as it may seem, some attention has been given to this by the Admiralty, whose prime duty and responsibility is to destroy any large sea-borne expedition before it reaches, or at the moment when it reaches, these shores. It would not be a good thing for me to go into details of this. It might suggest ideas to other people which they have not thought of, and they would not be likely to give us any of their ideas in exchange. All I will say is that untiring vigilance and mind-searching must be devoted to the subject, because the enemy is crafty and cunning and full of novel treacheries and stratagems. The House may be assured that the utmost ingenuity is being displayed and imagination is being evoked from large numbers of competent officers, well-trained in tactics and thoroughly up to date, to measure and counterwork novel possibilities. Untiring vigilance and untiring searching of the mind is being, and must be, devoted to the subject, because, remember, the enemy is crafty and there is no dirty trick he will not do.

Some people will ask why, then, was it that the British Navy was not able to prevent the movement of a large army from Germany into Norway across the Skagerrak? But the conditions in the Channel and in the North Sea are in no way like those which prevail in the Skagerrak. In the Skagerrak, because of the distance, we could give no air support to our surface ships, and consequently, lying as we did close to the enemy's main air power, we were compelled to use only our submarines. We could not enforce the decisive blockade or interruption which is possible from surface vessels. Our submarines took a heavy toll but could not, by themselves, prevent the invasion of Norway. In the Channel and in the North Sea, on the other hand, our superior naval surface forces, aided by our submarines, will operate with close and effective air assistance.

This brings me, naturally, to the great question of invasion from the air, and of the impending struggle between the British and German Air Forces. It seems quite clear that no invasion on a scale beyond the capacity of our land forces to crush speedily is likely to take place from the air until our Air Force has been definitely overpowered. In the meantime, there may be raids by parachute troops and attempted descents of airborne soldiers. We should be able to give those gentry a warm reception both in the air and on the ground, if they reach it in any condition to continue the dispute. But the great question is: Can we break Hitler's air weapon? Now, of course, it is a very great pity that we have not got an Air Force at least equal to that of the most powerful enemy within striking distance of these shores. But we have a very powerful Air Force which has proved itself far superior in quality, both in men and in many types of machine, to what we have met so far in the numerous and fierce air battles which have been fought with the Germans. In France, where we were at a considerable disadvantage and lost many machines on the ground when they were standing round the aerodromes, we were accustomed to inflict in the air losses of as much as two and two-and-a-half to one. In the fighting over Dunkirk, which was a sort of no-man's-land, we undoubtedly beat the German Air Force, and gained the mastery of the local air, inflicting here a loss of three or four to one day after day. Anyone who looks at the photographs which were published a week or so ago of the re-embarkation, showing the masses of troops assembled on the beach and forming an ideal target for hours at a time, must realize that this re-embarkation would not have been possible unless the enemy had resigned all hope of recovering air superiority at that time and at that place.

In the defence of this Island the advantages to the defenders will be much greater than they were in the fighting around Dunkirk. We hope to improve on the rate of three or four to one which was realized at Dunkirk; and in addition all our injured machines and their crews which get down safely-and, surprisingly, a very great many injured machines and men do get down safely in modern air fighting-all of these will fall, in an attack upon these Islands, on friendly. soil and live to fight another day; whereas all the injured enemy machines and their complements will be total losses as far as the war is concerned.

During the great battle in France, we gave very powerful and continuous aid to. the French Army, both by fighters and bombers; but in spite of every kind of pressure we never would allow the entire metropolitan fighter strength of the Air Force to be consumed. This decision was painful, but it was also right, because the fortunes of the battle in France could not have been decisively affected even if we had thrown in our entire fighter force. That battle was lost by the unfortunate strategical opening, by the extraordinary and unforseen power of the armored columns, and by the great preponderance of the German Army in numbers. Our fighter Air Force might easily have been exhausted as a mere accident in that great struggle, and then we should have found ourselves at the present time in a very serious plight. But as it is, I am happy to inform the House that our fighter strength is stronger at the present time relatively to the Germans, who have suffered terrible losses, than it has ever been; and consequently we believe ourselves possessed of the capacity to continue the war in the air under better conditions than we have ever experienced before. I look forward confidently to the exploits of our fighter pilots-these splendid men, this brilliant youth-who will have the glory of saving their native land, their island home, and all they love, from the most deadly of all attacks.

There remains, of course, the danger of bombing attacks, which will certainly be made very soon upon us by the bomber forces of the enemy. It is true that the German bomber force is superior in numbers to ours; but we have a very large bomber force also, which we shall use to strike at military targets in Germany without intermission. I do not at all underrate the severity of the ordeal which lies before us; but I believe our countrymen will show themselves capable of standing up to it, like the brave men of Barcelona, and will be able to stand up to it, and carry on in spite of it, at least as well as any other people in the world. Much will depend upon this; every man and every woman will have the chance to show the finest qualities of their race, and render the highest service to their cause. For all of us, at this time, whatever our sphere, our station, our occupation or our duties, it will be a help to remember the famous lines: He nothing common did or mean, Upon that memorable scene.

I have thought it right upon this occasion to give the House and the country some indication of the solid, practical grounds upon which we base our inflexible resolve to continue the war. There are a good many people who say, "Never mind. Win or lose, sink or swim, better die than submit to tyranny-and such a tyranny." And I do not dissociate myself from them. But I can assure them that our professional advisers of the three Services unitedly advise that we should carry on the war, and that there are good and reasonable hopes of final victory. We have fully informed and consulted all the self-governing Dominions, these great communities far beyond the oceans who have been built up on our laws and on our civilization, and who are absolutely free to choose their course, but are absolutely devoted to the ancient Motherland, and who feel themselves inspired by the same emotions which lead me to stake our all upon duty and honour. We have fully consulted them, and I have received from their Prime Ministers, Mr. Mackenzie King of Canada, Mr. Menzies of Australia, Mr. Fraser of New Zealand, and General Smuts of South Africa-that wonderful man, with his immense profound mind, and his eye watching from a distance the whole panorama of European affairs-I have received from all these eminent men, who all have Governments behind them elected on wide franchises, who are all there because they represent the will of their people, messages couched in the most moving terms in which they endorse our decision to fight on, and declare themselves ready to share our fortunes and to persevere to the end. That is what we are going to do.

We may now ask ourselves: In what way has our position worsened since the beginning of the war? It has worsened by the fact that the Germans have conquered a large part of the coast line of Western Europe, and many small countries have been overrun by them. This aggravates the possibilities of air attack and adds to our naval preoccupations. It in no way diminishes, but on the contrary definitely increases, the power of our long-distance blockade. Similarly, the entrance of Italy into the war increases the power of our long-distance blockade. We have stopped the worst leak by that. We do not know whether military resistance will come to an end in France or not, but should it do so, then of course the Germans will be able to concentrate their forces, both military and industrial, upon us. But for the reasons I have given to the House these will not be found so easy to apply. If invasion has become more imminent, as no doubt it has, we, being relieved from the task of maintaining a large army in France, have far larger and more efficient forces to meet it.

If Hitler can bring under his despotic control the industries of the countries he has conquered, this will add greatly to his already vast armament output. On the other hand, this will not happen immediately, and we are now assured of immense, continuous and increasing support in supplies and munitions of all kinds from the United States; and especially of aeroplanes and pilots from the Dominions and across the oceans coming from regions which are beyond the reach of enemy bombers.

I do not see how any of these factors can operate to our detriment on balance before the winter comes; and the winter will impose a strain upon the Nazi regime, with almost all Europe writhing and starving under its cruel heel, which, for all their ruthlessness, will run them very hard. We must not forget that from the moment when we declared war on the 3rd September it was always possible for Germany to turn all her Air Force upon this country, together with any other devices of invasion she might conceive, and that France could have done little or nothing to prevent her doing so. We have, therefore, lived under this danger, in principle and in a slightly modified form, during all these months. In the meanwhile, however, we have enormously improved our methods of defence, and we have learned what we had no right to assume at the beginning, namely, that the individual aircraft and the individual British pilot have a sure and definite superiority. Therefore, in casting up this dread balance sheet and contemplating our dangers with a disillusioned eye, I see great reason for intense vigilance and exertion, but none whatever for panic or despair.

During the first four years of the last war the Allies experienced nothing but disaster and disappointment. That was our constant fear: one blow after another, terrible losses, frightful dangers. Everything miscarried. And yet at the end of those four years the morale of the Allies was higher than that of the Germans, who had moved from one aggressive triumph to another, and who stood everywhere triumphant invaders of the lands into which they had broken. During that war we repeatedly asked ourselves the question: How are we going to win? and no one was able ever to answer it with much precision, until at the end, quite suddenly, quite unexpectedly, our terrible foe collapsed before us, and we were so glutted with victory that in our folly we threw it away.

We do not yet know what will happen in France or whether the French resistance will be prolonged, both in France and in the French Empire overseas. The French Government will be throwing away great opportunities and casting adrift their future if they do not continue the war in accordance with their Treaty obligations, from which we have not felt able to release them. The House will have read the historic declaration in which, at the desire of many Frenchmen-and of our own hearts-we have proclaimed our willingness at the darkest hour in French history to conclude a union of common citizenship in this struggle. However matters may go in France or with the French Government, or other French Governments, we in this Island and in the British Empire will never lose our sense of comradeship with the French people. If we are now called upon to endure what they have been suffering, we shall emulate their courage, and if final victory rewards our toils they shall share the gains, aye, and freedom shall be restored to all. We abate nothing of our just demands; not one jot or tittle do we recede. Czechs, Poles, Norwegians, Dutch, Belgians have joined their causes to our own. All these shall be restored.

What General Weygand called the Battle of France is over. I expect that the Battle of Britain is about to begin. Upon this battle depends the survival of Christian civilization. Upon it depends our own British life, and the long continuity of our institutions and our Empire. The whole fury and might of the enemy must very soon be turned on us. Hitler knows that he will have to break us in this Island or lose the war. If we can stand up to him, all Europe may be free and the life of the world may move forward into broad, sunlit uplands. But if we fail, then the whole world, including the United States, including all that we have known and cared for, will sink into the abyss of a new Dark Age made more sinister, and perhaps more protracted, by the lights of perverted science. Let us therefore brace ourselves to our duties, and so bear ourselves that, if the British Empire and its Commonwealth last for a thousand years, men will still say, "This was their finest hour."

Winston Churchill, *Broadcast on the Soviet-German War*

[June 22, 1941, London)

I have taken occasion to speak to you tonight because we have reached one of the climacterics of the war. In the first of these intense turning points, a year ago, France fell prostrate under the German hammer and we had to face the storm alone.

The second was when the Royal Air Force beat the Hun raiders out of the daylight air raid and thus warded off the Nazi invasion of our islands while we were still ill-armed and ill-prepared.

The third turning point was when the President and Congress of the United States passed the lease and lend enactment, devoting nearly 2,000,000,000 sterling of the wealth of the New World to help us defend our liberties and their own.

Those were the three climacterics.

The fourth is now upon us.

At 4 o'clock this morning Hitler attacked and invaded Russia. All his usual formalities of perfidy were observed with scrupulous technique. A non-aggression treaty had been solemnly signed and was in force between the two countries. No complaint had been made by Germany of its non-fulfillment. Under its cloak of false confidence the German armies drew up in immense strength along a line which stretched from the White Sea to the Black Sea and their air fleets and armoured divisions slowly and methodically took up their stations.

Then, suddenly, without declaration of war, without even an ultimatum, the German bombs rained down from the sky upon the Russian cities; the German troops violated the Russian frontiers and an hour later the German Ambassador, who till the night before was lavishing his assurances of friendship, almost of alliance, upon the Russians, called upon the Russian Foreign Minister to tell him that a state of war existed between Germany and Russia.

Thus was repeated on a far larger scale the same kind of outrage against every form of signed compact and international faith which we have witnessed in Norway, in Denmark, in Holland, in Belgium and which Hitler's accomplice and jackal, Mussolini, so faithfully imitated in the case of Greece.

All this was no surprise to me. In fact I gave clear and precise warnings to Stalin of what was coming. I gave him warnings, as I have given warnings to others before. I can only hope that these warnings did not fall unheeded.

All we know at present is that the Russian people are defending their native soil and that their leaders have called upon them to resist to the utmost.

Hitler is a monster of wickedness, insatiable in his lust for blood and plunder. Not content with having all Europe under his heel or else terrorized into various forms of abject submission, he must now carry his work of butchery and desolation among the vast multitudes of Russia and of Asia. The terrible military machine which we and the rest of the civilized world so foolishly, so supinely, so insensately allowed the Nazi gangsters to build up year by year from almost nothing-this machine cannot stand idle, lest it rust or fall to pieces. It must be in continual motion, grinding up human lives and trampling down the homes and the rights of hundreds of millions of men.

Moreover, it must be fed not only with flesh but with oil. So now this bloodthirsty guttersnipe must launch his mechanized armies upon new fields of slaughter, pillage and devastation. Poor as are the Russian peasants, workmen and soldiers, he must steal from them their daily bread. He must devour their harvests. He must rob them of the oil which drives their ploughs and thus produce a famine without example in human history.

And even the carnage and ruin which his victory, should he gain it-though he's not gained it yet-will bring upon the Russian people, will itself be only a stepping stone to the attempt to plunge four or five hundred millions who live in China and the 350,000,000 who live in India into that bottomless pit of human degradation over which the diabolic emblem of the swastika flaunts itself.

It is not too much to say here this pleasant summer evening that the lives and happiness of a thousand million additional human beings are now menaced with brutal Nazi violence. That is enough to make us hold our breath.

But presently I shall show you something else that lies behind and something that touches very nearly the life of Britain and of the United States.

The Nazi regime is indistinguishable from the worst features of Communism. It is devoid of all theme and principle except appetite and racial domination. It excels in all forms of human wickedness, in the efficiency of its cruelty and ferocious aggression. Noone has been a more consistent opponent of Communism than I have for the last twenty-five years. I will unsay no words that I've spoken about it. But all this fades away before the spectacle which is now unfolding.

The past, with its crimes, its follies and its tragedies, flashes away. I see the Russian soldiers standing on the threshold of their native land, guarding the fields which their fathers have tilled from time immemorial. I see them guarding their homes; their mothers and wives pray, ah yes, for there are times when all pray for the safety of their loved ones, for the return of the breadwinner, of the champion, of their protectors.

I see the 10,000 villages of Russia, where the means of existence was wrung so hardly from the soil, but where there are still primordial human joys, where maidens laugh and children play I see advancing upon all this, in hideous on-slaught, the Nazi war machine, with its clanking, heel-click-ing, dandified Prussian officers, its crafty expert agents, fresh from the cowing and tying down of a dozen countries. I see also the dull, drilled, docile brutish masses of the Hun sol-diery, plodding on like a swarm of crawling locusts. I see the German bombers and fighters in the sky, still smarting from many a British whipping, so delighted to find what they be-lieve is an easier and a safer prey. And behind all this glare, behind all this storm, I see that small group of villainous men who planned, organized and launched this cataract of horrors upon mankind.

And then my mind goes back across the years to the days when the Russian armies were our Allies against the same deadly foe when they fought with so much valor and con-stancy and helped to gain a victory, from all share in which, alas, they were, through no fault of ours, utterly cut off.

I have lived through all this and you will pardon me if I express my feelings and the stir of old memories. But now I have to declare the decision of His Majesty's Government, and I feel sure it is a decision in which the great Dominions will, in due course, concur. And that we must speak of now, at once, without a day's delay. I have to make the declara-tion, but can you doubt what our policy will be?

We have but one aim and one single irrevocable purpose. We are resolved to destroy Hitler and every vestige of the Nazi regime. From this nothing will turn us. Nothing. We will never parley; we will never negotiate with Hitler or any of his gang. We shall fight him by land; we shall fight him by sea; we shall fight him in the air, until, with God's help, we have rid the earth of his shadow and liberated its people from his yoke.

Any man or State who fights against Nazism will have our aid. Any man or State who marches with Hitler is our foe. This applies not only to organized States but to all representatives of that vile race of Quislings who make themselves the tools and agents of the Nazi regime against their fellow-countrymen and against the lands of their births. These Quislings, like the Nazi leaders themselves, if not disposed of by their fellow-countrymen, which would save trouble, will be delivered by us on the morrow of victory to the justice of the Allied tribunals. That is our policy and that is our declaration.

It follows, therefore, that we shall give whatever help we can to Russia and to the Russian people. We shall appeal to all our friends and Allies in every part of the world to take the same course and pursue it as we shall, faithfully and steadfastly to the end.

We have offered to the Government of Soviet Russia any technical or economic assistance which is in our power and which is likely to be of service to them. We shall bomb Germany by day as well as by night in ever-increasing measure, casting upon them month by month a heavier discharge of bombs and making the German people taste and gulp each month a sharper dose of the miseries they have showered upon mankind.

It is noteworthy that only yesterday the Royal Air Force, striking inland over France, cut down with very small loss to themselves twenty-eight of the Hun fighting machines in the air above the French soil they have invaded, defiled and profess to hold.

But this is only a beginning. From now henceforward the main expansion of our air force proceeds with gathering speed. In another six months the weight of the help we are receiving from the United States in war materials of all kinds, especially in heavy bombers, will begin to tell. This is no class war. It is a war in which the whole British Empire and Commonwealth of Nations is engaged without distinction of race, creed or party.

It is not for me to speak of the action of the United States, but this I will say: If Hitler imagines that his attack on Soviet Russia will cause the slightest division of aims or slackening of effort in the great democracies, who are resolved upon his doom, he is woefully mistaken. On the contrary, we shall be fortified and encouraged in our efforts to rescue mankind from his tyranny. We shall be strengthened and not weakened in our determination and in our resources.

This is no time to moralize upon the follies of countries and governments which have allowed themselves to be struck down one by one when by united action they could so easily have saved themselves and saved the world from this catastrophe.

But, when I spoke a few minutes ago of Hitler's blood-lust and the hateful appetites which have impelled or lured him on his Russian adventure, I said there was one deeper motive behind his outrage. He wishes to destroy the Russian power because he hopes that if he succeeds in this he will be able to bring back the main strength of his army and air force from the East and hurl it upon this island, which he knows he must conquer or suffer the penalty of his crimes.

His invasion of Russia is no more than a prelude to an attempted invasion of the British Isles. He hopes, no doubt, that all this may be accomplished before the Winter comes and that he can overwhelm Great Britain before the fleets and air power of the United States will intervene. He hopes that he may once again repeat upon a greater scale than ever before that process of destroying his enemies one by one, by which he has so long thrived and prospered, and that then the scene will be clear for the final act, without which all his conquests would be in vain, namely, the subjugation of the Western Hemisphere to his will and to his system.

The Russian danger is therefore our danger and the danger of the United States just as the cause of any Russian fighting for his hearth and home is the cause of free men and free peoples in every quarter of the globe.

Let us learn the lessons already taught by such cruel experience. Let us redouble our exertions and strike with united strength while life and power remain."

Winston Churchill, *Address to the United States Congress*

[December 26, 1941, Washington]

Members of the Senate and of the House of Representatives of the United States, I feel greatly honored that you should have thus invited me to enter the United States Senate Chamber and address the representatives of both branches of Congress. The fact that my American forebears have for so many generations played their part in the life of the United States, and that here I am, an Englishman, welcomed in your midst, makes this experience one of the most moving and thrilling in my life, which is already long and has not been entirely uneventful. I wish indeed that my mother, whose memory I cherish, across the vale of years, could have been here to see. By the way, I cannot help reflecting that if my father had been American and my mother British instead of the other way around, I might have got here on my own. In that case this would not have been the first time you would have heard my voice. In that case I should not have needed any invitation. But if I had it is hardly likely that it would have been unanimous. So perhaps things are better as they are.

I may confess, however, that I do not feel quite like a fish out of water in a legislative assembly where English is spoken. I am a child of the House of Commons. I was brought up in my father's house to believe in democracy. "Trust the people." That was his message. I used to see him cheered at meetings and in the streets by crowds of workingmen way back in those aristocratic Victorian days when as Disraeli said "the world was for the few, and for the very few."

Therefore I have been in full harmony all my life with the tides which have flowed on both sides of the Atlantic against privilege and monopoly and I have steered confidently towards the Gettysburg ideal of government of the people, by the people, for the people.

I owe my advancement entirely to the House of Commons, whose servant I am. In my country as in yours public men are proud to be the servants of the State and would be ashamed to be its masters. The House of Commons, if they thought the people wanted it, could, by a simple vote, remove me from my office. But I am not worrying about it at all.

As a matter of fact I am sure they will approve very highly of my journey here, for which I obtained the King's permission, in order to meet the President of the United States and to arrange with him for all that mapping out of our military plans and for all those intimate meetings of the high officers of the armed services in both countries which are indispensable for the successful prosecution of the war.

I should like to say first of all how much I have been impressed and encouraged by the breadth of view and sense of proportion which I have found in all quarters over here to which I have had access. Anyone who did not understand the size and solidarity of the foundations of the United States, might easily have expected to find an excited, disturbed, self-cantered atmosphere, with all minds fixed upon the novel, startling, and painful episodes of sudden war as they hit America. After all, the United States have been attacked and set upon by three most powerfully armed dictator states, the greatest military power in Europe, the greatest military power in Asia-Japan, Germany and Italy have all declared and are making war upon you, and the quarrel is opened which can only end in their overthrow or yours.

But here in Washington in these memorable days I have

found an Olympian fortitude which, far from being based upon complacency, is only the mask of an inflexible purpose and the proof of a sure, well-grounded confidence in the final outcome. We in Britain had the same feeling in our darkest days. We too were sure that in the end all would be well.

You do not, I am certain, underrate the severity of the ordeal to which you and we have still to be subjected. The forces ranged against us are enormous. They are bitter, they are ruthless. The wicked men and their factions, who have launched their peoples on the path of war and conquest, know that they will be called to terrible account if they cannot beat down by force of arms the peoples they have assailed. They will stop at nothing. They have a vast accumulation of war weapons of all kinds. They have highly trained and disciplined armies, navies and air services. They have plans and designs which have long been contrived and matured. They will stop at nothing that violence or treachery can suggest.

It is quite true that on our side our resources in manpower and materials are far greater than theirs. But only a portion of your resources are as yet mobilized and developed, and we both of us have much to learn in the cruel art of war. We have therefore without doubt a time of tribulation before us. In this same time, some ground will be lost which it will be hard and costly to regain. Many disappointments and unpleasant surprises await us. Many of them will afflict us before the full marshalling of our latent and total power can be accomplished.

For the best part of twenty years the youth of Britain and America have been taught that war was evil, which is true, and that it would never come again, which has been proved false. For the best part of twenty years, the youth of Germany, of Japan and Italy, have been taught that aggressive war is the noblest duty of the citizen and that it should be begun as soon as the necessary weapons and organization have been made. We have performed the duties and tasks of peace. They have plotted and planned for war. This naturally has placed us, in Britain, and now places you in the United States at a disadvantage which only time, courage and untiring exertion can correct.

We have indeed to be thankful that so much time has been granted to us. If Germany had tried to invade the British Isles after the French collapse in June, 1940, and if Japan had declared war on the British Empire and the United States at about the same date, no one can say what disasters and agonies might not have been our lot. But now, at the end of December, 1941, our transformation from easy-going peace to total war efficiency has made very great progress.

The broad flow of munitions in Great Britain has already begun. Immense strides have been made in the conversion of American industry to military purposes. And now that the United States is at war, it is possible for orders to be given every day which in a year or eighteen months hence will produce results in war power beyond anything which has been seen or foreseen in the dictator states.

Provided that every effort is made, that nothing is kept back, that the whole manpower, brain power, virility, valor and civic virtue of the English-speaking world, with all its galaxy of loyal, friendly or associated communities and states-provided that is bent unremittingly to the simple but supreme task, I think it would be reasonable to hope that the end of 1942 will see us quite definitely in a better position than we are now. And that the year 1943 will enable us to assume the initiative upon an ample scale.

Some people may be startled or momentarily depressed when, like your President, I speak of a long and a hard war. Our peoples would rather know the truth, somber though it be. And after all, when we are doing the noblest work in the world, not only defending our hearths and homes, but the cause of freedom in every land, the question of whether deliverance comes in 1942 or 1943 or 1944, falls into its proper place in the grand proportions of human history. Sure I am that this day, now, we are the masters of our fate. That the task which has been set us is not above our strength. That its pangs and toils are not beyond our endurance. As long as we have faith in our cause, and an unconquerable willpower, salvation will not be denied us. In the words of the Psalmist: "He shall not be afraid of evil tidings. His heart is fixed, trusting in the Lord."

Not all the tidings will be evil. On the contrary, mighty strokes of war have already been dealt against the enemy-the glorious defense of their native soil by the Russian armies and people; wounds have been inflicted upon the Nazi tyranny and system which have bitten deep and will fester and inflame not only in the Nazi body but in the Nazi mind. The boastful Mussolini has crumpled already. He is now but a lackey and a serf, the merest utensil of his master's will. He has inflicted great suffering and wrong upon his own industrious people. He has been stripped of all his African empire. Abyssinia has been liberated. Our Armies of the East, which were so weak and ill-equipped at the moment of French desertion, now control all the regions from Teheran to Bengazi, and from Aleppo and Cyprus to the sources of the Nile.

For many months we devoted ourselves to preparing to take the offensive in Libya. The very considerable battle which has been proceeding there the last six weeks in the desert, has been most fiercely fought on both sides. Owing to the difficulties of supply upon the desert flank, we were never able to bring numerically equal forces to bear upon the enemy. Therefore we had to rely upon superiority in the numbers and qualities of tanks and aircraft, British and American. For the first time, aided by these-for the first time we have fought the enemy with equal weapons. For the first time we have made the Hun feel the sharp edge of those tools with which he has enslaved Europe. The armed forces of the enemy in Cyrenaica amounted to about 150,000 men, of whom a third were Germans. General Auchinleck set out to destroy totally that armed force, and I have every reason to believe that his aim will be fully accomplished. I am so glad to be able to place before you, members of the Senate and of the House of Representatives, at this moment when you are entering the war, the proof that with proper weapons and proper organization, we are able to beat the life out of the savage Nazi.

What Hitlerism is suffering in Libya is only a sample and a foretaste of what we have got to give him and his accomplices wherever this war should lead us in every quarter of the Globe.

There are good tidings also from blue water. The lifeline of supplies which joins our two nations across the ocean, without which all would fail,-that lifeline is flowing steadily and freely in spite of all that the enemy can do. It is a fact that the British Empire, which many thought eighteen months ago was broken and ruined, is now incomparably stronger and is growing stronger with every month.

Lastly, if you will forgive me for saying it, to me the best tidings of all-the United States, united as never before, has drawn the sword for freedom and cast away the scabbard.

All these tremendous facts have led the subjugated peoples of Europe to lift up their heads again in hope. They have put aside forever the shameful temptation of resigning themselves to the conqueror's will. Hope has returned to the hearts of scores of millions of men and women, and with that hope there burns the flame of anger against the brutal, corrupt invader. And still more fiercely burn the fires of hatred and contempt for the filthy Quislings whom he has suborned.

In a dozen famous ancient states, now prostrate under

the Nazi yoke, the masses of the people, all classes and creeds, await the hour of liberation when they too will once again be able to play their part and strike their blows like men. That hour will strike. And its solemn peal will proclaim that night is past and that the dawn has come.

The onslaught upon us, so long and so secretly planned by Japan, has presented both our countries with grievous problems for which we could not be fully prepared. If people ask me, as they have a right to ask me in England, "Why is it that you have not got an ample equipment of modern aircraft and army weapons of all kinds in Malaya and in the East Indies?"-I can only point to the victory General Auchinleck has gained in the Libyan campaign. Had we diverted and dispersed our gradually-growing resources between Libya and Malaya, we should have been found wanting in both theaters.

If the United States has been found at a disadvantage at various points in the Pacific Ocean, we know well that that is to no small extent because of the aid which you have been giving to us in munitions for the defense of the British Isles and for the Libyan campaign, and above all because of your help in the Battle of the Atlantic, upon which all depends and which has in consequence been successfully and prosperously maintained.

Of course, it would have been much better, I freely admit, if we had had enough resources of all kinds to be at full strength at all threatened points. But considering how slowly and reluctantly we brought ourselves to large-scale preparations, and how long these preparations take, we had no right to expect to be in such a fortunate position.

The choice of how to dispose of our hitherto limited resources had to be made by Britain in time of war, and by the United States in time of peace. And I believe that history will pronounce that upon the whole, and it is upon the whole that these matters must be judged, that the choice made was right. Now that we are together, now that we are linked in a righteous comrade-ship of arms, now that our two considerable nations, each in perfect unity, have joined all their life-energies in a common resolve-a new scene opens upon which a steady light will glow and brighten.

Many people have been astonished that Japan should in a single day have plunged into war against the United States and the British Empire. We all wonder why, if this dark design with its laborious and intricate preparations had been so long filling their secret minds, they did not choose our moment of weakness eighteen months ago. Viewed quite dispassionately, in spite of the losses we have suffered and the further punishment we shall have to take, it certainly appears an irrational act. It is of course only prudent to assume that they have made very careful calculations and think they see their way through. Nevertheless, there may be another explanation.

We know that for many years past the policy of Japan has been dominated by secret societies of subalterns and junior officers of the army and navy, who have enforced their will upon successive Japanese cabinets and parliaments by the assassination of any Japanese statesmen who opposed or who did not sufficiently further their aggressive policy. It may be that these societies, dazzled and dizzy with their own schemes of aggression and the prospect of early victories, have forced their country-against its better judgment-into war. They have certainly embarked upon a very considerable undertaking.

After the outrages they have committed upon us at Pearl Harbor, in the Pacific Islands, in the Philippines, in Malaya and the Dutch East Indies, they must now know that the stakes for which they have decided to play are mortal. When we look at the resources of the United States and the British Empire compared to those of Japan; when we remember those of China, which have so long valiantly withstood invasion and tyranny-and when also we observe the Russian menace which hangs over Japan-it becomes still more difficult to reconcile Japanese action with prudence or even with sanity. What kind of a people do they think we are? Is it possible that they do not realize that we shall never cease to persevere against them until they have been taught a lesson which they and the world will never forget?

Members of the Senate, and members of the House of Representatives, I will turn for one moment more from the turmoil and convulsions of the present to the broader spaces of the future. Here we are together, facing a group of mighty foes who seek our ruin. Here we are together, defending all that to free men is dear. Twice in a single generation the catastrophe of world war has fallen upon us. Twice in our lifetime has the long arm of fate reached out across the oceans to bring the United States into the forefront of the battle.

If we had kept together after the last war, if we had taken common measures for our safety, this renewal of the curse need never have fallen upon us. Do we not owe it to ourselves, to our children, to tormented mankind, to make sure that these catastrophes do not engulf us for the third time?

It has been proved that pestilences may break out in the Old World which carry their destructive ravages into the New World, from which, once they are afoot, the New World can not escape. Duty and prudence alike command first that the germ-centers of hatred and revenge should be constantly and vigilantly served and treated in good time, and that an adequate organization should be set up to make sure that the pestilence can be controlled at its earliest beginnings, before it spreads and rages throughout the entire earth.

Five or six years ago it would have been easy, without shedding a drop of blood, for the United States and Great Britain to have insisted on the fulfilment of the disarmament clauses of the treaties which Germany signed after the Great War. And that also would have been the opportunity for assuring to the Germans those materials-those raw ma-terials-which we declared in the Atlantic Charter should not be denied to any nation, victor or vanquished. The chance has passed, it is gone. Prodigious hammer-strokes have been needed to bring us together today.

If you will allow me to use other language, I will say that he must indeed have a blind soul who cannot see that some great purpose and design is being worked out here below of which we have the honor to be the faithful servants. It is not given to us to peer into the mysteries of the future. Still, I avow my hope and faith, sure and inviolate, that in the days to come the British and American peoples will, for their own safety and for the good of all, walk together in majesty, in justice and in peace."

Winston Churchill, *An Iron Curtain has descend*

[March 5, 1946, London]

NOTE This speech may be regarded as the most important Churchill delivered as Leader of the Opposition (1945-1951). It contains certain phrases- "the special relationship," "the sinews of peace" - which at once entered into general use, and which have survived. But it is the passage on "the iron curtain" which attracted immediate international attention, and had incalculable impact upon public opinion in the United States and in Western Europe. Russian historians date the beginning of the Cold War from this speech. In its phraseology, in its intricate drawing together of several themes to an electrifying climax- this speech may be regarded as a technical classic.

I am glad to come to Westminster College this afternoon, and am complimented that you should give me a degree. The name "Westminster" is somehow familiar to me.

I seem to have heard of it before. Indeed, it was at Westminster that I received a very large part of my education in politics, dialectic, rhetoric, and one or two other things. In fact we have both been educated at the same, or similar, or, at any rate, kindred establishments.

It is also an honour, perhaps almost unique, for a private visitor to be introduced to an academic audience by the President of the United States. Amid his heavy burdens, duties, and responsibilities-unsought but not recoiled from-the President has travelled a thousand miles to dignify and magnify our meeting here to-day and to give me an opportunity of addressing this kindred nation, as well as my own countrymen across the ocean, and perhaps some other countries too. The President has told you that it is his wish, as I am sure it is yours, that I should have full liberty to give my true and faithful counsel in these anxious and baffling times. I shall certainly avail myself of this freedom, and feel the more right to do so because any private ambitions I may have cherished in my younger days have been satisfied beyond my wildest dreams. Let me, however, make it clear that I have no official mission or status of any kind, and that I speak only for myself. There is nothing here but what you see.

I can therefore allow my mind, with the experience of a lifetime, to play over the problems which beset us on the morrow of our absolute victory in arms, and to try to make sure with what strength I have that what has been gained with so much sacrifice and suffering shall be preserved for the future glory and safety of mankind.

The United States stands at this time at the pinnacle of world power. It is a solemn moment for the American Democracy. For with primacy in power is also joined an awe inspiring accountability to the future. If you look around you, you must feel not only the sense of duty done but also you must feel anxiety lest you fall below the level of achievement. Opportunity is here now, clear and shining for both our countries. To reject it or ignore it or fritter it away will bring upon us all the long reproaches of the after-time. It is necessary that constancy of mind, persistency of purpose, and the grand simplicity of decision shall guide and rule the conduct of the English-speaking peoples in peace as they did in war. We must, and I believe we shall, prove ourselves equal to this severe requirement.

When American military men approach some serious situation they are wont to write at the head of their directive the words "over-all strategic concept." There is wisdom in this, as it leads to clarity of thought. What then is the over-all strategic concept which we should inscribe today? It is nothing less than the safety and welfare, the freedom and progress, of all the homes and families of all the men and women in all the lands. And here I speak particularly of the myriad cottage or apartment homes where the wage-earner strives amid the accidents and difficulties of life to guard his wife and children from privation and bring the family up in the fear of the Lord, or upon ethical conceptions which often play their potent part.

To give security to these countless homes, they must be shielded from the two giant marauders, war and tyranny. We all know the frightful disturbances in which the ordinary family is plunged when the curse of war swoops down upon the bread-winner and those for whom he works and contrives. The awful ruin of Europe, with all its vanished glories, and of large parts of Asia glares us in the eyes. When the designs of wicked men or the aggressive urge of mighty States dissolve over large areas the frame of civilised society, humble folk are confronted with difficulties with which they cannot cope. For them all is distorted, all is broken, even ground to pulp.

When I stand here this quiet afternoon I shudder to visualise what is actually happening to millions now and what is going to happen in this period when famine stalks the earth. None can compute what has been called "the unestimated sum of human pain." Our supreme task and duty is to guard the homes of the common people from the horrors and miseries of another war. We are all agreed on that.

Our American military colleagues, after having proclaimed their "over-all strategic concept" and computed available resources, always proceed to the next step-namely, the method. Here again there is widespread agreement. A world organisation has already been erected for the prime purpose of preventing war, UNO, the successor of the League of Nations, with the decisive addition of the United States and all that that means, is already at work. We must make sure that its work is fruitful, that it is a reality and not a sham, that it is a force for action, and not merely a frothing of words, that it is a true temple of peace in which the shields of many nations can some day be hung up, and not merely a cockpit in a Tower of Babel. Before we cast away the solid assurances of national armaments for self-preservation we must be certain that our temple is built, not upon shifting sands or quagmires, but upon the rock. Anyone can see with his eyes open that our path will be difficult and also long, but if we persevere together as we did in the two world wars-though not, alas, in the interval between them-I cannot doubt that we shall achieve our common purpose in the end.

I have, however, a definite and practical proposal to make for action. Courts and magistrates may be set up but they cannot function without sheriffs and constables. The United Nations Organisation must immediately begin to be equipped with an international armed force. In such a matter we can only go step by step, but we must begin now. I propose that each of the Powers and States should be invited to delegate a certain number of air squadrons to the service of the world organisation. These squadrons would be trained and prepared in their own countries, but would move around in rotation from one country to another. They would wear the uniform of their own countries but with different badges. They would not be required to act against their own nation, but in other respects they would be directed by the world organisation. This might be started on a modest scale and would grow as confidence grew. I wished to see this done after the First World War, and I devoutly trust it may be done forthwith.

It would nevertheless be wrong and imprudent to entrust the secret knowledge or experience of the atomic bomb, which the United States, Great Britain, and Canada now share, to the world organisation, while it is still in its infancy. It would be criminal madness to cast it adrift in this still agitated and un-united world. No one in any country has slept less well in their beds because this knowledge and the method and the raw materials to apply it, are at present largely retained in American hands. I do not believe we should all have slept so soundly had the positions been reversed and if some Communist or neo-Fascist State monopolised for the time being these dread agencies. The fear of them alone might easily have been used to enforce totalitarian systems upon the free democratic world, with consequences appalling to human imagination. God has willed that this shall not be and we have at least a breathing space to set our house in order before this peril has to be encountered: and even then, if no effort is spared, we should still possess So formidable a superiority as to impose effective deterrents upon its employment, or threat of employment, by others. Ultimately, when the essential brotherhood of man is truly embodied and expressed in a world organisation with all the necessary practical safeguards to make it effective, these powers would naturally be confided to that world organisation.

Now I come to the second danger of these two marauders which threatens the cottage, the home, and the ordinary people-namely, tyranny. We cannot be blind to the fact that the liberties enjoyed by individual citizens throughout the British Empire are not valid in a considerable number of countries, some of which are very powerful. In these States control is enforced upon the common people by various kinds of all-embracing police governments. The power of the State is exercised without restraint, either by dictators or by compact oligarchies operating through a privileged party and a political police. It is not our duty at this time when difficulties are so numerous to interfere forcibly in the internal affairs of countries which we have not conquered in war. But we must never cease to proclaim in fearless tones the great principles of freedom and the rights of man which are the joint inheritance of the English-speaking world and which through Magna Carta, the Bill of Rights, the Habeas

Corpus, trial by jury, and the English common law find their most famous expression in the American Declaration of Independence.

All this means that the people of any country have the right, and should have the power by constitutional action, by free unfettered elections, with secret ballot, to choose or change the character or form of government under which they dwell; that freedom of speech and thought should reign; that courts of justice, independent of the executive, unbiased by any party, should administer laws which have received the broad assent of large majorities or are consecrated by time and custom. Here are the title deeds of freedom which should lie in every cottage home. Here is the message of the British and American peoples to mankind. Let us preach what we practise – let us practise what we preach.

I have now stated the two great dangers which menace the homes of the people: War and Tyranny. I have not yet spoken of poverty and privation which are in many cases the prevailing anxiety. But if the dangers of war and tyranny are removed, there is no doubt that science and co-operation can bring in the next few years to the world, certainly in the next few decades newly taught in the sharpening school of war, an expansion of material well-being beyond anything that has yet occurred in human experience. Now, at this sad and breathless moment, we are plunged in the hunger and distress which are the aftermath of our stupendous struggle; but this will pass and may pass quickly, and there is no reason except human folly or sub-human crime which should deny to all the nations the inauguration and enjoyment of an age of plenty. I have often used words which I learned fifty years ago from a great Irish-American orator, a friend of mine, Mr. Bourke Cockran. "There is enough for all. The earth is a generous mother; she will provide in plentiful abundance food for all her children if they will but cultivate her soil in justice and in peace." So far I feel that we are in full agreement.

Now, while still pursuing the method of realising our overall strategic concept, I come to the crux of what I have travelled here to Say. Neither the sure prevention of war, nor the continuous rise of world organisation will be gained without what I have called the fraternal association of the English-speaking peoples. This means a special relationship between the British Commonwealth and Empire and the United States. This is no time for generalities, and I will venture to be precise. Fraternal association requires not only the growing friendship and mutual understanding between our two vast but kindred Systems of society, but the continuance of the intimate relationship between our military advisers, leading to common study of potential dangers, the similarity of weapons and manuals of instructions, and to the interchange of officers and cadets at technical colleges. It should carry with it the continuance of the present facilities for mutual security by the joint use of all Naval and Air Force bases in the possession of either country all over the world. This would perhaps double the mobility of the American Navy and Air Force. It would greatly expand that of the British Empire Forces and it might well lead, if and as the world calms down, to important financial savings. Already we use together a large number of islands; more may well be entrusted to our joint care in the near future.

The United States has already a Permanent Defence Agreement with the Dominion of Canada, which is so devotedly attached to the British Commonwealth and Empire. This Agreement is more effective than many of those which have often been made under formal alliances. This principle should be extended to all British Commonwealths with full reciprocity. Thus, whatever happens, and thus only, shall we be secure ourselves and able to work together for the high and simple causes that are dear to us and bode no ill to any.

Eventually there may come-I feel eventually there will come-the principle of common citizenship, but that we may be content to leave to destiny, whose outstretched arm many of us can already clearly see.

There is however an important question we must ask ourselves. Would a special relationship between the United States and the British Commonwealth be inconsistent with our over-riding loyalties to the World Organisation? I reply that, on the contrary, it is probably the only means by which that organisation will achieve its full stature and strength. There are already the special United States relations with Canada which I have just mentioned, and there are the special relations between the United States and the South American Republics. We British have our twenty years Treaty of Collaboration and Mutual Assistance with Soviet Russia. I agree with Mr. Bevin, the Foreign Secretary of Great Britain, that it might well be a fifty years Treaty so far as we are concerned. We aim at nothing but mutual assistance and collaboration. The British have an alliance with Portugal unbroken since 1384, and which produced fruitful results at critical moments in the late war. None of these clash with the general interest of a world agreement, or a world organisation; on the contrary they help it. "In my father's house are many mansions." Special associations between members of the United Nations which have no aggressive point against any other country, which harbour no design incompatible with the Charter of the United Nations, far from being harmful, are beneficial and, as I believe, indispensable.

I spoke earlier of the Temple of Peace. Workmen from all countries must build that temple. If two of the workmen know each other particularly well and are old friends, if their families are inter-mingled, and if they have "faith in each other's purpose, hope in each other's future and charity towards each other's shortcomings"-to quote some good words I read here the other day-why cannot they work together at the common task as friends and partners? Why cannot they share their tools and thus increase each other's working powers? Indeed they must do so or else the temple may not be built, or, being built, it may collapse, and we shall all be proved again unteachable and have to go and try to learn again for a third time in a school of war, incomparably more rigorous than that from which we have just been released. The dark ages may return, the Stone Age may return on the gleaming wings of science, and what might now shower immeasurable material blessings upon mankind, may even bring about its total destruction. Beware, I say; time may be short. Do not let us take the course of allowing events to drift along until it is too late. If there is to be a fraternal association of the kind I have described, with all the extra strength and security which both our countries can derive from it, let us make sure that that great fact is known to the world, and that it plays its part in steadying and stabilising the foundations of peace. There is the path of wisdom. Prevention is better than cure.

A shadow has fallen upon the scenes so lately lighted by the Allied victory. Nobody knows what Soviet Russia and its Communist international organisation intends to do in the immediate future, or what are the limits, if any, to their expansive and proselytising tendencies. I have a strong admiration and regard for the valiant Russian people and for my wartime comrade, Marshal Stalin. There is deep sympathy and goodwill in Britain-and I doubt not here also-towards the peoples of all the Russias and a resolve to persevere through many differences and rebuffs in establishing lasting friendships. We understand the Russian need to be secure on her western frontiers by the removal of all possibility of German aggression. We welcome Russia to her rightful place among the leading nations of the world. We welcome her flag upon the seas. Above all, we welcome constant, frequent and growing contacts between the Russian people and our own people on both sides of the Atlantic. It is my duty however, for I am sure you would wish me to state the facts as I see them to you, to place before you certain facts about the present position in Europe.

From Stettin in the Baltic to Trieste in the Adriatic, an iron curtain has descended across the Continent. Behind that line lie all the capitals of the ancient states of Central and Eastern Europe. Warsaw, Berlin, Prague, Vienna, Budapest, Belgrade, Bucharest and Sofia, all these famous cities and the populations around them lie in what I must call the Soviet sphere, and all are subject in one form or another, not only to Soviet influence but to a very high and, in many cases, increasing measure of control from Moscow. Athens alone-Greece with its immortal glories-is free to decide its future at an election under British, American and French observation. The Russian-dominated Polish Government has been encouraged to make enormous and wrongful inroads upon Germany, and mass expulsions of millions of Germans on a scale grievous and undreamed-of are now taking place. The Communist parties, which were very small in all these Eastern States of Europe, have been raised to pre-eminence and power far beyond their numbers and are seeking everywhere to obtain totalitarian control. Police governments are prevailing in nearly every case, and so far, except in Czechoslovakia, there is no true democracy.

Turkey and Persia are both profoundly alarmed and disturbed at the claims which are being made upon them and at the pressure being exerted by the Moscow Government. An attempt is being made by the Russians in Berlin to build up a quasi-Communist party in their zone of Occupied Germany by showing special favours to groups of left-wing German leaders. At the end of the fighting last June, the American and British Armies withdrew westwards, in accordance with an earlier agreement, to a depth at some points of 150 miles upon a front of nearly four hundred miles, in order to allow our Russian allies to occupy this vast expanse of territory which the Western Democracies had conquered.

If now the Soviet Government tries, by separate action, to build up a pro-Communist Germany in their areas, this will cause new serious difficulties in the British and American zones, and will give the defeated Germans the power of putting themselves up to auction between the Soviets and the Western Democracies. Whatever conclusions may be drawn from these facts-and facts they are-this is certainly not the Liberated Europe we fought to build up. Nor is it one which contains the essentials of permanent peace.

The safety of the world requires a new unity in Europe, from which no nation should be permanently outcast. It is from the quarrels of the strong parent races in Europe that the world wars we have witnessed, or which occurred in former times, have sprung. Twice in our own lifetime we have seen the United States, against their wishes and their traditions, against arguments, the force of which it is impossible not to comprehend, drawn by irresistible forces, into these wars in time to secure the victory of the good cause, but only after frightful slaughter and devastation had occurred. Twice the United States has had to send several millions of its young men across the Atlantic to find the war; but now war can find any nation, wherever it may dwell between dusk and dawn. Surely we should work with conscious purpose for a grand pacification of Europe, within the structure of the United Nations and in accordance with its Charter. That I feel is an open cause of policy of very great importance.

In front of the iron curtain which lies across Europe are other causes for anxiety. In Italy the Communist Party is seriously hampered by having to Support the Communist-trained Marshal Tito's claims to former Italian territory at the head of the Adriatic. Nevertheless the future of Italy hangs in the balance. Again one cannot imagine a regenerated Europe without a strong France. All my public life I have worked for a Strong France and I never lost faith in her destiny, even in the darkest hours. I will not lose faith now. However, in a great number of countries, far from the Russian frontiers and throughout the world, Communist fifth columns are established and work in complete unity and absolute obedience to the directions they receive from the Communist centre. Except in the British Commonwealth and in the United States where Communism is in its infancy, the Communist parties or fifth columns constitute a growing challenge and peril to Christian civilisation. These are sombre facts for anyone to have to recite on the morrow of a victory gained by so much splendid comradeship in arms and in the cause of freedom and democracy; but we should be most unwise not to face them squarely while time remains.

The outlook is also anxious in the Far East and especially in Manchuria. The Agreement which was made at Yalta, to which I was a party, was extremely favourable to Soviet Russia, but it was made at a time when no one could say that the German war might not extend all through the summer and autumn of 1945 and when the Japanese war was expected to last for a further 18 months from the end of the German war. In this country you are all so well-informed about the Far East, and such devoted friends of China, that I do not need to expatiate on the situation there.

I have felt bound to portray the shadow which, alike in the west and in the east, falls upon the world. I was a high minister at the time of the Versailles Treaty and a close friend of Mr. Lloyd-George, who was the head of the British delegation at Versailles. I did not myself agree with many things that were done, but I have a very Strong impression in my mind of that situation, and I find it painful to contrast it with that which prevails now. In those days there were high hopes and unbounded confidence that the wars were over, and that the League of Nations would become all-powerful. I do not see or feel that same confidence or even the same hopes in the haggard world at the present time.

On the other hand I repulse the idea that a new war is inevitable; still more that it is imminent. It is because I am sure that our fortunes are still in our own hands and that we hold the power to save the future, that I feel the duty to speak out now that I have the occasion and the opportunity to do so. I do not believe that Soviet Russia desires war. What they desire is the fruits of war and the indefinite expansion of their power and doctrines. But what we have to consider here to-day while time remains, is the permanent prevention of war and the establishment of conditions of freedom and democracy as rapidly as possible in all countries. Our difficulties and dangers will not be removed by closing our eyes to them. They will not be removed by mere waiting to see what happens; nor will they be removed by a policy of appeasement. What is needed is a settlement, and the longer this is delayed, the more difficult it will be and the greater our dangers will become.

From what I have seen of our Russian friends and Allies during the war, I am convinced that there is nothing they admire so much as strength, and there is nothing for which they have less respect than for weakness, especially military weakness. For that reason the old doctrine of a balance of power is unsound. We cannot afford, if we can help it, to work on narrow margins, offering temptations to a trial of strength. If the Western Democracies stand together in strict adherence to the principles of the United Nations Charter, their influence for furthering those principles will be immense and no one is likely to molest them. If however they become divided or falter in their duty and if these all-important years are allowed to slip away then indeed catastrophe may overwhelm us all.

Last time I saw it all coming and cried aloud to my own fellow-countrymen and to the world, but no one paid any attention. Up till the year 1933 or even 1935, Germany might have been saved from the awful fate which has overtaken her and we might all have been spared the miseries Hitler let loose upon mankind. There never was a war in all history easier to prevent by timely action than the one which has just desolated such great areas of the globe. It could have been prevented in my belief without the firing of a single shot, and Germany might be powerful, prosperous and honoured to-day; but no one would listen and one by one we were all sucked into the awful whirlpool. We surely must not let that happen again. This can only be achieved by reaching now, in 1946, a good understanding on all points with Russia under the general authority of the United Nations Organisation and by the maintenance of that good understanding through many peaceful years, by the world instrument, supported by the whole strength of the English-speaking world and all its connections. There is the solution which I respectfully offer to you in this Address to which I have given the title "The Sinews of Peace."

Let no man underrate the abiding power of the British Empire and Commonwealth. Because you see the 46 millions in our island harassed about their food supply, of which they only grow one half, even in war-time, or because we have difficulty in restarting our industries and export trade after six years of passionate war effort, do not suppose that we shall not come through these dark years of privation as we have come through the glorious years of agony, or that half a century from now, you will not see 70 or 80 millions of Britons spread about the world and united in defence of our traditions, our way of life, and of the world causes which you and we espouse. If the population of the English-speaking Commonwealths be added to that of the United States with all that such co-operation implies in the air, on the sea, all over the globe and in science and in industry, and in moral force, there will be no quivering, precarious balance of power to offer its temptation to ambition or adventure. On the contrary, there will be an overwhelming assurance of security. If we adhere faithfully to the Charter of the United Nations and walk forward in sedate and sober strength seeking no one's land or treasure, seeking to lay no arbitrary control upon the thoughts of men; if all British moral and material forces and convictions are joined with your own in fraternal association, the high-roads of the future will be clear, not only for us but for all, not only for our time, but for a century to come."

Edward VIII, *Farewell Address*

[December 11, 1936, London]

NOTE Edward VIII (1894-1972) became King of England upon the death of his father, George V, on January 20, 1936. Nearly 42-years-old and a bachelor, Edward then made known his desire to marry an American woman named Wallis Warfield Simpson, whom he had known since 1931. He sought the approval of his family, the Church of England, and the political establishment to marry her, but met with strong opposition. She had been married twice before and her second divorce was still pending.
The love affair and possible royal marriage resulted in sensational newspaper headlines around the world and created a storm of controversy, but did not sway Edward. On December 10, 1936, King Edward VIII submitted his abdication and it was endorsed by Parliament the next day. He thus became the only British monarch ever to resign voluntarily. His younger brother, George VI, took the throne and immediately gave Edward the title, Duke of Windsor. The Duke and Simpson were married in France on June 3, 1937 and lived in Paris.
The speech below is from December 11th, when Edward publicly announced his decision via radio to a worldwide audience.

At long last I am able to say a few words of my own. I have never wanted to withhold anything, but until now it has not been constitutionally possible for me to speak.

A few hours ago I discharged my last duty as King and Emperor, and now that I have been succeeded by my brother, the Duke of York, my first words must be to declare my allegiance to him. This I do with all my heart.

You all know the reasons which have impelled me to renounce the throne. But I want you to understand that in making up my mind I did not forget the country or the empire, which, as Prince of Wales and lately as King, I have for twenty-five years tried to serve.

But you must believe me when I tell you that I have found it impossible to carry the heavy burden of responsibility and to discharge my duties as King as I would wish to do without the help and support of the woman I love.

And I want you to know that the decision I have made has been mine and mine alone. This was a thing I had to judge entirely for myself. The other person most nearly concerned has tried up to the last to persuade me to take a different course.

I have made this, the most serious decision of my life, only upon the single thought of what would, in the end, be best for all.

This decision has been made less difficult to me by the sure knowledge that my brother, with his long training in the public affairs of this country and with his fine qualities, will be able to take my place forthwith without interruption or injury to the life and progress of the empire. And he has one matchless blessing, enjoyed by so many of you, and not bestowed on me – a happy home with his wife and children.

During these hard days I have been comforted by her majesty my mother and by my family. The ministers of the crown, and in particular, Mr. Baldwin, the Prime Minister, have always treated me with full consideration. There has never been any constitutional difference between me and them, and between me and Parliament. Bred in the constitutional tradition by my father, I should never have allowed any such issue to arise.

Ever since I was Prince of Wales, and later on when I occupied the throne, I have been treated with the greatest kindness by all classes of the people wherever I have lived or journeyed throughout the empire. For that I am very grateful.

I now quit altogether public affairs and I lay down my burden. It may be some time before I return to my native land, but I shall always follow the fortunes of the British race and empire with profound interest, and if at any time in the future I can be found of service to his majesty in a private station, I shall not fail.

And now, we all have a new King. I wish him and you, his people, happiness and prosperity with all my heart. God bless you all! God save the King!

Elizabeth II, *We Will Meet Again*

[April 5, 2020, Windsor]

NOTE In a rare speech, Her Majesty Queen Elizabeth II (1926-2022) delivers a special message to the United Kingdom and the Commonwealth during the coronavirus pandemic; and echoes the words of Vera Lynn's wartime song, 'We will meet again.'

I'm speaking to you at what I know is an increasingly challenging time, a time of disruption in the life of our country, a disruption that has brought grief to some, financial difficulties to many, and enormous changes to the daily lives of us all. I want to thank everyone on the NHS frontline, as well as care workers and those carrying out essential roles who selflessly continue their day-to-day duties outside the home in support of us all. I'm sure the nation will join me in assuring you that what you do is appreciated, and every hour of your hard work brings us closer to a return to more normal times. I also want to thank those of you who are staying at home, thereby helping to protect the vulnerable, and sparing many families the pain already felt by those who have lost loved ones.

Together we are tackling this disease, and I want to reassure you that if we remain united and resolute, then we will overcome it. I hope in the years to come everyone will be able to take pride in how they responded to this challenge, and those who come after us will say the Britons of this generation were as strong as any, that the attributes of self-discipline, of quiet, good-humoured resolve, and of fellow feeling still characterise this country. The pride in who we are is not a part of our past, it defines our present and our future.

The moments when the United Kingdom has come together to applaud its care and essential workers will be remembered as an expression of our national spirit, and its symbol will be the rainbows drawn by children. Across the Commonwealth and around the world, we have seen heartwarming stories of people coming together to help others, be it through delivering food parcels and medicines, checking on neighbours, or converting businesses to help the relief effort. And though self-isolating may at times be hard, many people of all faiths and of none are discovering that it presents an opportunity to slow down, pause and reflect in prayer or meditation.

It reminds me of the very first broadcast I made in 1940, helped by my sister. We as children spoke from here at Windsor to children who had been evacuated from their homes and sent away for their own safety. Today, once again, many will feel a painful sense of separation from their loved ones, but now as then, we know deep down that it is the right thing to do. While we have faced challenges before, this one is different. This time we join with all nations across the globe in a common endeavour. Using the great advances of science and our instinctive compassion to heal, we will succeed, and that success will belong to every one of us. We should take comfort that while we may have more still to endure, better days will return. We will be with our friends again. We will be with our families again. We will meet again. But for now, I send my thanks and warmest good wishes to you all.

William Faulkner, *Acceptance Speech for the Nobel Prize in Literature*

[December 10, 1950, Stockholm]

NOTE William Faulkner (1897-1962), born in New Albany, Mississippi, was the son of a family proud of their prominent role in the history of the south. His major work began with the publication of *The Sound and the Fury* in 1929. *As I Lay Dying* (1930), *Sanctuary* (1931), *Light in August* (1932), *Absalom, Absalom!* (1936) and *The Wild Palms* (1939) are the key works of his great creative period leading up to *Intruder in the Dust* (1948). Faulkner was awarded the Nobel Prize for Literature in 1949 and the Pulitzer Prize for *The Reivers* just before his death in July 1962.

I feel that this award was not made to me as a man, but to my work – a life's work in the agony and sweat of the human spirit, not for glory and least of all for profit, but to create out of the materials of the human spirit something which did not exist before. So this award is only mine in trust. It will not be difficult to find a dedication for the money part of it commensurate with the purpose and significance of its origin. But I would like to do the same with the acclaim too, by using this moment as a pinnacle from which I might be listened to by the young men and women already dedicated to the same anguish and travail, among whom is already that one who will some day stand here where I am standing.

Our tragedy today is a general and universal physical fear so long sustained by now that we can even bear it. There are no longer problems of the spirit. There is only the question: When will I be blown up? Because of this, the young man or woman writing today has forgotten the problems of the human heart in conflict with itself which alone can make good writing because only that is worth writing about, worth the agony and the sweat.

He must learn them again. He must teach himself that the basest of all things is to be afraid; and, teaching himself that, forget it forever, leaving no room in his workshop for anything but the old verities and truths of the heart, the old universal truths lacking which any story is ephemeral and doomed – love and honor and pity and pride and compassion and sacrifice. Until he does so, he labors under a curse. He writes not of love but of lust, of defeats in which nobody loses anything of value, of victories without hope and, worst of all, without pity or compassion. His griefs grieve on no universal bones, leaving no scars. He writes not of the heart but of the glands.

Until he relearns these things, he will write as though he stood among and watched the end of man. I decline to accept the end of man. It is easy enough to say that man is immortal simply because he will endure: that when the last ding-dong of doom has clanged and faded from the last worthless rock hanging tideless in the last red and dying evening, that even then there will still be one more sound: that of his puny inexhaustible voice, still talking. I refuse to accept this. I believe that man will not merely endure: he will prevail. He is immortal, not because he alone among creatures has an inexhaustible voice, but because he has a soul, a spirit capable of compassion and sacrifice and endurance. The poet's, the writer's, duty is to write about these things. It is his privilege to help man endure by lifting his heart, by reminding him of the courage and honor and hope and pride and compassion and pity and sacrifice which have been the glory of his past. The poet's voice need not merely be the record of man, it can be one of the props, the pillars to help him endure and prevail.

George VI, *With God's Help, We Shall Prevail*

[September 3, 1939, London]

NOTE This is the King's Speech which George VI broadcast to his people in Britain, and throughout the Empire, immediately after Britain's Declaration of War against Germany on September 3, 1939. Soon after the King delivered this speech, other Dominion governments also declared war against Germany. The impact of the war upon the King, George VI, was incalculable. He died, at the age of 56, in February of 1952. He was succeeded by his daughter, Elizabeth II. The much-loved monarch struggled with public speaking. The story of how he overcame his stammer is the subject of an award-winning film, "The King's Speech."

In this grave hour, perhaps the most fateful in our history, I send to every household of my peoples, both at home and overseas, this message, spoken with the same depth of feeling for each one of you as if I were able to cross your threshold and speak to you myself.

For the second time in the lives of most of us we are at war.

Over and over again we have tried to find a peaceful way out of the differences between ourselves and those who are now our enemies. But it has been in vain. We have been forced into a conflict. For we are called, with our allies, to meet the challenge of a principle which, if it were to prevail, would be fatal to any civilized order in the world.

It is the principle which permits a state, in the selfish pursuit of power, to disregard its treaties and its solemn pledges; which sanctions the use of force, or threat of force, against the sovereignty and independence of other states.

Such a principle, stripped of all disguise, is surely the mere primitive doctrine that "might is right"; and if this principle were established throughout the world, the freedom of our own country and of the whole of the British Commonwealth of Nations would be in danger. But far more than this – the peoples of the world would be kept in the bondage of fear, and all hopes of settled peace and of the security of justice and liberty among nations would be ended.

This is the ultimate issue which confronts us. For the sake of all that we ourselves hold dear, and of the world order and peace, it is unthinkable that we should refuse to meet the challenge.

It is to this high purpose that I now call my people at home and my peoples across the seas, who will make our cause their own. I ask them to stand calm and firm and united in this time of trial. The task will be hard. There may be dark days ahead, and war can no longer be confined to the battlefield. But we can only do the right as we see the right, and reverently commit our cause to God.

If one and all we keep resolutely faithful to it, ready for whatever service or sacrifice it may demand, then, with God's help, we shall prevail.

May He bless and keep us all.

Ernest Hemingway, *Acceptance Speech for the Nobel Prize in Literature*

[October 1954, Oslo]

NOTE Ernest Hemingway (1899-1961) was born in Illinois and began his career as a reporter before enlisting as an ambulance driver at the Italian front in World War I. Known first for short stories, he sealed his literary reputation with his novels, including *The Sun Also Rises, A Farewell to Arms, For Whom the Bell Tolls*, and *The Old Man and the Sea*. Winner of the Nobel Prize in Literature in 1954.

Having no facility for speech-making and no command of oratory nor any domination of rhetoric, I wish to thank the administrators of the generosity of Alfred Nobel for this Prize.

No writer who knows the great writers who did not receive the Prize can accept it other than with humility. There is no need to list these writers. Everyone here may make his own list according to his knowledge and his conscience.

It would be impossible for me to ask the Ambassador of my country to read a speech in which a writer said all of the things which are in his heart. Things may not be immediately discernible in what a man writes, and in this sometimes he is fortunate; but eventually they are quite clear and by these and the degree of alchemy that he possesses he will endure or be forgotten.

Writing, at its best, is a lonely life. Organizations for writers palliate the writer's loneliness but I doubt if they improve his writing. He grows in public stature as he sheds his loneliness and often his work deteriorates. For he does his work alone and if he is a good enough writer he must face eternity, or the lack of it, each day.

For a true writer each book should be a new beginning where he tries again for something that is beyond attainment. He should always try for something that has never been done or that others have tried and failed. Then sometimes, with great luck, he will succeed.

How simple the writing of literature would be if it were only necessary to write in another way what has been well written. It is because we have had such great writers in the past that a writer is driven far out past where he can go, out to where no one can help him.

I have spoken too long for a writer. A writer should write what he has to say and not speak it. Again I thank you.

Adolf Hitler, *First Radio Address*

[February 1, 1933, Berlin]

NOTE On February 1, 1933, two days after he was appointed chancellor, Adolf Hitler (1889-1945) spoke over the radio to the German people about his vision for the future of the country.

Over fourteen years have passed since that unhappy day when the German people, blinded by promises made by those at home and abroad, forgot the highest values of our past, of the Reich, of its honor and its freedom, and thereby lost everything. Since those days of treason, the Almighty has withdrawn his blessing from our nation. Discord and hatred have moved in. Filled with the deepest distress, millions of the best German men and women from all walks of life see the unity of the nation disintegrating in a welter of egotistical political opinions, economic interests, and ideological conflicts.

As so often in our history, Germany, since the day the revolution broke out, presents a picture of heartbreaking disunity. We did not receive the equality and fraternity which was promised us; instead we lost our freedom. The breakdown of the unity of mind and will of our nation at home was followed by the collapse of its political position abroad.

We have a burning conviction that the German people in 1914 went into the great battle without any thought of personal guilt [for the start of the war] and weighed down only by the burden of having to defend the Reich from attack, to defend the freedom and material existence of the

German people. In the appalling fate that has dogged us since November 1918 we see only the consequence of our inward collapse. But the rest of the world is no less shaken by great crises. The historical balance of power, which at one time contributed not a little to the understanding of the necessity for solidarity among the nations, with all the economic advantages resulting therefrom, has been destroyed.

The delusion that some are the conquerors and others the conquered destroys the trust between nations and thereby also destroys the world economy. But the misery of our people is terrible! The starving industrial proletariat [working class] have become unemployed in their millions, while the whole middle and artisan class have been made paupers. If the German farmer also is involved in this collapse we shall be faced with a catastrophe of vast proportions. For in that case, there will collapse not only a Reich, but also a 2000-year-old inheritance of the highest works of human culture and civilization.

All around us are symptoms portending this breakdown. With an unparalleled effort of will and of brute force the Communist method of madness is trying as a last resort to poison and undermine an inwardly shaken and uprooted nation. They seek to drive it towards an epoch which would correspond even less to the promises of the Communist speakers of today than did the epoch now drawing to a close to the promises of the same emissaries in November 1918.

Starting with the family, and including all notions of honor and loyalty, nation and fatherland, culture and economy, even the eternal foundations of our morals and our faith—nothing is spared by this negative, totally destructive ideology... One year of Bolshevism would destroy Germany. The richest and most beautiful areas of world civilization would be transformed into chaos and a heap of ruins. Even the misery of the past decade and a half could not be compared with the affliction of a Europe in whose heart the red flag of destruction had been planted. The thousands of injured, the countless dead which this battle has already cost Germany may stand as a presage of the disaster.

In these hours of overwhelming concern for the existence and the future of the German nation, the venerable World War leader [President Paul von Hindenburg] appealed to us men of the nationalist parties and associations to fight under him again as once we did at the front, but now loyally united for the salvation of the Reich at home. The revered President of the Reich having with such generosity joined hands with us in a common pledge, we nationalist leaders would vow before God, our conscience and our people that we shall doggedly and with determination fulfill the mission entrusted to us as the National Government.

It is an appalling inheritance which we are taking over.

The task before us is the most difficult which has faced German statesmen in living memory. But we all have unbounded confidence, for we believe in our nation and in its eternal values. Farmers, workers, and the middle class must unite to contribute the bricks wherewith to build the new Reich.

The National Government will therefore regard it as its first and supreme task to restore to the German people unity of mind and will. It will preserve and defend the foundations on which the strength of our nation rests. It will take under its firm protection Christianity as the basis of our morality, and the family as the nucleus of our nation and our state. Standing above estates [groups that make up society's social hierarchy] and classes, it will bring back to our people the consciousness of its racial and political unity and the obligations arising therefrom. It wishes to base the education of German youth on respect for our great past and pride in our old traditions [...] Germany must not and will not sink into Communist anarchy.

In place of our turbulent instincts, it will make national

discipline govern our life. In the process it will take into account all the institutions which are the true safeguards of the strength and power of our nation.

The National Government will carry out the great task of reorganizing our national economy with two big Four-Year Plans:

Saving the German farmer so that the nation's food supply and thus the life of the nation shall be secured.

Saving the German worker by a massive and comprehensive attack on unemployment.

In fourteen years the November parties have ruined the German farmer. In fourteen years they created an army of millions of unemployed. The National Government will carry out the following plan with iron resolution and dogged perseverance. Within four years the German farmer must be saved from pauperism. Within four years unemployment must be completely overcome [...] Our concern to provide daily bread will be equally a concern for the fulfillment of the responsibilities of society to those who are old and sick. The best safeguard against any experiment which might endanger the currency lies in economical administration, the promotion of work, and the preservation of agriculture, as well as in the use of individual initiative.

In foreign policy, the National Government will see its highest mission in the preservation of our people's right to an independent life and in the regaining thereby of their freedom. The determination of this Government to put an end to the chaotic conditions in Germany is a step towards the integration into the community of nations of a state having equal status and therefore equal rights with the rest. In so doing, the Government is aware of its great obligation to support, as the Government of a free and equal nation, that maintenance and consolidation of peace which the world needs today more than ever before. May all others understand our position and so help to ensure that this sincere desire for the welfare of Europe and of the whole world shall find fulfillment.

Despite our love for our Army as the bearer of our arms and the symbol of our great past, we should be happy if the world, by restricting its armaments, made unnecessary any increase in our own weapons.

But if Germany is to experience this political and economic revival and conscientiously to fulfill its duties towards other nations, a decisive act is required: We must overcome the demoralization of Germany by the Communists.

We, men of this Government, feel responsible to German history for the reconstitution of a proper national body so that we may finally overcome the insanity of class and class warfare. We do not recognize classes, but only the German people, its millions of farmers, citizens and workers who together will either overcome this time of distress or succumb to it.

With resolution and fidelity to our oath, seeing the powerlessness of the present Reichstag to shoulder the task we advocate, we wish to commit it to the whole German people.

We therefore appeal now to the German people to sign this act of mutual reconciliation. The Government of the National Uprising [the Nazi-led government] wishes to set to work, and it will work. It has not for fourteen years brought ruin to the German nation; it wants to lead it to the summit. It is determined to make amends in four years for the liabilities of fourteen years. But it cannot subject the work of reconstruction to the will of those who were responsible for the breakdown.

The Marxist parties [political parties including the Social Democrats] and their followers had fourteen years to prove their abilities. The result is a heap of ruins. Now, German people, give us four years and then judge us.

Let us begin, loyal to the command of the Field-Marshal.

May Almighty God favor our work, shape our will in the right way, bless our vision and bless us with the trust of our people. We have no desire to fight for ourselves; only for Germany.

Steve Jobs, *Stay Hungry, Stay Foolish*

[June 12, 2005, Stanford]

NOTE Steve Jobs (1955-2011) was a charismatic pioneer of the personal computer era. With Steve Wozniak, Jobs founded Apple Inc. in 1976 and transformed the company into a world leader in telecommunications.
Steve Jobs delivered this commencement address at Stanford University. It has become one of the most famous speeches of recent decades.

I am honored to be with you today at your commencement from one of the finest universities in the world. I never graduated from college. Truth be told, this is the closest I've ever gotten to a college graduation. Today I want to tell you three stories from my life. That's it. No big deal. Just three stories.

The first story is about connecting the dots.

I dropped out of Reed College after the first 6 months, but then stayed around as a drop-in for another 18 months or so before I really quit. So why did I drop out?

It started before I was born. My biological mother was a young, unwed college graduate student, and she decided to put me up for adoption. She felt very strongly that I should be adopted by college graduates, so everything was all set for me to be adopted at birth by a lawyer and his wife. Except that when I popped out they decided at the last minute that they really wanted a girl. So my parents, who were on a waiting list, got a call in the middle of the night asking: "We have an unexpected baby boy; do you want him?" They said: "Of course." My biological mother later found out that my mother had never graduated from college and that my father had never graduated from high school. She refused to sign the final adoption papers. She only relented a few months later when my parents promised that I would someday go to college.

And 17 years later I did go to college. But I naively chose a college that was almost as expensive as Stanford, and all of my working-class parents' savings were being spent on my college tuition. After six months, I couldn't see the value in it. I had no idea what I wanted to do with my life and no idea how college was going to help me figure it out. And here I was spending all of the money my parents had saved their entire life. So I decided to drop out and trust that it would all work out OK. It was pretty scary at the time, but looking back it was one of the best decisions I ever made. The minute I dropped out I could stop taking the required classes that didn't interest me, and begin dropping in on the ones that looked interesting.

It wasn't all romantic. I didn't have a dorm room, so I slept on the floor in friends' rooms, I returned coke bottles for the 5¢ deposits to buy food with, and I would walk the 7 miles across town every Sunday night to get one good meal a week at the Hare Krishna temple. I loved it. And much of what I stumbled into by following my curiosity and intuition turned out to be priceless later on. Let me give you one example:

Reed College at that time offered perhaps the best calligraphy instruction in the country. Throughout the campus every poster, every label on every drawer, was beautifully hand calligraphed. Because I had dropped out and didn't have to take the normal classes, I decided to take a calligraphy class to learn how to do this. I learned about serif and san serif typefaces, about varying the amount of space between different letter combinations, about what makes great typography great. It was beautiful, historical, artistically subtle in a way that science can't capture, and I found it fascinating.

None of this had even a hope of any practical application in my life. But ten years later, when we were designing the first Macintosh computer, it all came back to me. And we designed it all into the Mac. It was the first computer with beautiful typography. If I had never dropped in on that single course in college, the Mac would have never had multiple typefaces or proportionally spaced fonts. And since Windows just copied the Mac, it's likely that no personal computer would have them. If I had never dropped out, I would have never dropped in on this calligraphy class, and personal computers might not have the wonderful typography that they do. Of course it was impossible to connect the dots looking forward when I was in college. But it was very, very clear looking backwards ten years later.

Again, you can't connect the dots looking forward; you can only connect them looking backwards. So you have to trust that the dots will somehow connect in your future. You have to trust in something – your gut, destiny, life, karma, whatever. This approach has never let me down, and it has made all the difference in my life.

My second story is about love and loss.

I was lucky – I found what I loved to do early in life. Woz and I started Apple in my parents garage when I was 20. We worked hard, and in 10 years Apple had grown from just the two of us in a garage into a $2 billion company with over 4000 employees. We had just released our finest creation – the Macintosh – a year earlier, and I had just turned 30. And then I got fired. How can you get fired from a company you started? Well, as Apple grew we hired someone who I thought was very talented to run the company with me, and for the first year or so things went well. But then our visions of the future began to diverge and eventually we had a falling out. When we did, our Board of Directors sided with him. So at 30 I was out. And very publicly out. What had been the focus of my entire adult life was gone, and it was devastating.

I really didn't know what to do for a few months. I felt that I had let the previous generation of entrepreneurs down – that I had dropped the baton as it was being passed to me. I met with David Packard and Bob Noyce and tried to apologize for screwing up so badly. I was a very public failure, and I even thought about running away from the valley. But something slowly began to dawn on me – I still loved what I did. The turn of events at Apple had not changed that one bit. I had been rejected, but I was still in love. And so I decided to start over.

I didn't see it then, but it turned out that getting fired from Apple was the best thing that could have ever happened to me. The heaviness of being successful was replaced by the lightness of being a beginner again, less sure about everything. It freed me to enter one of the most creative periods of my life.

During the next five years, I started a company named NeXT, another company named Pixar, and fell in love with an amazing woman who would become my wife. Pixar went on to create the worlds first computer animated feature film, Toy Story, and is now the most successful animation studio in the world. In a remarkable turn of events, Apple bought NeXT, I returned to Apple, and the technology we developed at NeXT is at the heart of Apple's current renaissance. And Laurene and I have a wonderful family together.

I'm pretty sure none of this would have happened if I hadn't been fired from Apple. It was awful tasting medicine, but I guess the patient needed it. Sometimes life hits you in the head with a brick. Don't lose faith. I'm convinced that the only thing that kept me going was that I loved what I did. You've got to find what you love. And that is as true for your work as it is for your lovers. Your work is going to fill a large part of your life, and the only way to be truly satisfied is to do what you believe is great work. And the only way to do great work is to love what you do. If you haven't found it yet, keep looking. Don't settle. As with all matters of the heart, you'll know when you find it. And, like any great relationship, it just gets better and better as the years roll on. So keep looking until you find it. Don't settle.

My third story is about death.

When I was 17, I read a quote that went something like: "If you live each day as if it was your last, someday you'll most certainly be right." It made an impression on me, and since then, for the past 33 years, I have looked in the mirror every morning and asked myself: "If today were the last day of my life, would I want to do what I am about to do today?" And whenever the answer has been "No" for too many days in a row, I know I need to change something.

Remembering that I'll be dead soon is the most important tool I've ever encountered to help me make the big choices in life. Because almost everything – all external expectations, all pride, all fear of embarrassment or failure – these things just fall away in the face of death, leaving only what is truly important. Remembering that you are going to die is the best way I know to avoid the trap of thinking you have something to lose. You are already naked. There is no reason not to follow your heart.

About a year ago I was diagnosed with cancer. I had a scan at 7:30 in the morning, and it clearly showed a tumor on my pancreas. I didn't even know what a pancreas was. The doctors told me this was almost certainly a type of cancer that is incurable, and that I should expect to live no longer than three to six months. My doctor advised me to go home and get my affairs in order, which is doctor's code for prepare to die. It means to try to tell your kids everything you thought you'd have the next 10 years to tell them in just a few months. It means to make sure everything is buttoned up so that it will be as easy as possible for your family. It means to say your goodbyes.

I lived with that diagnosis all day. Later that evening I had a biopsy, where they stuck an endoscope down my throat, through my stomach and into my intestines, put a needle into my pancreas and got a few cells from the tumor. I was sedated, but my wife, who was there, told me that when they viewed the cells under a microscope the doctors started crying because it turned out to be a very rare form of pancreatic cancer that is curable with surgery. I had the surgery and I'm fine now.

This was the closest I've been to facing death, and I hope it's the closest I get for a few more decades. Having lived through it, I can now say this to you with a bit more certainty than when death was a useful but purely intellectual concept: No one wants to die. Even people who want to go to heaven don't want to die to get there. And yet death is the destination we all share.

No one has ever escaped it. And that is as it should be, because Death is very likely the single best invention of Life. It is Life's change agent. It clears out the old to make way for the new. Right now the new is you, but someday not too long from now, you will gradually become the old and be cleared away. Sorry to be so dramatic, but it is quite true.

Your time is limited, so don't waste it living someone else's life. Don't be trapped by dogma – which is living with the results of other people's thinking. Don't let the noise of others' opinions drown out your own inner voice. And most important, have the courage to follow your heart and intuition. They somehow already know what you truly want to become. Everything else is secondary.

When I was young, there was an amazing publication called The Whole Earth Catalog, which was one of the bibles of my generation. It was created by a fellow named Stewart Brand not far from here in Menlo Park, and he brought it to life with his poetic touch. This was in the late 1960's, before personal computers and desktop publishing, so it was all made with typewriters, scissors, and polaroid cameras. It was sort of like Google in paperback form, 35 years before Google came along: it was idealistic, and overflowing with neat tools and great notions.

Stewart and his team put out several issues of The Whole Earth Catalog, and then when it had run its course, they put out a final issue. It was the mid-1970s, and I was your age. On the back cover of their final issue was a photograph of an early morning country road, the kind you might find yourself hitchhiking on if you were so adventurous. Beneath it were the words: "Stay Hungry. Stay Foolish." It was their farewell message as they signed off.

Stay Hungry. Stay Foolish. And I have always wished that for myself. And now, as you graduate to begin anew, I wish that for you. Stay Hungry. Stay Foolish.

Thank you all very much.

John F. Kennedy, *Presidential Inaugural Address*

[January 20, 1961, Washington]

NOTE John Fitzgerald Kennedy (1917-1963), often referred to by his initials JFK and also known as Jack Kennedy, was an American politician who served as the 35th president of the United States (the youngest) from 1961 until his assassination near the end of his third year in office.
John Fitzgerald Kennedy is remembered for his moving and inspirational oratory. Unlike Ronald Reagan or Margaret Thatcher who were conviction speakers with ideological messages, John Kennedy's platform was more inspiring, pragmatic and liberal. His Inaugural Address and his speech at the Berlin Wall are examples of this.

We observe today not a victory of party, but a celebration of freedom – symbolizing an end, as well as a beginning – signifying renewal, as well as change. For I have sworn before you and Almighty God the same solemn oath our forebears prescribed nearly a century and three-quarters ago.

The world is very different now. For man holds in his mortal hands the power to abolish all forms of human poverty and all forms of human life. And yet the same revolutionary beliefs for which our forebears fought are still at issue around the globe – the belief that the rights of man come not from the generosity of the state, but from the hand of God.

We dare not forget today that we are the heirs of that first revolution.

Let the word go forth from this time and place, to friend and foe alike, that the torch has been passed to a new generation of Americans – born in this century, tempered by war, disciplined by a hard and bitter peace, proud of our ancient heritage, and unwilling to witness or permit the slow undoing of those human rights to which this nation has always been committed, and to which we are committed today at home and around the world.

Let every nation know, whether it wishes us well or ill, that we shall pay any price, bear any burden, meet any hardship, support any friend, oppose any foe, to assure the survival and the success of liberty.

This much we pledge – and more.

To those old allies whose cultural and spiritual origins we share, we pledge the loyalty of faithful friends. United there is little we cannot do in a host of cooperative ventures. Divided there is little we can do – for we dare not meet a powerful challenge at odds and split asunder.

To those new states whom we welcome to the ranks of the free, we pledge our word that one form of colonial control shall not have passed away merely to be replaced by a far more iron tyranny. We shall not always expect to find them supporting our view. But we shall always hope to find them strongly supporting their own freedom – and to remember that, in the past, those who foolishly sought power by riding the back of the tiger ended up inside.

To those people in the huts and villages of half the globe struggling to break the bonds of mass misery, we pledge our best efforts to help them help themselves, for whatever period is required – not because the Communists may be doing it, not because we seek their votes, but because it is right. If a free society cannot help the many who are poor, it cannot save the few who are rich.

To our sister republics south of our border, we offer a special pledge: to convert our good words into good deeds, in a new alliance for progress, to assist free men and free governments in casting off the chains of poverty. But this peaceful revolution of hope cannot become the prey of hostile powers. Let all our neighbors know that we shall join with them to oppose aggression or subversion anywhere in the Americas. And let every other power know that this hemisphere intends to remain the master of its own house.

To that world assembly of sovereign states, the United Nations, our last best hope in an age where the instruments of war have far outpaced the instruments of peace, we renew our pledge of support — to prevent it from becoming merely a forum for invective, to strengthen its shield of the new and the weak, and to enlarge the area in which its writ may run.

Finally, to those nations who would make themselves our adversary, we offer not a pledge but a request: that both sides begin anew the quest for peace, before the dark powers of destruction unleashed by science engulf all humanity in planned or accidental self-destruction.

We dare not tempt them with weakness. For only when our arms are sufficient beyond doubt can we be certain beyond doubt that they will never be employed.

But neither can two great and powerful groups of nations take comfort from our present course — both sides overburdened by the cost of modern weapons, both rightly alarmed by the steady spread of the deadly atom, yet both racing to alter that uncertain balance of terror that stays the hand of mankind's final war.

So let us begin anew — remembering on both sides that civility is not a sign of weakness, and sincerity is always subject to proof. Let us never negotiate out of fear, but let us never fear to negotiate.

Let both sides explore what problems unite us instead of belaboring those problems which divide us.

Let both sides, for the first time, formulate serious and precise proposals for the inspection and control of arms, and bring the absolute power to destroy other nations under the absolute control of all nations.

Let both sides seek to invoke the wonders of science instead of its terrors. Together let us explore the stars, conquer the deserts, eradicate disease, tap the ocean depths, and encourage the arts and commerce.

Let both sides unite to heed, in all corners of the earth, the command of Isaiah – to "undo the heavy burdens, and [to] let the oppressed go free."

And, if a beachhead of cooperation may push back the jungle of suspicion, let both sides join in creating a new endeavor – not a new balance of power, but a new world of law – where the strong are just, and the weak secure, and the peace preserved.

All this will not be finished in the first one hundred days. Nor will it be finished in the first one thousand days; nor in the life of this Administration; nor even perhaps in our lifetime on this planet. But let us begin.

In your hands, my fellow citizens, more than mine, will rest the final success or failure of our course. Since this country was founded, each generation of Americans has been summoned to give testimony to its national loyalty. The graves of young Americans who answered the call to service surround the globe.

Now the trumpet summons us again – not as a call to bear arms, though arms we need – not as a call to battle, though embattled we are – but a call to bear the burden of a long twilight struggle, year in and year out, "rejoicing in hope; patient in tribulation," a struggle against the common enemies of man: tyranny, poverty, disease, and war itself.

Can we forge against these enemies a grand and global alliance, North and South, East and West, that can assure a more fruitful life for all mankind? Will you join in that historic effort?

In the long history of the world, only a few generations have been granted the role of defending freedom in its hour of maximum danger. I do not shrink from this responsibility – I welcome it. I do not believe that any of us would exchange places with any other people or any other generation.

The energy, the faith, the devotion which we bring to this endeavor will light our country and all who serve it. And the glow from that fire can truly light the world.

And so, my fellow Americans, ask not what your country can do for you; ask what you can do for your country.

My fellow citizens of the world, ask not what America will do for you, but what together we can do for the freedom of man.

Finally, whether you are citizens of America or citizens of the world, ask of us here the same high standards of strength and sacrifice which we ask of you. With a good conscience our only sure reward, with history the final judge of our deeds, let us go forth to lead the land we love, asking His blessing and His help, but knowing that here on earth God's work must truly be our own.

John F. Kennedy, *Cuban Missile Crisis Address to the Nation*

[October 22, 1962, Washington]

NOTE In October 1962, an American U-2 spy plane secretly photographed nuclear missile sites being built by the Soviet Union on the island of Cuba. President Kennedy did not want the Soviet Union and Cuba to know that he had discovered the missiles. He met in secret with his advisors for several days to discuss the problem. After many long and difficult meetings, Kennedy decided to place a naval blockade, or a ring of ships, around Cuba. The aim of this "quarantine," as he called it, was to prevent the Soviets from bringing in more military supplies. He demanded the removal of the missiles already there and the destruction of the sites. On October 22, President Kennedy spoke to the nation about the crisis in a televised address. In his speech he reports the establishment of offensive missile sites presumably intended to launch a nuclear offensive against Western nations.

This Government, as promised, has maintained the closest surveillance of the Soviet military buildup on the island of Cuba. Within the past week, unmistakable evidence has established the fact that a series of offensive missile sites is now in preparation on that imprisoned island. The purpose of these bases can be none other than to provide a nuclear strike capability against the Western Hemisphere.

Upon receiving the first preliminary hard information of this nature last Tuesday morning at 9 A.M., I directed that our surveillance be stepped up. And having now confirmed and completed our evaluation of the evidence and our decision on a course of action, this Government feels obliged to report this new crisis to you in fullest detail.

The characteristics of these new missile sites indicate two

distinct types of installations. Several of them include medium range ballistic missiles, capable of carrying a nuclear warhead for a distance of more than 1,000 nautical miles. Each of these missiles, in short, is capable of striking Washington, D. C., the Panama Canal, Cape Canaveral, Mexico City, or any other city in the southeastern part of the United States, in Central America, or in the Caribbean area.

Additional sites not yet completed appear to be designed for intermediate range ballistic missiles – capable of traveling more than twice as far – and thus capable of striking most of the major cities in the Western Hemisphere, ranging as far north as Hudson Bay, Canada, and as far south as Lima, Peru. In addition, jet bombers, capable of carrying nuclear weapons, are now being uncrated and assembled in Cuba, while the necessary air bases are being prepared.

This urgent transformation of Cuba into an important strategic base – by the presence of these large, long-range, and clearly offensive weapons of sudden mass destruction – constitutes an explicit threat to the peace and security of all the Americas, in flagrant and deliberate defiance of the Rio Pact of 1947, the traditions of this nation and hemisphere, the joint resolution of the 87th Congress, the Charter of the United Nations, and my own public warnings to the Soviets on September 4 and 13. This action also contradicts the repeated assurances of Soviet spokesmen, both publicly and privately delivered, that the arms buildup in Cuba would retain its original defensive character, and that the Soviet Union had no need or desire to station strategic missiles. on the territory of any other nation.

The size of this undertaking makes clear that it has been planned for some months. Yet, only last month, after I had made clear the distinction between any introduction of ground-to-ground missiles and the existence of defensive antiaircraft missiles, the Soviet Government publicly stated on September 11 that, and I quote, "the armaments and military equipment sent to Cuba are designed exclusively for defensive purposes," that there is, and I quote the Soviet Government, "there is no need for the Soviet Government to shift its weapons for a retaliatory blow to any other country, for instance Cuba," and that, and I quote their government, "the Soviet Union has so powerful rockets to carry these nuclear warheads that there is no need to search for sites for them beyond the boundaries of the Soviet Union."

That statement was false. Only last Thursday, as evidence of this rapid offensive buildup was already in my hand, Soviet Foreign Minister Gromyko told me in my office that he was instructed to make it clear once again, as he said his government had already done, that Soviet assistance to Cuba, and I quote, "pursued solely the purpose of contributing to the defense capabilities of Cuba," that, and I quote him, "training by Soviet specialists of Cuban nationals in handling defensive armaments was by no means offensive, and if it were otherwise," Mr. Gromyko went on, "the Soviet Government would never become involved in rendering such assistance."

That statement also was false. Neither the United States of America nor the world community of nations can tolerate deliberate deception and offensive threats on the part of any nation, large or small. We no longer live in a world where only the actual firing of weapons represents a sufficient challenge to a nation's security to constitute maximum peril. Nuclear weapons are so destructive and ballistic missiles are so swift, that any substantially increased possibility of their use or any sudden change in their deployment may well be regarded as a definite threat to peace.

For many years, both the Soviet Union and the United States, recognizing this fact, have deployed strategic nuclear weapons with great care, never upsetting the precarious status quo which insured that these weapons would not be used in the absence of some vital challenge. Our own strategic missiles have never been transferred to the territory of any other nation under a cloak of secrecy and deception; and our history – unlike that of the Soviets since the end of World War II – demonstrates that we have no desire to dominate or conquer any other nation or impose our system upon its people. Nevertheless, American citizens have become adjusted to living daily on the bull's-eye of Soviet missiles located inside the U.S.S.R. or in submarines.

In that sense, missiles in Cuba add to an already clear and present danger – although it should be noted the nations of Latin America have never previously been subjected to a potential nuclear threat. But this secret, swift, extraordinary buildup of Communist missiles – in an area well known to have a special and historical relationship to the United States and the nations of the Western Hemisphere, in violation of Soviet assurances, and in defiance of American and hemispheric policy – this sudden, clandestine decision to station strategic weapons for the first time outside of Soviet soil – is a deliberately provocative and unjustified change in the status quo which cannot be accepted by this country, if our courage and our commitments are ever to be trusted again by either friend or foe.

The 1930's taught us a clear lesson: aggressive conduct, if allowed to go unchecked and unchallenged, ultimately leads to war. This nation is opposed to war. We are also true to our word. Our unswerving objective, therefore, must be to prevent the use of these missiles against this or any other country, and to secure their withdrawal or elimination from the Western Hemisphere.

Our policy has been one of patience and restraint, as befits a peaceful and powerful nation which leads a worldwide alliance. We have been determined not to be diverted from our central concerns by mere irritants and fanatics. But now further action is required, and it is under way; and these actions may only be the beginning. We will not prematurely or unnecessarily risk the costs of worldwide nuclear war in which even the fruits of victory would be ashes in our mouth; but neither will we shrink from that risk at any time it must be faced.

Acting, therefore, in the defense of our own security and of the entire Western Hemisphere, and under the authority entrusted to me by the Constitution as endorsed by the Resolution of the Congress, I have directed that the following initial steps be taken immediately:

First: To halt this offensive buildup a strict quarantine on all offensive military equipment under shipment to Cuba is being initiated. All ships of any kind bound for Cuba from whatever nation or port will, if found to contain cargoes of offensive weapons, be turned back. This quarantine will be extended, if needed, to other types of cargo and carriers. We are not at this time, however, denying the necessities of life as the Soviets attempted to do in their Berlin blockade of 1948.

Second: I have directed the continued and increased close surveillance of Cuba and its military buildup. The foreign ministers of the OAS [Organization of American States], in their communiqué' of October 6, rejected secrecy on such matters in this hemisphere. Should these offensive military preparations continue, thus increasing the threat to the hemisphere, further action will be justified. I have directed the Armed Forces to prepare for any eventualities; and I trust that in the interest of both the Cuban people and the Soviet technicians at the sites, the hazards to all concerned of continuing this threat will be recognized.

Third: It shall be the policy of this nation to regard any nuclear missile launched from Cuba against any nation in the Western Hemisphere as an attack by the Soviet Union on the United States, requiring a full retaliatory response upon the Soviet Union.

Fourth: As a necessary military precaution, I have

reinforced our base at Guantanamo, evacuated today the dependents of our personnel there, and ordered additional military units to be on a standby alert basis.

Fifth: We are calling tonight for an immediate meeting of the Organization of Consultation under the Organization of American States, to consider this threat to hemispheric security and to invoke articles 6 and 8 of the Rio Treaty in support of all necessary action. The United Nations Charter allows for regional security arrangements, and the nations of this hemisphere decided long ago against the military presence of outside powers. Our other allies around the world have also been alerted.

Sixth: Under the Charter of the United Nations, we are asking tonight that an emergency meeting of the Security Council be convoked without delay to take action against this latest Soviet threat to world peace. Our resolution will call for the prompt dismantling and withdrawal of all offensive weapons in Cuba, under the supervision of U.N. observers, before the quarantine can be lifted.

Seventh and finally: I call upon Chairman Khrushchev to halt and eliminate this clandestine, reckless, and provocative threat to world peace and to stable relations between our two nations. I call upon him further to abandon this course of world domination, and to join in an historic effort to end the perilous arms race and to transform the history of man. He has an opportunity now to move the world back from the abyss of destruction by returning to his government's own words that it had no need to station missiles outside its own territory, and withdrawing these weapons from Cuba by refraining from any action which will widen or deepen the present crisis, and then by participating in a search for peaceful and permanent solutions.

This nation is prepared to present its case against the Soviet threat to peace, and our own proposals for a peaceful world, at any time and in any forum – in the OAS, in the

United Nations, or in any other meeting that could be useful – without limiting our freedom of action. We have in the past made strenuous efforts to limit the spread of nuclear weapons. We have proposed the elimination of all arms and military bases in a fair and effective disarmament treaty. We are prepared to discuss new proposals for the removal of tensions on both sides, including the possibilities of a genuinely independent Cuba, free to determine its own destiny. We have no wish to war with the Soviet Union – for we are a peaceful people who desire to live in peace with all other peoples.

But it is difficult to settle or even discuss these problems in an atmosphere of intimidation. That is why this latest Soviet threat – or any other threat which is made either independently or in response to our actions this week– must and will be met with determination. Any hostile move anywhere in the world against the safety and freedom of peoples to whom we are committed, including in particular the brave people of West Berlin, will be met by whatever action is needed.

Finally, I want to say a few words to the captive people of Cuba, to whom this speech is being directly carried by special radio facilities. I speak to you as a friend, as one who knows of your deep attachment to your fatherland, as one who shares your aspirations for liberty and justice for all. And I have watched and the American people have watched with deep sorrow how your nationalist revolution was betrayed – and how your fatherland fell under foreign domination. Now your leaders are no longer Cuban leaders inspired by Cuban ideals. They are puppets and agents of an international conspiracy which has turned Cuba against your friends and neighbors in the Americas, and turned it into the first Latin American country to become a target for nuclear war – the first Latin American country to have these weapons on its soil.

These new weapons are not in your interest. They contribute nothing to your peace and well-being. They can only undermine it. But this country has no wish to cause you to suffer or to impose any system upon you. We know that your lives and land are being used as pawns by those who deny your freedom. Many times in the past, the Cuban people have risen to throw out tyrants who destroyed their liberty. And I have no doubt that most Cubans today look forward to the time when they will be truly free – free from foreign domination, free to choose their own leaders, free to select their own system, free to own their own land, free to speak and write and worship without fear or degradation. And then shall Cuba be welcomed back to the society of free nations and to the associations of this hemisphere.

My fellow citizens, let no one doubt that this is a difficult and dangerous effort on which we have set out. No one can foresee precisely what course it will take or what costs or casualties will be incurred. Many months of sacrifice and self-discipline lie ahead – months in which both our patience and our will will be tested, months in which many threats and denunciations will keep us aware of our dangers. But the greatest danger of all would be to do nothing.

The path we have chosen for the present is full of hazards, as all paths are; but it is the one most consistent with our character and courage as a nation and our commitments around the world. The cost of freedom is always high, but Americans have always paid it. And one path we shall never choose, and that is the path of surrender or submission.

Our goal is not the victory of might, but the vindication of right; not peace at the expense of freedom, but both peace and freedom, here in this hemisphere, and, we hope, around the world. God willing, that goal will be achieved.

Thank you and good night.

John F. Kennedy, *Ich bin ein Berliner*

[June 26, 1963, Berlin]

NOTE "Ich bin ein Berliner" is a speech given in West Berlin. Twenty-two months earlier, East Germany had erected the Berlin Wall to prevent mass emigration to West Berlin. The speech was aimed as much at the Soviet Union as it was at West Berliners. It is one of the best-known speeches of the Cold War and among the most famous anti-communist speeches.

I am proud to come to this city as the guest of your distinguished Mayor, who has symbolized throughout the world the fighting spirit of West Berlin. And I am proud to visit the Federal Republic with your distinguished Chancellor who for so many years has committed Germany to democracy and freedom and progress, and to come here in the company of my fellow American, General Clay, who has been in this city during its great moments of crisis and will come again if ever needed.

Two thousand years ago the proudest boast was "civis Romanus sum". Today, in the world of freedom, the proudest boast is "Ich bin ein Berliner".

I appreciate my interpreter translating my German!

There are many people in the world who really don't understand, or say they don't, what is the great issue between the free world and the Communist world. Let them come to Berlin. There are some who say that communism is the wave of the future. Let them come to Berlin. And there are some who say in Europe and elsewhere we can work with the Communists. Let them come to Berlin. And there are even a few who say that it is true that communism is an evil system, but it permits us to make economic progress. Lass' sie nach Berlin kommen. Let them come to Berlin.

Freedom has many difficulties and democracy is not perfect, but we have never had to put a wall up to keep our people in, to prevent them from leaving us. I want to say, on behalf of my countrymen, who live many miles away on the other side of the Atlantic, who are far distant from you, that they take the greatest pride that they have been able to share with you, even from a distance, the story of the last 18 years. I know of no town, no city, that has been besieged for 18 years that still lives with the vitality and the force, and the hope and the determination of the city of West Berlin. While the wall is the most obvious and vivid demonstration of the failures of the Communist system, for all the world to see, we take no satisfaction in it, for it is, as your Mayor has said, an offense not only against history but an offense against humanity, separating families, dividing husbands and wives and brothers and sisters, and dividing a people who wish to be joined together.

What is true of this city is true of Germany – real, lasting peace in Europe can never be assured as long as one German out of four is denied the elementary right of free men, and that is to make a free choice. In 18 years of peace and good faith, this generation of Germans has earned the right to be free, including the right to unite their families and their nation in lasting peace, with good will to all people. You live in a defended island of freedom, but your life is part of the main. So let me ask you as I close, to lift your eyes beyond the dangers of today, to the hopes of tomorrow, beyond the freedom merely of this city of Berlin, or your country of Germany, to the advance of freedom everywhere, beyond the wall to the day of peace with justice, beyond yourselves and ourselves to all mankind.

Freedom is indivisible, and when one man is enslaved, all are not free. When all are free, then we can look forward to that day when this city will be joined as one and this country and this great Continent of Europe in a peaceful and hopeful globe. When that day finally comes, as it will, the people of West Berlin can take sober satisfaction in the fact that they were in the front lines for almost two decades.

All free men, wherever they may live, are citizens of Berlin, and, therefore, as a free man, I take pride in the words "Ich bin ein Berliner".

Martin L. King, Jr., *I Have a Dream*

[August 28, 1963, Washington]

NOTE Martin Luther King, Jr. (1929-1968) was a Baptist minister and social activist who led the civil rights movement in the United States from the mid-1950s until his death by assassination in 1968. His leadership was fundamental to that movement's success in ending the legal segregation of African Americans in the South and other parts of the United States. King rose to national prominence as head of the Southern Christian Leadership Conference, which promoted nonviolent tactics, such as the massive March on Washington (1963), to achieve civil rights. "I Have a Dream" is a public speech that was delivered during the March on Washington for Jobs and Freedom on August 28, 1963. In the speech, King called for civil and economic rights and an end to racism in the United States. Delivered to over 250,000 civil rights supporters from the steps of the Lincoln Memorial in Washington, D.C., the speech was a defining moment of the civil rights movement and among the most iconic speeches in American history.

I am happy to join with you today in what will go down in history as the greatest demonstration for freedom in the history of our nation.

Five score years ago, a great American, in whose symbolic shadow we stand today, signed the Emancipation Proclamation. This momentous decree came as a great beacon light of hope to millions of Negro slaves who had been seared in the flames of withering injustice. It came as a joyous daybreak to end the long night of their captivity.

But one hundred years later, the Negro still is not free. One hundred years later, the life of the Negro is still sadly crippled by the manacles of segregation and the chains of discrimination. One hundred years later, the Negro lives on a lonely island of poverty in the midst of a vast ocean of material prosperity. One hundred years later, the Negro is still languished in the corners of American society and finds himself an exile in his own land. And so we've come here today to dramatize a shameful condition.

In a sense we've come to our nation's capital to cash a check. When the architects of our republic wrote the magnificent words of the Constitution and the Declaration of Independence, they were signing a promissory note to which every American was to fall heir. This note was a promise that all men, yes, black men as well as white men, would be guaranteed the "unalienable Rights" of "Life, Liberty and the pursuit of Happiness." It is obvious today that America has defaulted on this promissory note, insofar as her citizens of color are concerned. Instead of honoring this sacred obligation, America has given the Negro people a bad check, a check which has come back marked "insufficient funds."

But we refuse to believe that the bank of justice is bankrupt. We refuse to believe that there are insufficient funds in the great vaults of opportunity of this nation. And so, we've come to cash this check, a check that will give us upon demand the riches of freedom and the security of justice.

We have also come to this hallowed spot to remind America of the fierce urgency of Now. This is no time to engage in the luxury of cooling off or to take the tranquilizing drug of gradualism. Now is the time to make real the promises of democracy. Now is the time to rise from the dark and desolate valley of segregation to the sunlit path of racial justice. Now is the time to lift our nation from the quicksands of racial injustice to the solid rock of brotherhood. Now is the time to make justice a reality for all of God's children.

It would be fatal for the nation to overlook the urgency

of the moment. This sweltering summer of the Negro's legitimate discontent will not pass until there is an invigorating autumn of freedom and equality. Nineteen sixty-three is not an end, but a beginning. And those who hope that the Negro needed to blow off steam and will now be content will have a rude awakening if the nation returns to business as usual. And there will be neither rest nor tranquility in America until the Negro is granted his citizenship rights. The whirlwinds of revolt will continue to shake the foundations of our nation until the bright day of justice emerges.

But there is something that I must say to my people, who stand on the warm threshold which leads into the palace of justice: In the process of gaining our rightful place, we must not be guilty of wrongful deeds. Let us not seek to satisfy our thirst for freedom by drinking from the cup of bitterness and hatred. We must forever conduct our struggle on the high plane of dignity and discipline. We must not allow our creative protest to degenerate into physical violence. Again and again, we must rise to the majestic heights of meeting physical force with soul force.

The marvelous new militancy which has engulfed the Negro community must not lead us to a distrust of all white people, for many of our white brothers, as evidenced by their presence here today, have come to realize that their destiny is tied up with our destiny. And they have come to realize that their freedom is inextricably bound to our freedom.

We cannot walk alone.

And as we walk, we must make the pledge that we shall always march ahead.

We cannot turn back.

There are those who are asking the devotees of civil rights, "When will you be satisfied?" We can never be satisfied as long as the Negro is the victim of the unspeakable horrors of police brutality. We can never be satisfied as long as our bodies, heavy with the fatigue of travel, cannot gain lodging in the motels of the highways and the hotels of the cities. We cannot be satisfied as long as the negro's basic mobility is from a smaller ghetto to a larger one. We can never be satisfied as long as our children are stripped of their self-hood and robbed of their dignity by signs stating: "For Whites Only." We cannot be satisfied as long as a Negro in Mississippi cannot vote and a Negro in New York believes he has nothing for which to vote. No, no, we are not satisfied, and we will not be satisfied until "justice rolls down like waters, and righteousness like a mighty stream."

I am not unmindful that some of you have come here out of great trials and tribulations. Some of you have come fresh from narrow jail cells. And some of you have come from areas where your quest – quest for freedom left you battered by the storms of persecution and staggered by the winds of police brutality. You have been the veterans of creative suffering. Continue to work with the faith that unearned suffering is redemptive. Go back to Mississippi, go back to Alabama, go back to South Carolina, go back to Georgia, go back to Louisiana, go back to the slums and ghettos of our northern cities, knowing that somehow this situation can and will be changed.

Let us not wallow in the valley of despair, I say to you today, my friends.

And so even though we face the difficulties of today and tomorrow, I still have a dream. It is a dream deeply rooted in the American dream.

I have a dream that one day this nation will rise up and live out the true meaning of its creed: "We hold these truths to be self-evident, that all men are created equal."

I have a dream that one day on the red hills of Georgia, the sons of former slaves and the sons of former slave owners will be able to sit down together at the table of brotherhood.

I have a dream that one day even the state of Mississippi, a state sweltering with the heat of injustice, sweltering with the heat of oppression, will be transformed into an oasis of freedom and justice.

I have a dream that my four little children will one day live in a nation where they will not be judged by the color of their skin but by the content of their character.

I have a dream today!

I have a dream that one day, down in Alabama, with its vicious racists, with its governor having his lips dripping with the words of "interposition" and "nullification" – one day right there in Alabama little black boys and black girls will be able to join hands with little white boys and white girls as sisters and brothers.

I have a dream today!

I have a dream that one day every valley shall be exalted, and every hill and mountain shall be made low, the rough places will be made plain, and the crooked places will be made straight; "and the glory of the Lord shall be revealed and all flesh shall see it together."2

This is our hope, and this is the faith that I go back to the South with.

With this faith, we will be able to hew out of the mountain of despair a stone of hope. With this faith, we will be able to transform the jangling discords of our nation into a beautiful symphony of brotherhood. With this faith, we will be able to work together, to pray together, to struggle together, to go to jail together, to stand up for freedom together, knowing that we will be free one day.

And this will be the day – this will be the day when all of God's children will be able to sing with new meaning:

> My country 'tis of thee, sweet land of liberty, of thee I sing.
> Land where my fathers died, land of the Pilgrim's pride,
> From every mountainside, let freedom ring!

And if America is to be a great nation, this must become true.

And so let freedom ring from the prodigious hilltops of New Hampshire.

> Let freedom ring from the mighty mountains of New York.
> Let freedom ring from the heightening Alleghenies of Pennsylvania.
> Let freedom ring from the snow-capped Rockies of Colorado.
> Let freedom ring from the curvaceous slopes of California.

But not only that:

> Let freedom ring from Stone Mountain of Georgia.
> Let freedom ring from Lookout Mountain of Tennessee.
> Let freedom ring from every hill and molehill of Mississippi.
> From every mountainside, let freedom ring.

And when this happens, and when we allow freedom ring, when we let it ring from every village and every hamlet, from every state and every city, we will be able to speed up that day when all of God's children, black men and white men, Jews and Gentiles, Protestants and Catholics, will be able to join hands and sing in the words of the old Negro spiritual:

> Free at last! Free at last!
> Thank God Almighty, we are free at last!

Martin L. King Jr., *Acceptance Speech for the Nobel Peace Prize*

[December 10, 1964, Oslo]

I accept the Nobel Prize for Peace at a moment when 22 million Negroes of the United States of America are engaged in a creative battle to end the long night of racial injustice. I accept this award on behalf of a civil rights movement which is moving with determination and a majestic scorn for risk and danger to establish a reign of freedom and a rule of justice. I am mindful that only yesterday in Birmingham, Alabama, our children, crying out for brotherhood, were answered with fire hoses, snarling dogs and even death. I am mindful that only yesterday in Philadelphia, Mississippi, young people seeking to secure the right to vote were brutalized and murdered. And only yesterday more than 40 houses of worship in the State of Mississippi alone were bombed or burned because they offered a sanctuary to those who would not accept segregation. I am mindful that debilitating and grinding poverty afflicts my people and chains them to the lowest rung of the economic ladder.

Therefore, I must ask why this prize is awarded to a movement which is beleaguered and committed to unrelenting struggle; to a movement which has not won the very peace and brotherhood which is the essence of the Nobel Prize.

After contemplation, I conclude that this award which I receive on behalf of that movement is a profound recognition that nonviolence is the answer to the crucial political and moral question of our time – the need for man to overcome oppression and violence without resorting to violence and oppression. Civilization and violence are antithetical concepts. Negroes of the United States, following the people of India, have demonstrated that nonviolence is not sterile passivity, but a powerful moral force which makes for social transformation. Sooner or later all the people of the world will have to discover a way to live together in peace, and thereby transform this pending cosmic elegy into a creative psalm of brotherhood. If this is to be achieved, man must evolve for all human conflict a method which rejects revenge, aggression and retaliation. The foundation of such a method is love.

The tortuous road which has led from Montgomery, Alabama to Oslo bears witness to this truth. This is a road over which millions of Negroes are travelling to find a new sense of dignity. This same road has opened for all Americans a new era of progress and hope. It has led to a new Civil Rights Bill, and it will, I am convinced, be widened and lengthened into a super highway of justice as Negro and white men in increasing numbers create alliances to overcome their common problems.

I accept this award today with an abiding faith in America and an audacious faith in the future of mankind. I refuse to accept despair as the final response to the ambiguities of history. I refuse to accept the idea that the "isness" of man's present nature makes him morally incapable of reaching up for the eternal "oughtness" that forever confronts him. I refuse to accept the idea that man is mere flotsam and jetsam in the river of life, unable to influence the unfolding events which surround him. I refuse to accept the view that mankind is so tragically bound to the starless midnight of racism and war that the bright daybreak of peace and brotherhood can never become a reality.

I refuse to accept the cynical notion that nation after nation must spiral down a militaristic stairway into the hell of thermonuclear destruction. I believe that unarmed truth and unconditional love will have the final word in reality. This is why right temporarily defeated is stronger than evil triumphant. I believe that even amid today's mortar bursts and whining bullets, there is still hope for a brighter tomorrow. I believe that wounded justice, lying prostrate on the blood-flowing streets of our nations, can be lifted from this dust of shame to reign supreme among the children of men. I have the audacity to believe that peoples everywhere can have three meals a day for their bodies, education and culture for their minds, and dignity, equality and freedom for their spirits. I believe that what self-centered men have torn down men other-centered can build up. I still believe that one day mankind will bow before the altars of God and be crowned triumphant over war and bloodshed, and nonviolent redemptive good will proclaim the rule of the land. "And the lion and the lamb shall lie down together and every man shall sit under his own vine and fig tree and none shall be afraid." I still believe that We Shall overcome!

This faith can give us courage to face the uncertainties of the future. It will give our tired feet new strength as we continue our forward stride toward the city of freedom. When our days become dreary with low-hovering clouds and our nights become darker than a thousand midnights, we will know that we are living in the creative turmoil of a genuine civilization struggling to be born.

Today I come to Oslo as a trustee, inspired and with renewed dedication to humanity. I accept this prize on behalf of all men who love peace and brotherhood. I say I come as a trustee, for in the depths of my heart I am aware that this prize is much more than an honor to me personally.

Every time I take a flight, I am always mindful of the many people who make a successful journey possible – the known pilots and the unknown ground crew.

So you honor the dedicated pilots of our struggle who

have sat at the controls as the freedom movement soared into orbit. You honor, once again, Chief Lutuli of South Africa, whose struggles with and for his people, are still met with the most brutal expression of man's inhumanity to man. You honor the ground crew without whose labor and sacrifices the jet flights to freedom could never have left the earth. Most of these people will never make the headline and their names will not appear in Who's Who. Yet when years have rolled past and when the blazing light of truth is focused on this marvellous age in which we live – men and women will know and children will be taught that we have a finer land, a better people, a more noble civilization – because these humble children of God were willing to suffer for righteousness' sake.

I think Alfred Nobel would know what I mean when I say that I accept this award in the spirit of a curator of some precious heirloom which he holds in trust for its true owners – all those to whom beauty is truth and truth beauty – and in whose eyes the beauty of genuine brotherhood and peace is more precious than diamonds or silver or gold.

Abraham Lincoln, *The "House Divided Against Itself" Speech*

[June 16, 1858, Springfield]

NOTE Abraham Lincoln (1809-1865), 16th president of the United States (1861-65), preserved the Union during the American Civil War and brought about the emancipation of enslaved people in the United States. Among American heroes, Lincoln continues to have a unique appeal for his fellow countrymen and also for people of other lands. This charm derives from his remarkable life story-the rise from humble origins, the dramatic death-and from his distinctively human and humane personality as well as from his historical role as savior of the Union and emancipator of enslaved people. His relevance endures and grows especially because of his eloquence as a spokesman for democracy.
This speech - delivered at the Illinois Republican State Convention at Springfield, on June 16, 1858, after he had been chosen the party candidate for the United States Senate, as the successor of Stephen A. Douglas - practically initiated the famous debate between Lincoln and Douglas, which followed during the political campaign of that year.

If we could first know where we are, and whither we are tending, we could better judge what to do, and how to do it. We are now far into the fifth year since a policy was initiated with the avowed object, and confident promise, of putting an end to slavery agitation. Under the operation of that policy, that agitation not only has not ceased, but has constantly augmented. In my opinion, it will not cease until a crisis shall have been reached and passed. "A house divided against itself can not stand." I believe this government can not endure permanently half slave and half free. I do not expect the Union to be dissolved; I do not expect the house to fall; but I do expect that it will cease to be divided. It will become all one thing, or all the other. Either the opponents of slavery will arrest the further spread of it, and place it where the public mind shall rest in the belief that it is in the course of ultimate extinction; or its advocates will push it forward till it shall become alike lawful in all the States, old as well as new, North as well as South. Have we no tendency to the latter condition? Let any one who doubts carefully contemplate that now almost complete legal combination-piece of machinery, so to speak–compounded of the Nebraska doctrine and the Dred Scott decision.

Put this and that together, and we have another nice little niche, which we may, ere long, see filled with another Supreme Court decision, declaring that the Constitution of the United States does not permit a State to exclude slavery from its limits. And this may especially be expected if the doctrine of "care not whether slavery be voted down or voted up," shall gain upon the public mind sufficiently to give promise that such a decision can be maintained when made.

Such a decision is all that slavery now lacks of being alike lawful in all the States. Welcome or unwelcome, such decision is probably coming, and will soon be upon us, unless the power of the present political dynasty shall be met and overthrown. We shall lie down pleasantly dreaming that the people of Missouri are on the verge of making their State free, and we shall awake to the reality, instead, that the Supreme Court has made Illinois a slave State. To meet and overthrow that dynasty is the work before all those who would prevent that consummation. That is what we have to do. How can we best do it?

There are those who denounce us openly to their own friends, and yet whisper to us softly that Senator Douglas is the aptest instrument there is with which to effect that object. They wish us to infer all, from the fact that he now has a little quarrel with the present head of the dynasty; and that he has regularly voted with us on a single point, upon which he and we have never differed. They remind us that he is a great man and that the largest of us are very small ones. Let this be granted. "But a living dog is better than a dead lion." Judge Douglas, if not a dead lion, for this work, is at least a caged and toothless one.

How can he oppose the advance of slavery? He does not care anything about it. His avowed mission is impressing the "public heart" to care nothing about it. A leading Douglas Democratic newspaper thinks Douglas's superior talent will be needed to resist the revival of the African slave-trade. Does Douglas believe an effort to revive that trade is approaching? He has not said so. Does he really think so? But if it is, how can he resist it? For years he has labored to prove it a sacred right of white men to take negro slaves into the new Territories. Can he possibly show that it is less a sacred right to buy them where they can be bought cheapest? And unquestionably they can be bought cheaper in Africa than in Virginia.

He has done all in his power to reduce the whole question of slavery to one of a mere right of property; and as such, how can he oppose the foreign slave-trade? How can he refuse that trade in that "property" shall be "perfectly free," unless he does it as a protection to the home production? And as the home producers will probably ask the protection, he will be wholly without a ground of opposition.

Senator Douglas holds, we know, that a man may rightfully be wiser to-day than he was yesterday—that he may rightfully change when he finds himself wrong. But can we, for that reason run ahead, and infer that he will make any particular change, of which he himself has given no intimation? Can we safely base our action upon any such vague inference? Now, as ever, I wish not to misrepresent Judge Douglas's position, question his motives, or do aught that can be personally offensive to him. Whenever, if ever, he and we can come together on principle, so that our cause may have assistance from his great ability, I hope to have interposed no adventitious obstacle. But, clearly, he is not now with us–he does not pretend to be, he does not promise ever to be.

Our cause, then, must be entrusted to, and conducted by, its own undoubted friends–those whose hands are free, whose hearts are in the work–who do care for the result. Two years ago the Republicans of the nation mustered over thirteen hundred thousand strong. We did this under the single impulse of resistance to a common danger. With every external circumstance against us, of strange, discordant, and even hostile elements, we gathered from the four winds, and formed and fought the battle through, under the constant hot fire of a disciplined, proud, and pampered enemy. Did we brave all then, to falter now?–now, when that same enemy is wavering, dissevered, and belligerent! The result is not doubtful. We shall not fail–if we stand firm, we shall not fail. Wise counsels may accelerate, or mistakes delay it; but, sooner or later, the victory is sure to come.

Abraham Lincoln, *Farewell Address at Springfield*

[February 11, 1861, Springfield]

NOTE One of Abraham Lincoln's most beloved short speeches, the extemporaneous Farewell Address was given on February 11, 1861, the day he left his hometown for Washington. The scene was the Springfield, Illinois Great Western railroad depot, now a restored private office with a public exhibit area.

My friends, no one, not in my situation, can appreciate my feeling of sadness at this parting. To this place and the kindness of this people I owe everything. Here I have lived a quarter of a century and have passed from a young to an old man. Here my children have been born and one is buried.

I now leave, not knowing when or whether ever I may return, with a task before me greater than that which rested upon Washington. Without the assistance of that Divine Being who ever attended him I can not succeed. With that assistance I can not fail.

Trusting in Him who can go with me and remain with you and be everywhere for good, let us confidently hope that all will yet be well. To His care commending you, as I hope in your prayers you will commend me, I bid you an affectionate farewell.

Abraham Lincoln, *First Inaugural Address*

[March 4, 1861, Washington]

NOTE Abraham Lincoln's first inaugural address was delivered on Monday, March 4, 1861, as part of his taking of the oath of office for his first term as the sixteenth President of the United States. The speech was primarily addressed to the people of the South, and was intended to succinctly state Lincoln's intended policies and desires toward that section, where seven states had seceded from the Union and formed the Confederate States of America.

In compliance with a custom as old as the government itself, I appear before you to address you briefly, and to take in your presence the oath prescribed by the Constitution of the United States to be taken by the president "before he enters on the execution of his office."

I do not consider it necessary at present for me to discuss those matters of administration about which there is no special anxiety or excitement.

Apprehension seems to exist, among the people of the Southern States, that by the accession of a Republican administration their property and their peace and personal security are to be endangered. There never has been any reasonable cause for such apprehension. Indeed, the most ample evidence to the contrary has all the while existed and been open to their inspection. It is found in nearly all the published speeches of him who now addresses you. I do but quote from one of those speeches when I declare that "I have no purpose, directly or indirectly, to interfere with the institution of slavery in the States where it exists. I believe I have no lawful right to do so, and I have no inclination to do so."

Those who nominated and elected me did so with full knowledge that I had made this and many similar declarations, and had never recanted them. And more than this, they placed in the platform for my acceptance, and as a law to themselves and to me, the clear and emphatic resolution which I now read:

"Resolved, That the maintenance inviolate of the rights of the States, and especially the right of each State to order and control its own domestic institutions according to its judgment exclusively, is essential to the balance of power on which the perfection and endurance of our political fabric depend, and we denounce the lawless invasion by armed force of the soil of any State or Territory, no matter under what pretext, as among the gravest of crimes."

I now reiterate these sentiments; and, in doing so, I only press upon the public attention the most conclusive evidence of which the case is susceptible, that the property, peace, and security of no section are to be in any wise endangered by the now incoming administration. I add, too, that all the protection which, consistently with the Constitution and the laws, can be given, will be cheerfully given to all the States, when lawfully demanded, for whatever cause, as cheerfully to one section as to another.

There is much controversy about the delivering up of fugitives from service or order. The clause I now read is as plainly written in the Constitution as any other of its provisions:

"No person hold to service or labor in one State, under the laws thereof, escaping into another, shall, in consequence of any law or regulation therein, be discharged from such service or labor, but shall be delivered up on claim of the party to whom such service or labor may be due."

It is scarcely questioned that this provision was intended by those who made it for the reclaiming of what we call fugitive slaves; and the intention of the lawgiver is the law. All members of Congress swear their support to the whole Constitution—to this provision as much as any other. To the proposition, then, that slaves whose cases come within the terms of this clause, "shall be delivered up," their oaths are unanimous. Now, if they would make the effort in good temper, could they not, with nearly equal unanimity, frame and pass a law by means of which to keep good that unanimous oath?

There is some difference of opinion whether this clause should be enforced by national or State authority, but surely that difference is not a very material one. If the slave is to be surrendered, it can be of but little consequence to him, or to others, by what authority it is done. And should any one, in any case, be content that his oath should go unkept, on a mere unsubstantial controversy as to how it shall be kept?

Again, in any law upon this subject, ought not all the safeguards of liberty known in civilized and humane jurisprudence to be introduced, so that a free man be not, in any case, surrendered as a slave? And might it not be well, at the same time, to provide by law for the enforcement of that clause of the Constitution which guarantees that "the citizens of each State shall be entitled to all privileges and immunities of citizens in the several States?"

I take the official oath to-day with no mental reservation, and with no purpose to construe the Constitution or laws by any hypercritical rules. And while I do not choose now to specify particular acts of Congress as proper to be enforced, I do suggest that it will be much safer for all, both in official and private stations, to conform to and abide by all those acts which stand unrepealed, than to violate any of them, trusting to find impunity in having them held to be unconstitutional.

It is seventy-two years since the first inauguration of a president under our national Constitution. During that period, fifteen different and greatly distinguished citizens have, in succession, administered the executive branch of the government. They have conducted it through many perils, and generally with great success. Yet, with all this scope for precedent, I now enter upon the same task for the brief constitutional term of four years, under great and peculiar difficulty. A disruption of the federal Union, heretofore only menaced, is now formidably attempted.

I hold that in contemplation of universal law, and of the Constitution, the Union of these States is perpetual. Perpetuity is implied, if not expressed, in the fundamental law of all national governments. It is safe to assert that no government proper ever had a provision in its organic law for its own termination. Continue to execute all the express provisions of our national government, and the Union will endure for ever—it being impossible to destroy it, except by some action not provided for in the instrument itself.

Again, if the United States be not a government proper, but an association of States in the nature of contract merely, can it, as a contract, be peaceably unmade by less than all the parties who made it? One party to a contract may violate it—break it, so to speak; but does it not require all to lawfully rescind it?

Descending from these general principles, we find the proposition that, in legal contemplation, the Union is perpetual, confirmed by the history of the Union itself. The Union is much older than the Constitution. It was formed, in fact, by the Articles of Association in 1774. It was matured and continued by the Declaration of Independence in 1776. It was further matured, and the faith of all the then thirteen States expressly plighted and engaged that it should be perpetual, by the Articles of Confederation in 1778. And, finally, in 1787, one of the declared objects for ordaining and establishing the Constitution was "to form a more perfect union."

But if destruction of the Union, by one, or by a part only,

of the States, be lawfully possible, the Union is less perfect than before, the Constitution having lost the vital element of perpetuity.

It follows, from these views, that no State, upon its own mere motion, can lawfully get out of the Union; that resolves and ordinances to that effect are legally void; and that acts of violence within any State or States, against the authority of the United States, are insurrectionary or revolutionary, according to circumstances.

I therefore consider that, in view of the Constitution and the laws, the Union is unbroken, and to the extent of my ability I shall take care, as the Constitution itself expressly enjoins upon me, that the laws of the Union be faithfully executed in all the States. Doing this, I deem to be only a simple duty on my part; and I shall perform it, so far as practicable, unless my rightful masters, the American people, shall withhold the requisite means, or, in some authoritative manner, direct the contrary. I trust this will not be regarded as a menace, but only as the declared purpose of the Union that it will constitutionally defend and maintain itself. In doing this there need be no bloodshed or violence; and there shall be none, unless it be forced upon the national authority. The power confided to me will be used to hold, occupy, and possess the property and places belonging to the government, and to collect the duties and imposts; but beyond what may be necessary for these objects, there will be no invasion, no using of force against or among the people anywhere. Where hostility to the United States, in any interior locality, shall be so great and universal as to prevent competent resident citizens from holding the federal offices, there will be no attempt to force obnoxious strangers among the people for that object. While the strict legal right may exist in the government to enforce the exercise of these offices, the attempt to do so would be so irritating, and so nearly impracticable withal, that I deem it better to forego, for the time, the uses of such offices.

The mails, unless repelled, will continue to be furnished in all parts of the Union. So far as possible, the people everywhere shall have that sense of perfect security which is most favorable to calm thought and reflection. The course here indicated will be followed, unless current events and experience shall show a modification or change to be proper, and in every case and exigency my best discretion will be exercised, according to circumstances actually existing, and with a view and a hope of a peaceful solution of the national troubles, and the restoration of fraternal sympathies and affections.

That there are persons in one section or another who seek to destroy the Union at all events, and are glad of any pretext to do it, I will neither affirm nor deny; but if there be such, I need address no word to them. To those, however, who really love the Union, may I not speak?

Before entering upon so grave a matter as the destruction of our national fabric, with all its benefits, its memories, and its hopes, would it not be wise to ascertain why we do it? Will you hazard so desperate a step while there is any possibility that any portion of the certain ills you fly from have no real existence? Will you, while the certain ills you fly to are greater than all the real ones you fly from—will you risk the commission of so fearful a mistake?

All profess to be content in the Union, if all constitutional rights can be maintained. Is it true, then, that any right, plainly written in the Constitution, has been denied? I think not. Happily the human mind is so constituted that no party can reach to the audacity of doing this. Think, if you can, of a single instance in which a plainly written provision of the Constitution has ever been denied. If, by the mere force of numbers, a majority should derive a minority of any clearly written constitutional right, it might, in a moral point of view, justify revolution—certainly would if such right were a vital one. But such is not our case. All the vital rights of minorities and of individuals are so plainly assured to them by affirmations and negations, guarantees and prohibitions in the Constitution, that controversies never arise concerning them. But no organic law can ever be framed with a provision specifically applicable to every question which may occur in practical administration. No foresight can anticipate, nor any document of reasonable length contain, express provisions for all possible questions. Shall fugitives from labor be surrendered by national or State authority? The Constitution does not expressly say. May Congress prohibit slavery in the Territories? The Constitution does not expressly say. Must Congress protect slavery in the Territories? The Constitution does not expressly say.

From questions of this class spring all our constitutional controversies, and we divide upon them into majorities and minorities. If the minority will not acquiesce, the majority must, or the government must cease. There is no other alternative; for continuing the government is acquiescence on one side or the other. If a minority in such case will secede rather than acquiesce, they make a precedent which, in turn, will divide and ruin them; for a minority of their own will secede from them whenever a majority refuses to be controlled by such a minority. For instance, why may not any portion of a new confederacy, a year or two hence, arbitrarily secede again, precisely as portions of the present Union now claim to secede from it? All who cherish disunion sentiments are now being educated to the exact temper of doing this.

Is there such perfect identity of interests among the States to compose a new Union, as to produce harmony only, and prevent renewed secession?

Plainly, the central idea of secession is the essence of anarchy. A majority held in restraint by constitutional checks and limitations, and always changing easily with deliberate changes of popular opinions and sentiments, is the only true sovereign of a free people. Whoever rejects it, does, of necessity, fly to anarchy or to despotism. Unanimity is impossible; the rule of a minority, as a permanent arrangement, is wholly inadmissible; so that, rejecting the majority principle, anarchy or despotism, in some form, is all that is left.

Physically speaking, we can not separate. We can not remove our respective sections from each other, nor build an impassable wall between them. A husband and wife may be divorced, and go out of the presence and beyond the reach of each other; but the different parts of our country can not do this. They can not but remain face to face, and intercourse, either amicable or hostile, must continue between them. It is impossible, then, to make that intercourse more advantageous or more satisfactory after separation than before. Can aliens make treaties easier than friends can make laws? Can treaties be more faithfully enforced between aliens than laws can among friends? Suppose you go to war; you can not fight always, and when after much loss on both sides and no gain on either you cease fighting, the identical old questions as to terms of intercourse are again upon you.

This country, with its institutions, belongs to the people who inhabit it. Whenever they shall grow weary of the existing government they can exercise their constitutional right of amending it, or their revolutionary right to dismember or overthrow it. I can not be ignorant of the fact that many worthy and patriotic citizens are desirous of having the national Constitution amended.... I understand a proposed amendment to the Constitution—which amendment, however, I have not seen—has passed Congress, to the effect that the federal government shall never interfere with the domestic institutions of the States, including that of persons held to service. To avoid misconstruction of what I have said, I depart from my purpose not to speak of particular amendments, so far as to say that, holding such a provision now to be implied constitutional law, I have no objections to its being made express and irrevocable.

The chief magistrate derives all his authority from the people, and they have conferred none upon him to fix terms for the separation of the States. The people themselves can do this also if they choose, but the executive, as such, has nothing to do with it. His duty is to administer the present government as it came to his hands, and to transmit it, unimpaired by him, to his successor. Why should there not be a patient confidence in the ultimate justice of the people? Is there any better or equal hope in the world? In our present differences is either party without faith of being in the right? If the Almighty Ruler of nations, with his eternal truth and justice, be on your side of the North, or yours of the South, that truth and that justice will surely prevail, by the judgment of this great tribunal of the American people. By the frame of the government under which we live, the same people have wisely given their public servants but little power for mischief, and have with equal wisdom provided for the return of that little to their own hands at very short intervals. While the people retain their virtue and vigilance, no administration, by any extreme of wickedness or folly, can very seriously injure the government in the short space of four years.

My countrymen, one and all, think calmly and well upon this whole subject. Nothing valuable can be lost by taking time. If there be an object to hurry any of you in hot haste to a step which you would never take deliberately, that object will be frustrated by taking time; but no good object can be frustrated by it. Such of you as are now dissatisfied still have the old Constitution unimpaired, and on the sensitive point, the laws of your own framing under it; while the new administration will have no immediate power, if it would, to change either. If it were admitted that you who are dissatisfied hold the right side in this dispute there is still no single good reason for precipitate action. Intelligence, patriotism, Christianity, and a firm reliance on Him who has never yet forsaken this favored land are still competent to adjust in the best way all our present difficulty. In your hands, my dissatisfied fellow countrymen, and not in mine, are the momentous issues of civil war. The government will not assail you. You can have no conflict without being yourselves the aggressors. You have no oath registered in heaven to destroy the government, while I shall have the most solemn one to "preserve, protect, and defend" it.

I am loath to close. We are not enemies, but friends. We must not be enemies. Though passion may have strained, it must not break, our bonds of affection. The mystic chords of memory, stretching from every battle-field and patriot grave to every living heart and hearthstone all over this broad land, will yet swell the chorus of the Union when again touched, as surely they will be, by the better angels of our nature.

Abraham Lincoln, *Address at Gettysburg*

[November 19, 1863, Gettysburg]

NOTE The Battle of Gettysburg was fought between July 1 and July 3, 1863. It was one of the bloodiest battles of the United States Civil War, with over 51,000 casualties-soldiers killed, injured, or otherwise lost to action-combined. Around 3,100 U.S. troops were killed, while 3,900 Confederates died. The U.S. victory there marked the turning point of the war. President Lincoln was asked to deliver a message at the dedication of the Gettysburg Civil War Cemetery on November 19, 1863. The featured speaker for the occasion was Edward Everett, a former dean of Harvard University, and one of the most famous orators of his day. He spoke for two hours.
Despite (or perhaps because of) its brevity, since the speech was delivered, it has come to be recognized as one of the most powerful statements in the English language and, in fact, one of the most important expressions of freedom and liberty in any language.
There are five known copies of the speech in Lincoln's handwriting, each with a slightly different text, and named for the people who first received them: Nicolay, Hay, Everett, Bancroft and Bliss. Two copies apparently were written before delivering the speech, one of which probably was the reading copy. The remaining ones were produced months later for soldier benefit events.
Ever since Lincoln wrote it in 1864, this version (Bliss Copy) has been the most often reproduced, notably on the walls of the Lincoln Memorial in Washington. It is named after Colonel Alexander Bliss, stepson of historian George Bancroft.

Fourscore and seven years ago our fathers brought forth upon this continent a new nation, conceived in liberty, and dedicated to the proposition that all men are created equal.

Now we are engaged in a great civil war, testing whether that nation, or any nation so conceived and so dedicated, can long endure. We are met on a great battle-field of that war. We have come to dedicate a portion of that field 2 as a final resting-place for those who here gave their lives that that nation might live. It is altogether fitting and proper that we should do this.

But in a larger sense, we can not dedicate–we can not consecrate–we can not hallow this ground. The brave men, living and dead, who struggled here, have consecrated it far above our poor 3 power to add or detract. The world will little note, nor long remember, what we say here, but it can never forget what they did here. It is for us, the living, rather, to be dedicated here to the unfinished work which 4 they who fought here thus far so nobly advanced. It is rather for us to be here dedicated to the great task remaining before us–that from these honored dead we take increased devotion to that cause for which they gave the last full measure of devotion–that we here highly resolve that these 5 dead shall not have died in vain–that this nation, under God, shall 6 have a new birth of freedom and that government of the people, by the people, and for the people, shall not perish from the earth.

Abraham Lincoln, *Second Inaugural Address*

[March 4, 1865, Washington]

NOTE Abraham Lincoln delivered his second inaugural address on Saturday, March 4, 1865, during his second inauguration as President of the United States. At a time when victory over secessionists in the American Civil War was within days and slavery in all of the U.S. was near an end, Lincoln did not speak of happiness, but of sadness.
The address is inscribed, along with the Gettysburg Address, in the Lincoln Memorial.

At this second appearing to take the oath of the presidential office, there is less occasion for an extended address than there was at first. Then a statement, somewhat in detail, of a course to be pursued seemed very fitting and proper. Now, at the expiration of four years, during which public declarations have been constantly called forth on every point and phase of the great contest which still absorbs the attention and engrosses the energies of the nation, little that is new could be presented.

The progress of our arms, upon which all else chiefly depends, is as well known to the public as to myself, and it is, I trust, reasonably satisfactory and encouraging to all. With high hope for the future, no prediction in regard to it is ventured.

On the occasion corresponding to this four years ago, all thoughts were anxiously directed to an impending civil war. All dreaded it; all sought to avoid it. While the inaugural address was being delivered from this place, devoted altogether to saving the Union without war, insurgent agents were in the city seeking to destroy it with war–seeking to dissolve the Union and divide the effects by negotiation. Both parties deprecated war, but one of them would make war rather than let the nation survive, and the other would accept war rather than let it perish, and the war came. One-eighth of the whole population were colored slaves, not distributed generally over the Union, but localized in the Southern part of it.

These slaves constituted a peculiar and powerful interest. All knew that this interest was somehow the cause of the war. To strengthen, perpetuate, and extend this interest was the object for which the insurgents would rend the Union by war, while the government claimed no right to do more than to restrict the Territorial enlargement of it.

Neither party expected for the war the magnitude or the duration which it has already attained. Neither anticipated that the cause of the conflict might cease when, or even before the conflict itself should cease. Each looked for an easier triumph, and a result less fundamental and astounding. Both read the same Bible and pray to the same God, and each invokes His aid against the other. It may seem strange that any men should dare to ask a just God's assistance in wringing their bread from the sweat of other men's faces, but let us judge not, that we be not judged. The prayer of both could not be answered. That of neither has been answered fully. The Almighty has His own purposes. "Woe unto the world because of offenses, for it must needs be that offenses come; but woe to that man by whom the offenses cometh!"

If we shall suppose that American slavery is one of those offenses which, in the providence of God, must needs come, but which having continued through His appointed time, He now wills to remove, and that He gives to both North and South this terrible war as the woe due to those by whom the offense came, shall we discern there any departure from those divine attributes which the believers in a living God always ascribe to Him? Fondly do we hope, fervently do we pray, that this mighty scourge of war may speedily pass away. Yet if God wills that it continue until all the wealth piled by the bondsman's two hundred and fifty years of unrequited toil shall be sunk, and until every drop of blood drawn with the lash shall be paid by another drawn with the sword, as was said three thousand years ago, so still it must be said, that the judgments of the Lord are true and righteous altogether.

With malice toward none, with charity for all, with firmness in the right as God gives us to see the right, let us finish the work we are in, to bind up the nation's wounds, to care for him who shall have borne the battle, and for his widow and his orphans, to do all which may achieve and cherish a just and a lasting peace among ourselves and with all nations.

Douglas MacArthur, *Duty, Honor, Country: Sylvanus Thayer Award Acceptance Address*

[May 12, 1962, West Point]

NOTE The address by General of the Army Douglas MacArthur (1880-1964) to the cadets of the U.S. Military Academy in accepting the Sylvanus Thayer Award on 12 May 1962 is a memorable tribute to the ideals that inspired that great American soldier. General MacArthur's service to his country spanned the years from 1903, when he was graduated from the Military Academy, to 5 April 1964, when he died in Washington. He was recognized early in his career as a brilliant officer and was advanced to brigadier general in 1918. Twelve years later he was named Chief of Staff of the Army, and in 1937 he retired. Recalled to active duty during World War II, he was commander of the Southwest Pacific Area during the greater part of the war. His wartime triumphs were followed by service as supreme commander of the Allied occupation forces in Japan.

As I was leaving the hotel this morning, a doorman asked me, "Where are you bound for, General?" And when I replied, "West Point," he remarked, "Beautiful place. Have you ever been there before?"

No human being could fail to be deeply moved by such a tribute as this [Thayer Award]. Coming from a profession I have served so long, and a people I have loved so well, it fills me with an emotion I cannot express. But this award is not intended primarily to honor a personality, but to symbolize a great moral code — the code of conduct and chivalry of those who guard this beloved land of culture and ancient descent. That is the animation of this medallion. For all eyes and for all time, it is an expression of the ethics of the American soldier. That I should be integrated in this way with so noble an ideal arouses a sense of pride and yet of humility which will be with me always.

Duty, Honor, Country: Those three hallowed words reverently dictate what you ought to be, what you can be, what you will be. They are your rallying points: to build courage when courage seems to fail; to regain faith when there seems to be little cause for faith; to create hope when hope becomes forlorn.

Unhappily, I possess neither that eloquence of diction, that poetry of imagination, nor that brilliance of metaphor to tell you all that they mean.

The unbelievers will say they are but words, but a slogan, but a flamboyant phrase. Every pedant, every demagogue, every cynic, every hypocrite, every troublemaker, and I am sorry to say, some others of an entirely different character, will try to downgrade them even to the extent of mockery and ridicule.

But these are some of the things they do: They build your basic character. They mold you for your future roles as the custodians of the nation's defense. They make you strong enough to know when you are weak, and brave enough to face yourself when you are afraid. They teach you to be proud and unbending in honest failure, but humble and gentle in success; not to substitute words for actions, not to seek the path of comfort, but to face the stress and spur of difficulty and challenge; to learn to stand up in the storm but to have compassion on those who fall; to master yourself before you seek to master others; to have a heart that is clean, a goal that is high; to learn to laugh, yet never forget how to weep; to reach into the future yet never neglect the past; to be serious yet never to take yourself too seriously; to be modest so that you will remember the simplicity of true greatness, the open mind of true wisdom, the meekness of true strength.

They give you a temper of the will, a quality of the

imagination, a vigor of the emotions, a freshness of the deep springs of life, a temperamental predominance of courage over timidity, of an appetite for adventure over love of ease. They create in your heart the sense of wonder, the unfailing hope of what next, and the joy and inspiration of life. They teach you in this way to be an officer and a gentleman.

And what sort of soldiers are those you are to lead? Are they reliable? Are they brave? Are they capable of victory? Their story is known to all of you. It is the story of the American man-at-arms. My estimate of him was formed on the battlefield many, many years ago, and has never changed. I regarded him then as I regard him now – as one of the world's noblest figures, not only as one of the finest military characters, but also as one of the most stainless. His name and fame are the birthright of every American citizen. In his youth and strength, his love and loyalty, he gave all that mortality can give.

He needs no eulogy from me or from any other man. He has written his own history and written it in red on his enemy's breast. But when I think of his patience under adversity, of his courage under fire, and of his modesty in victory, I am filled with an emotion of admiration I cannot put into words. He belongs to history as furnishing one of the greatest examples of successful patriotism. He belongs to posterity as the instructor of future generations in the principles of liberty and freedom. He belongs to the present, to us, by his virtues and by his achievements. In 20 campaigns, on a hundred battlefields, around a thousand campfires, I have witnessed that enduring fortitude, that patriotic self-abnegation, and that invincible determination which have carved his statue in the hearts of his people. From one end of the world to the other he has drained deep the chalice of courage.

As I listened to those songs [from the glee club], in memory's eye I could see those staggering columns of the

First World War, bending under soggy packs, on many a weary march from dripping dusk to drizzling dawn, slogging ankle-deep through the mire of shell-shocked roads, to form grimly for the attack, blue-lipped, covered with sludge and mud, chilled by the wind and rain, driving home to their objective, and for many, to the judgment seat of God.

I do not know the dignity of their birth, but I do know the glory of their death. They died unquestioning, uncomplaining, with faith in their hearts, and on their lips the hope that we would go on to victory. Always, for them: Duty, Honor, Country; always their blood and sweat and tears, as we sought the way and the light and the truth.

And 20 years after, on the other side of the globe, again the filth of murky foxholes, the stench of ghostly trenches, the slime of dripping dugouts; those boiling suns of relentless heat, those torrential rains of devastating storms; the loneliness and utter desolation of jungle trails; the bitterness of long separation from those they loved and cherished; the deadly pestilence of tropical disease; the horror of stricken areas of war; their resolute and determined defense, their swift and sure attack, their indomitable purpose, their complete and decisive victory – always victory. Always through the bloody haze of their last reverberating shot, the vision of gaunt, ghastly men reverently following your password of:

Duty, Honor, Country.

The code which those words perpetuate embraces the highest moral laws and will stand the test of any ethics or philosophies ever promulgated for the uplift of mankind. Its requirements are for the things that are right, and its restraints are from the things that are wrong.

The soldier, above all other men, is required to practice the greatest act of religious training – sacrifice.

In battle and in the face of danger and death, he discloses those divine attributes which his Maker gave when he created man in his own image. No physical courage and no brute instinct can take the place of the Divine help which alone can sustain him.

However horrible the incidents of war may be, the soldier who is called upon to offer and to give his life for his country is the noblest development of mankind.

You now face a new world – a world of change. The thrust into outer space of the satellite, spheres, and missiles mark the beginning of another epoch in the long story of mankind. In the five or more billions of years the scientists tell us it has taken to form the earth, in the three or more billion years of development of the human race, there has never been a more abrupt or staggering evolution. We deal now not with things of this world alone, but with the illimitable distances and as yet unfathomed mysteries of the universe. We are reaching out for a new and boundless frontier.

We speak in strange terms: of harnessing the cosmic energy; of making winds and tides work for us; of creating unheard synthetic materials to supplement or even replace our old standard basics; to purify sea water for our drink; of mining ocean floors for new fields of wealth and food; of disease preventatives to expand life into the hundreds of years; of controlling the weather for a more equitable distribution of heat and cold, of rain and shine; of space ships to the moon; of the primary target in war, no longer limited to the armed forces of an enemy, but instead to include his civil populations; of ultimate conflict between a united human race and the sinister forces of some other planetary galaxy; of such dreams and fantasies as to make life the most exciting of all time.

And through all this welter of change and development, your mission remains fixed, determined, inviolable: it is to win our wars.

Everything else in your professional career is but corollary to this vital dedication. All other public purposes, all other public projects, all other public needs, great or small, will find others for their accomplishment. But you are the ones who are trained to fight. Yours is the profession of arms, the will to win, the sure knowledge that in war there is no substitute for victory; that if you lose, the nation will be destroyed; that the very obsession of your public service must be:

Duty, Honor, Country.

Others will debate the controversial issues, national and international, which divide men's minds; but serene, calm, aloof, you stand as the Nation's war-guardian, as its life-guard from the raging tides of international conflict, as its gladiator in the arena of battle. For a century and a half you have defended, guarded, and protected its hallowed traditions of liberty and freedom, of right and justice.

Let civilian voices argue the merits or demerits of our processes of government; whether our strength is being sapped by deficit financing, indulged in too long, by federal paternalism grown too mighty, by power groups grown too arrogant, by politics grown too corrupt, by crime grown too rampant, by morals grown too low, by taxes grown too high, by extremists grown too violent; whether our personal liberties are as thorough and complete as they should be. These great national problems are not for your professional participation or military solution. Your guidepost stands out like a ten-fold beacon in the night:

Duty, Honor, Country.

You are the leaven which binds together the entire fabric of our national system of defense. From your ranks come the great captains who hold the nation's destiny in their hands the moment the war tocsin sounds. The Long Gray Line has never failed us. Were you to do so, a million ghosts in olive drab, in brown khaki, in blue and gray, would rise from their white crosses thundering those magic words:

Duty, Honor, Country.

This does not mean that you are war mongers.

On the contrary, the soldier, above all other people, prays for peace, for he must suffer and bear the deepest wounds and scars of war.

But always in our ears ring the ominous words of Plato, that wisest of all philosophers: "Only the dead have seen the end of war."1

The shadows are lengthening for me. The twilight is here. My days of old have vanished, tone and tint. They have gone glimmering through the dreams of things that were. Their memory is one of wondrous beauty, watered by tears, and coaxed and caressed by the smiles of yesterday. I listen vainly, but with thirsty ears, for the witching melody of faint bugles blowing reveille, of far drums beating the long roll. In my dreams I hear again the crash of guns, the rattle of musketry, the strange, mournful mutter of the battlefield.

But in the evening of my memory, always I come back to West Point.

Always there echoes and re-echoes: Duty, Honor, Country.

Today marks my final roll call with you, but I want you to know that when I cross the river my last conscious thoughts will be of The Corps, and The Corps, and The Corps.

I bid you farewell.

Malcolm X, *The Ballot or the Bullet*

[April 12, 1964, Detroit]

NOTE Malcolm X (1925-1965) was an American Muslim minister and human rights activist who was a prominent figure during the civil rights movement. A spokesman for the Nation of Islam until 1964, he was a vocal advocate for Black empowerment and the promotion of Islam within the Black community.

Mr. Moderator, Rev. Cleage, brothers and sisters and friends, and I see some enemies. In fact, I think we'd be fooling ourselves if we had an audience this large and didn't realize that there were some enemies present.

This afternoon we want to talk about the ballot or the bullet. The ballot or the bullet explains itself. But before we get into it, since this is the year of the ballot or the bullet, I would like to clarify some things that refer to me personally, concerning my own personal position.

I'm still a Muslim. That is, my religion is still Islam. My religion is still Islam. I still credit Mr. Muhammad for what I know and what I am. He's the one who opened my eyes. At present I am the minister of the newly founded Muslim Mosque Incorporated, which has its offices in the Theresa Hotel right in the heart of Harlem, that's the black belt in New York City. And when we realize that Adam Clayton Powell, is a Christian minister, he has Abyssinian Baptist Church, but at the same time he's more famous for his political struggling. And Dr. King is a Christian minister from Atlanta Georgia, or in Atlanta Georgia, but he's become more famous for being involved in the civil rights struggle. There's another in New York, Rev. Galamison, I don't know if you've heard of him out here, he's a Christian minister from Brooklyn, but has become famous for his fight against the segregated school system in Brooklyn. Rev. Cleage, right here, is a Christian minister, here in Detroit, he's head of the Freedom Now Party. All of these are Christian ministers …all of these are Christian ministers but they don't come to us as Christian ministers, they come to us as fighters in some other category.

I am a Muslim minister. The same as they are Christian ministers, I'm a Muslim minister. And I don't believe in fighting today on any one front, but on all fronts. In fact, I'm a Black Nationalist freedom fighter. Islam is my religion but I believe my religion is my personal business. It governs my personal life, my personal morals. And my religious philosophy is personal between me and the God in whom I believe, just as the religious philosophy of these others is between them and the God in whom they believe. And this is best this way. Were we to come out here discussing religion, we'd have too many differences from the out start and we could never get together.

So today, though Islam is my religious philosophy, my political, economic and social philosophy is black nationalism. You and I – As I say, if we bring up religion, we'll have differences, we'll have arguments, and we'll never be able to get together. But if we keep our religion at home, keep our religion in the closet, keep our religion between ourselves and our God, but when we come out here we have a fight that's common to all of us against a enemy who is common to all of us.

The political philosophy of black nationalism only means that the black man should control the politics and the politicians in his own community. The time when white people can come in our community and get us to vote for them so that they can be our political leaders and tell us what to do and what not to do is long gone.

By the same token, the time when that same white man, knowing that your eyes are too far open, can send another Negro in the community, and get you and me to support him, so that he can use him to lead us astray, those days are long gone too.

The political philosophy of black nationalism only means that if you and I are going to live in a black community – and that's where we're going to live, 'cause as soon as you move into one of their….soon as you move out of the black community into their community, it's mixed for a period of time, but they're gone and you're right there all by yourself again.

We must, we must understand the politics of our community and we must know what politics is supposed to produce. We must know what part politics play in our lives. And until we become politically mature, we will always be misled, led astray, or deceived or maneuvered into supporting someone politically who doesn't have the good of our community at heart. So the political philosophy of black nationalism only means that we will have to carry on a program, a political program, of reeducation – to open our people's eyes, make us become more politically conscious, politically mature. And then, we will – whenever we are ready to cast our ballot, that ballot will be cast for a man of the community, who has the good of the community at heart.

The economic philosophy of black nationalism only means that we should own and operate and control the economy of our community. You would never have found— you can't open up a black store in a white community. White man won't even patronize you. And he's not wrong. He got sense enough to look out for himself. It's you who don't have sense enough to look out for yourself.

The white man, the white man is too intelligent to let someone else come and gain control of the economy of his community. But you will let anybody come in and control the economy of your community, control the housing, control the education, control the jobs, control the businesses, under the pretext that you want to integrate. Nah, you're out of your mind.

The political … the economic philosophy of black nationalism only means that we have to become involved in a program of reeducation, to educate our people into the importance of knowing that when you spend your dollar out of the community in which you live, the community in which you spend your money becomes richer and richer, the community out of which you take your money becomes poorer and poorer. And because these Negroes, who have been misled, misguided, are breaking their necks to take their money and spend it with the Man, the Man is becoming richer and richer, and you're becoming poorer and poorer. And then what happens? The community in which you live becomes a slum. It becomes a ghetto. The conditions become rundown. And then you have the audacity to complain about poor housing in a rundown community, while you're running down yourselves when you take your dollar out.

And you and I are in a double trap because not only do we lose by taking our money someplace else and spending it, when we try and spend it in our own community we're trapped because we haven't had sense enough to set up stores and control the businesses of our community. The man who is controlling the stores in our community is a man who doesn't look like we do. He's a man who doesn't even live in the community. So you and I, even when we try and spend our money on the block where we live or the area where we live, we're spending it with a man who, when the sun goes down, takes that basket full of money in another part of the town.

So we're trapped, trapped, double-trapped, triple-trapped. Any way we go, we find that we're trapped. Any every kind of solution that someone comes up with is just another trap. But the political and economic philosophy of black nationalism…the economic philosophy of black nationalism shows our people the importance of setting up these little stores, and developing them and expanding them into larger operations. Woolworth didn't start out big like they are today; they started out with a dime store, and expanded, and expanded, and expanded until today they are all over the country and all over the world and they getting some of everybody's money.

Now this is what you and I – General Motors, the same way, it didn't start out like it is. It started out just a little rat-race type operation. And it expanded and it expanded until today it's where it is right now. And you and I have to make a start. And the best place to start is right in the community where we live.

So our people not only have to be reeducated to the importance of supporting black business, but the black man himself has to be made aware of the importance of going into business. And once you and I go into business, we own and operate at least the businesses in our community. What we will be doing is developing a situation, wherein, we will actually be able to create employment for the people in the community. And once you can create some employment in the community where you live, it will eliminate the necessity of you and me having to act ignorantly and disgracefully, boycotting and picketing some cracker someplace else trying to beg him for a job.

Anytime you have to rely upon your enemy for a job, you're in bad shape. When you – and he is your enemy. You wouldn't be in this country if some enemy hadn't kidnapped you and brought you here. On the other hand, some of you think you came here on the Mayflower.

So as you can see, brothers and sisters, today – this afternoon it is not our intention to discuss religion. We're going to forget religion. If we bring up religion we'll be in an argument. And the best way to keep away from arguments and differences, as I said earlier, put your religion at home, in the closet, keep it between you and your God. Because if it hasn't done anything more for you than it has, you need to forget it anyway.

Whether you are a Christian or a Muslim or a nationalist, we all have the same problem. They don't hang you because you're a Baptist; they hang you 'cause you're black. They don't attack me because I'm a Muslim. They attack me 'cause I'm black. They attacked all of us for the same reason. All of us catch hell from the same enemy. We're all in the same bag, in the same boat.

We suffer political oppression, economic exploitation and social degradation. All of 'em from the same enemy. The government has failed us. You can't deny that. Any time you're living in the 20th century, 1964, and you walking around here singing "We Shall Overcome," the government has failed you. This is part of what's wrong with you, you do too much singing. Today it's time to stop singing and start swinging.

You can't sing up on freedom. But you can swing up on some freedom. Cassius Clay can sing. But singing didn't help him to become the heavyweight champion of the world. Swinging helped him.

So this government has failed us. The government itself has failed us. And the white liberals who have been posing as our friends have failed us. And once we see that all of these other sources to which we've turned have failed, we stop turning to them and turn to ourselves. We need a self-help program, a do-it-yourself philosophy, a do-it-right-now philosophy, a it's-already-too-late philosophy. This is what you and I need to get with. And the only time – the only way we're going to solve our problem is with a self-help program. Before we can get a self-help program started, we have to have a self-help philosophy. Black nationalism is a self-help philosophy.

What's so good about it – you can stay right in the church where you are and still take black nationalism as your philosophy. You can stay in any kind of civic organization that you belong to and still take black nationalism as your philosophy. You can be an atheist and still take black nationalism as your philosophy. This is a philosophy that eliminates the necessity for division and argument, 'cause if you're black, you should be thinking black. And if you're black and you not thinking black at this late date, well, I'm sorry for you.

Once you change your philosophy, you change your thought pattern. Once you change your thought pattern you change your attitude. Once you change your attitude it changes your behavior pattern. And then you go on into some action. As long as you got a sit-down philosophy you'll have a sit-down thought pattern. And as long as you think that old sit-down thought, you'll be in some kind of sit-down action. They'll have you sitting in everywhere.

It's not so good to refer to what you're going to do as a sit-in. That right there castrates you. Right there it brings you down. What goes with it? What – think of the image of someone sitting. An old woman can sit. An old man can sit. A chump can sit, a coward can sit, anything can sit. Well, you and I been sitting long enough and it's time for us today to start doing some standing and some fighting to back that up.

When we look at other parts of this Earth upon which we live, we find that black, brown, red and yellow people in Africa and Asia are getting their independence. They're not getting it by singing, 'We Shall Overcome." No, they're getting it through nationalism. It is nationalism that brought about the independence of the people in Asia. Every nation in Asia gained its independence through the philosophy of nationalism. Every nation on the African continent that has gotten its independence brought it about through the philosophy of nationalism. And it will take black nationalism to bring about the freedom of 22 million Afro-Americans, here in this country, where we have suffered colonialism for the past 400 years.

America is just as much a colonial power as England ever was. America is just as much a colonial power as France ever was. In fact, America is more so a colonial power than they, because she is a hypocritical colonial power behind it. What is 20th – what, what do you call second-class citizenship? Why, that's colonization. Second-class citizenship is nothing but 20th slavery. How you gonna to tell me you're a second-class citizen? They don't have second-class citizenship in any other government on this Earth. They just have slaves and people who are free! Well, this country is a hypocrite! They try and make you think they set you free by calling you a second-class citizen. No, you're nothing but a 20th century slave.

Just as it took nationalism to remove colonialism from Asia and Africa, it'll take black nationalism today to remove colonialism from the backs and the minds of twenty-two million Afro-Americans here in this country. And 1964 looks like it might be the year of the ballot or the bullet.

Why does it look like it might be the year of the ballot or the bullet? Because Negroes have listened to the trickery and the lies and the false promises of the white man now for too long, and they're fed up. They've become disenchanted. They've become disillusioned. They've become dissatisfied. And all of this has built up frustrations in the black community that makes the black community throughout America today more explosive than all of the atomic bombs the Russians can ever invent. Whenever you got a racial powder keg sitting in your lap, you're in more trouble than if you had an atomic powder keg sitting in your lap. When a racial powder keg goes off, it doesn't care who it knocks out the way. Understand this, it's dangerous.

And in 1964, this seems to be the year. Because what can the white man use, now, to fool us? After he put down that March on Washington – and you see all through that now, he tricked you, had you marching down to Washington. Had you marching back and forth between the feet of a dead man named Lincoln and another dead man named George Washington, singing, "We Shall Overcome."

He made a chump out of you. He made a fool out of you. He made you think you were going somewhere and you end up going nowhere but between Lincoln and Washington.

So today our people are disillusioned. They've become disenchanted. They've become dissatisfied. And in their frustrations they want action. And in 1964 you'll see this young black man, this new generation, asking for the ballot or the bullet. That old Uncle Tom action is outdated. The young generation don't want to hear anything about "the odds are against us." What do we care about odds?

When this country here was first being founded, there were thirteen colonies. The whites were colonized. They were fed up with this taxation without representation. So some of them stood up and said, "Liberty or death!" I went to a white school over here in Mason, Michigan. The white man made the mistake of letting me read his history books. He made the mistake of teaching me that Patrick Henry was a patriot, and George Washington – wasn't nothing non-violent about ol' Pat, or George Washington. "Liberty or death" is was what brought about the freedom of whites in this country from the English.

They didn't care about the odds. Why, they faced the wrath of the entire British Empire. And in those days, they used to say that the British Empire was so vast and so powerful that the sun would never set on it. This is how big it was, yet these thirteen little scrawny states, tired of taxation without representation, tired of being exploited and oppressed and degraded, told that big British Empire, "Liberty or death." And here you have 22 million Afro-Americans, black people today, catching more hell than Patrick Henry ever saw.

And I'm here to tell you in case you don't know it – that you got a new, you got a new generation of black people in this country who don't care anything whatsoever about odds. They don't want to hear you ol' Uncle Tom, handkerchief-heads talking about the odds. No! This is a new generation. If they're going to draft these young black men, and send them over to Korea or to South Vietnam to face 800 million Chinese... If you're not afraid of those odds, you shouldn't be afraid of these odds.

Why is America – why does this loom to be such an explosive political year? Because this is the year of politics. This is the year when all of the white politicians are going to come into the Negro community. You never see them until election time. You can't find them until election time. They're going to come in with false promises. And as they make these false promises they're going to feed our frustrations, and this will only serve to make matters worse. I'm no politician. I'm not even a student of politics. I'm not a Republican, nor a Democrat, nor an American – and got sense enough to know it.

I'm one of the 22 million black victims of the Democrats. One of the 22 million black victims of the Republicans and one of the 22 million black victims of Americanism. And when I speak, I don't speak as a Democrat or a Republican, nor an American. I speak as a victim of America's so-called democracy. You and I have never seen democracy – all we've seen is hypocrisy.

When we open our eyes today and look around America, we see America not through the eyes of someone who has enjoyed the fruits of Americanism. We see America through the eyes of someone who has been the victim of Americanism. We don't see any American dream. We've experienced only the American nightmare. We haven't benefited from America's democracy. We've only suffered from America's hypocrisy. And the generation that's coming up now can see it. And are not afraid to say it. If you go to jail, so what? If you're black, you were born in jail.

If you black you were born in jail, in the North as well as the South. Stop talking about the South. As long as you south of the Canadian border, you South. Don't call Governor Wallace a Dixie governor, Romney is a Dixie Governor.

Twenty-two million black victims of Americanism are waking up and they are gaining a new political consciousness, becoming politically mature. And as they become — develop this political maturity, they're able to see the recent trends in these political elections. They see that the whites are so evenly divided that every time they vote, the race is so close they have to go back and count the votes all over again. Which means that any block, any minority that has a block of votes that stick together is in a strategic position. Either way you go, that's who gets it. You're in a position to determine who'll go to the White House and who'll stay in the doghouse.

You're the one who has that power. You can keep Johnson in Washington D.C., or you can send him back to his Texas cotton patch. You're the one who sent Kennedy to Washington. You're the one who put the present Democratic administration in Washington, D.C. The whites were evenly divided. It was the fact that you threw 80 percent of your votes behind the Democrats that put the Democrats in the White House.

When you see this, you can see that the Negro vote is the key factor. And despite the fact that you are in a position to be the determining factor, what do you get out of it? The Democrats have been in Washington, D.C. only because of the Negro vote. They've been down there four years. And they're – all other legislation they wanted to bring up they've brought it up, and gotten it out of the way, and now they bring up you. And now they bring up you! You put them first and they put you last. Because you're a chump! A political chump.

In Washington, D.C., in the House of Representatives there are 257 who are Democrats. Only 177 are Republican. In the Senate there are 67 Democrats. Only 33 are Republicans. The party that you backed controls two-thirds of the House of Representatives and the Senate and still they can't keep their promise to you. 'Cause you're a chump.

Any time you throw your weight behind a political party that controls two-thirds of the government, and that party can't keep the promise that it made to you during election-time, and you're dumb enough to walk around continuing to identify yourself with that party, you're not only a chump but you're a traitor to your race.

What kind of alibi do come up with? They try and pass the buck to the Dixiecrats. Now, back during the days when you were blind, deaf and dumb, ignorant, politically imma-ture, naturally you went along with that. But today, as your eyes come open, and you develop political maturity, you're able to see and think for yourself, and you can see that a Dixiecrat is nothing but a Democrat – in disguise.

You look at the structure of the government that controls this country, is controlled by 16 senatorial committees and 20 congressional committees. Of the 16 senatorial commit-tees that run the government, 10 of them are in the hands of southern segregationists. Of the 20 congressional com-mittees that run the government, 12 of them are in the hands of southern segregationists. And they're going to tell you and me that the South lost the war?

You, today, are in the hands of a government of segregationists. Racists, white supremacists, who belong to the Democratic party but disguise themselves as Dixiecrats. A Dixiecrat is nothing but a Democrat. Whoever runs the Democrats is also the father of the Dixiecrats. And the father of all of them is sitting in the White House. I say, and I'll say it again, you got a president who's nothing but a southern segregationist from the state of Texas. They'll lynch in Texas as quick as they'll lynch you in Mississippi. Only in Texas they lynch you with a Texas accent, in Mississippi they lynch you with a Mississippi accent.

The first thing the cracker does when he comes in power, he takes all the Negro leaders and invites them for coffee. To show that he's all right. And those Uncle Toms can't pass up the coffee. They come away from the coffee table telling you and me that this man is all right . 'Cause he's from the South and since he's from the South he can deal with the South. Look at the logic that they're using. What about Eastland? He's from the South. Why not make him the president? If Johnson is a good man 'cause he's from Texas, and being from Texas will enable him to deal with the South, Eastland can deal with the South better than Johnson!

Oh, I say you been misled. You been had. You been took. I was in Washington a couple of weeks ago while the senators were filibustering and I noticed in the back of the Senate a huge map, and on this map it showed the distribution of Negroes in America. And surprisingly, the same senators that were involved in the filibuster were from the states where there were the most Negroes. Why were they filibustering the civil rights legislation? Because the civil rights legislation is supposed to guarantee boarding rights to Negroes from those states. And those senators from those states know that if the Negroes in those states can vote, those senators are down the drain. The representatives of those states go down the drain.

And in the Constitution of this country it has a stipulation, wherein, whenever the rights, the voting rights of people in a certain district are violated, then the representative who's from that particular district, according to the Constitution, is supposed to be expelled from the Congress. Now, if this particular aspect of the Constitution was enforced, why, you wouldn't have a cracker in Washington, D.C.

But what would happen? When you expel the Dixiecrat, you're expelling the Democrat. When you destroy the power of the Dixiecrat, you are destroying the power of the Democratic Party. So how in the world can the Democratic Party in the South actually side with you, in sincerity, when all of its power is based in the South?

These Northern Democrats are in cahoots with the southern Democrats. They're playing a giant con game, a political con game. You know how it goes. One of 'em comes to you and make believe he's for you. And he's in cahoots with the other one that's not for you. Why? Because neither one of 'em is for you. But they got to make you go with one of 'em or the other.

So this is a con game, and this is what they've been doing with you and me all of these years. First thing, Johnson got off the plane when he become president, he ask, "Where's Dickey?" You know who Dickey is? Dickey is old southern cracker Richard Russell. Lookie here! Yes, Lyndon B. Johnson's best friend is the one who is a head, who's heading the forces that are filibustering civil rights legislation. You tell me how in the hell is he going to be Johnson's best friend? How can Johnson be his friend and your friend too? No, that man is too tricky. Especially if his friend is still ol' Dickey.

Whenever the Negroes keep the Democrats in power they're keeping the Dixiecrats in power. This is true! A vote for a Democrat is nothing but a vote for a Dixiecrat. I know you don't like me saying that. I'm not the kind of person who come here to say what you like. I'm going to tell you the truth whether you like it or not.

Up here in the North you have the same thing. The Democratic Party don't – they don't do it that way. They got a thing they call gerrymandering. They maneuver you out of power. Even though you can vote they fix it so you're voting for nobody. They got you going and coming. In the South they're outright political wolves, in the North they're political foxes. A fox and a wolf are both canine, both belong to the dog family. Now, you take your choice. You going to choose a northern dog or a southern dog? Because either dog you choose, I guarantee you, you'll still be in the doghouse.

This is why I say it's the ballot or the bullet. It's liberty or it's death. It's freedom for everybody or freedom for nobody. America today finds herself in a unique situation. Historically, revolutions are bloody, oh yes they are. They have never had a bloodless revolution. Or a non-violent revolution. That don't happen even in Hollywood You don't have a revolution in which you love your enemy. And you don't have a revolution in which you are begging the system of exploitation to integrate you into it. Revolutions overturn systems. Revolutions destroy systems.

A revolution is bloody, but America is in a unique position. She's the only country in history, in the position actually to become involved in a bloodless revolution. The Russian Revolution was bloody, Chinese Revolution was bloody, French Revolution was bloody, Cuban Revolution was bloody. And there was nothing more bloody than the American Revolution. But today, this country can become involved in a revolution that won't take bloodshed. All she's got to do is give the black man in this country everything that's due him, everything.

I hope that the white man can see this. 'Cause if you don't see it you're finished. If you don't see it you're going to become involved in some action in which you don't have a chance. We don't care anything about your atomic bomb; it's useless, because other countries have atomic bombs. When two or three different countries have atomic bombs, nobody can use them. So it means that the white man today is without a weapon. If you want some action you've got to come on down to Earth, and there's more black people on Earth than there are white people.

I only got a couple more minutes. The white man can never win another war on the ground. His days of war – victory – his days of battleground victory are over. Can I prove it? Yes. Take all the action that's going on this Earth right now that he's involved in. Tell me where he's winning – nowhere. Why, some rice farmers, some rice farmers! Some rice-eaters ran him out of Korea, yes they ran him out of Korea. Rice-eaters, with nothing but gym shoes and a rifle and a bowl of rice, took him and his tanks and his napalm and all that other action he's supposed to have and ran him across the Yalu. Why? Because the day that he can win on the ground has passed.

Up in French Indochina, those little peasants, rice-growers, took on the might of the French army and ran all the Frenchmen, you remember Dien Bien Phu! The same thing happened in Algeria, in Africa. They didn't have anything but a rifle. The French had all these highly mechanized instruments of warfare. But they put some guerilla action on. And a white man can't fight a guerilla warfare. Guerilla action takes heart, take nerve, and he doesn't have that. He's brave when he's got tanks. He's brave when he's got planes. He's brave when he's got bombs. He's brave when he's got a whole lot of company along with him. But you take that little man from Africa and Asia; turn him loose in the woods with a blade. A blade. That's all he needs. All he needs is a blade. And when the sun comes down – goes down and it's dark, it's even-Stephen.

So it's the, it's the ballot or the bullet. Today, our people can see that we're faced with a government conspiracy. This government has failed us. The senators who are filibustering concerning your and my rights, that's the government. Don't say it's southern senators, this is the government. This is a government filibuster. It's not a segregationist filibuster, it's a government filibuster. Any kind of activity that takes place on the floor of the Congress or the Senate, that's the government. Any kind of dilly-dallying, that's the government. Any kind of pussy-footing, that's the government. Any kind of act that's designed to delay or deprive you and me, right now, of getting full rights, that's the government that's responsible. And anytime you find the government involved in a conspiracy to violate the citizenship or the civil rights of a people in 1964, then you are wasting your time going to that government expecting redress. Instead you have to take that government to the world court and accuse it of genocide and all of the other crimes that it is guilty of today.

So those of us whose political and economic and social philosophy is black nationalism have become involved in the civil rights struggle. We have injected ourselves into the civil rights struggle. And we intend to expand it from the level of civil rights to the level of human rights. As long as you fight it on the level of civil rights, you're under Uncle Sam's jurisdiction. You're going to his court expecting him to correct the problem. He created the problem. He's the criminal! You don't take your case to the criminal, you take your criminal to court.

When the government of South Africa began to trample upon the human rights of the people of South Africa they were taken to the U.N. When the government of Portugal began to trample upon the rights of our brothers and sisters in Angola, it was taken before the U.N. Why, even the white man took the Hungarian question to the U.N. And just this week, Chief Justice Goldberg was crying over three million Jews in Russia, about their human rights – charging Russia with violating the U.N. Charter because of its mistreatment of the human rights of Jews in Russia. Now you tell me how can the plight of everybody on this Earth reach the halls of the United Nations and you have twenty-two million Afro-Americans whose churches are being bombed, whose little girls are being murdered, whose leaders are being shot down in broad daylight? Now you tell me why the leaders of this struggle have never taken [their case to the U.N.]

So our next move is to take the entire civil rights struggle – problem – into the United Nations and let the world see that Uncle Sam is guilty of violating the human rights of 22 million Afro-Americans right down to the year of 1964 and still has the audacity or the nerve to stand up and represent himself as the leader of the free world? Not only is he a crook, he's a hypocrite. Here he is standing up in front of other people, Uncle Sam, with the blood of your and mine mothers and fathers on his hands. With the blood dripping down his jaws like a bloody-jawed wolf. And still got the nerve to point his finger at other countries. In 1964 you can't even get civil rights legislation and this man has got the nerve to stand up and talk about South Africa or talk about Nazi Germany or talk about Portugal. No, no more days like those!

So I say in my conclusion, the only way we're going to solve it: we got to unite. We got to work together in unity and harmony. And black nationalism is the key. How we gonna overcome the tendency to be at each other's throats that always exists in our neighborhood? And the reason this tendency exists – the strategy of the white man has always been divide and conquer. He keeps us divided in order to conquer us. He tells you, I'm for separation and you for integration, and keep us fighting with each other. No, I'm not for separation and you're not for integration, what you and

I are for is freedom. Only, you think that integration will get you freedom; I think that separation will get me freedom. We both got the same objective, we just got different ways of getting' at it.

So I studied this man, Billy Graham, who preaches white nationalism. That's what he preaches. I say, that's what he preaches. The whole church structure in this country is white nationalism, you go inside a white church – that's what they preaching, white nationalism. They got Jesus white, Mary white, God white, everybody white – that's white nationalism.

So what he does – the way he circumvents the jealousy and envy that he ordinarily would incur among the heads of the church – whenever you go into an area where the church already is, you going to run into trouble. Because they got that thing, what you call it, syndicated ... they got a syndicate just like the racketeers have. I'm going to say what's on my mind because the preachers already proved to you that they got a syndicate. And when you're out in the rackets, whenever you're getting in another man's territory, you know, they gang up on you. And that's the same way with you. You run into the same thing. So how Billy Graham gets around that, instead of going into somebody else's territory, like he going to start a new church, he doesn't try and start a church, he just goes in preaching Christ. And he says anybody who believe in him, you go wherever you find him.

So, this helps all the churches, and since it helps all the churches, they don't fight him. Well, we going to do the same thing, only our gospel is black nationalism. His gospel is white nationalism, our gospel is black nationalism. And the gospel of black nationalism, as I told you, means you should control your own, the politics of your community, the economy of your community, and all of the society in which you live should be under your control. And once you... feel that this philosophy will solve your problem, go join any church where that's preached. Don't join any church where white nationalism is preached. Why, you can go to a Negro church and be exposed to white nationalism. 'Cause when you are on – when you walk in a Negro church and see a white Jesus and a white Mary and some white angels, that Negro church is preaching white nationalism.

But, when you go to a church and you see the pastor of that church with a philosophy and a program that's designed to bring black people together and elevate black people, join that church. Join that church. If you see where the NAACP is preaching and practicing that which is designed to make black nationalism materialize, join the NAACP. Join any kind of organization – civic, religious, fraternal, political or otherwise that's based on lifting the black man up and making him master of his own community.

Nelson Mandela, *First Speech*

[February 11, 1990, Cape Town, South Africa]

NOTE On February 11, 1990, after over 25 years of imprisonment, Nelson Mandela (1918-2013) was released from Victor Verster Prison, roughly 30 miles east of Cape Town, and he immediately went to the front steps of its City Hall for his first speech as a free man for a crowd of 50,000 people and a worldwide television audience. Here are photographs of the crowd and of Mandela giving his speech followed by extracts of what he said that day.

Amandla! Amandla! i-Afrika, mayibuye! [Power! Power! Africa it is ours!] My friends, comrades and fellow South Africans, I greet you all in the name of peace, democracy and freedom for all. I stand here before you not as a prophet but as a humble servant of you, the people.

Your tireless and heroic sacrifices have made it possible for me to be here today. I therefore place the remaining years of my life in your hands.

On this day of my release, I extend my sincere and warmest gratitude to the millions of my compatriots and those in every corner of the globe who have campaigned tirelessly for my release.

I extend special greetings to the people of Cape Town, the city which has been my home for three decades. Your mass marches and other forms of struggle have served as a constant source of strength to all political prisoners." He then extended salutations to the African National Congress and its leaders and allies and expressed "my deep appreciation for the strength given to me during my long and lonely years in prison by my beloved wife and family.

Today the majority of South Africans, black and white, recognize that apartheid has no future. It has to be ended by our own decisive mass actions in order to build peace and security. The mass campaigns of defiance and other actions of our organizations and people can only culminate in the establishment of democracy.

The apartheid destruction on our subcontinent is incalculable. The fabric of family life of millions of my people has been shattered. Millions are homeless and unemployed.

Our economy lies in ruins and our people are embroiled in political strife. Our resort to the armed struggle in 1960 with the formation of the military wing of the A.N.C., Umkonto We Sizwe, was a purely defensive action against the violence of apartheid.

The factors which necessitated the armed struggle still exist today. We have no option but to continue. We express the hope that a climate conducive to a negotiated settlement would be created soon so that there may no longer be the need for the armed struggle.

I am a loyal and disciplined member of the African National Congress. I am, therefore, in full agreement with all of its objectives, strategies and tactics.

The need to unite the people of our country is as important a task now as it always has been. No individual leader is able to take all these enormous tasks on his own. It is our task as leaders to place our views before our organization and to allow the democratic structures to decide on the way forward.

On the question of democratic practice, I feel duty bound to make the point that a leader of the movement is a person who has been democratically elected at a national conference. This is a principle which must be upheld without any exceptions.

Today, I wish to report to you that my talks with the Government have been aimed at normalizing the political situation in the country. We have not as yet begun discussing the basic demands of the struggle.

I wish to stress that I myself had at no time entered into negotiations about the future of our country, except to insist on a meeting between the A.N.C. and the Government.

Mr. de Klerk has gone further than any other Nationalist president in taking real steps to normalize the situation. However, there are further steps as outlined in the Harare Declaration that have to be met before negotiations on the basic demands of our people can begin.

I reiterate our call for inter alia the immediate ending of the state of emergency and the freeing of all, and not only some, political prisoners.

Only such a normalized situation which allows for free political activity can allow us to consult our people in order to obtain a mandate. The people need to be consulted on who will negotiate and on the content of such negotiations.

Negotiations cannot take place above the heads or behind the backs of our people. It is our belief that the future of our country can only be determined by a body which is democratically elected on a non-racial basis.

Negotiations on the dismantling of apartheid will have to address the overwhelming demand of our people for a democratic non-racial and unitary South Africa. There must be an end to white monopoly on political power.

And a fundamental restructuring of our political and economic systems to insure that the inequalities of apartheid are addressed and our society thoroughly democratized.

It must be added that Mr. de Klerk himself is a man of integrity who is acutely aware of the dangers of a public figure not honoring his undertakings. But as an organization, we base our policy and strategy on the harsh reality we are faced with, and this reality is that we are still suffering under the policies of the Nationalist Government.

Our struggle has reached a decisive moment. We call on

our people to seize this moment so that the process toward democracy is rapid and uninterrupted. We have waited too long for our freedom. We can no longer wait. Now is the time to intensify the struggle on all fronts.

To relax our efforts now would be a mistake which generations to come will not be able to forgive. The sight of freedom looming on the horizon should encourage us to redouble our efforts. It is only through disciplined mass action that our victory can "be assured.

We call on our white compatriots to join us in the shaping of a new South Africa. The freedom movement is the political home for you, too. We call on the international community to continue the campaign to isolate the apartheid regime.

To lift sanctions now would be to run the risk of aborting the process toward the complete eradication of apartheid. Our march to freedom is irreversible. We must not allow fear to stand in our way.

Universal suffrage on a common voters roll in a united democratic and non-racial South Africa is the only way to peace and racial harmony.

In conclusion, I wish to go to my own words during my trial in 1964. They are as true today as they were then: 'I have fought against white domination, and I have fought against black domination. I have cherished the idea of a democratic and free society in which all persons live together in harmony and with equal opportunities.'

It is an ideal which I hope to live for and to achieve. But if needs be, it is an ideal for which I am prepared to die. My friends, I have no words of eloquence to offer today except to say that the remaining days of my life are in your hands. I hope you will disperse with discipline. And not a single one of you should do anything which will make other people to say that we can't control our own people.

Nelson Mandela, *Presidential Inaugural Address*

[May 10, 1994, Pretoria]

NOTE Statement of the President of the African National Congress, Nelson Mandela, at his inauguration as President of the Democratic Republic of South Africa, Union Buildings, Pretoria, may 10 1994.

Today, all of us do, by our presence here, and by our celebrations in other parts of our country and the world, confer glory and hope to newborn liberty.

Out of the experience of an extraordinary human disaster that lasted too long, must be born a society of which all humanity will be proud.

Our daily deeds as ordinary South Africans must produce an actual South African reality that will reinforce humanity's belief in justice, strengthen its confidence in the nobility of the human soul and sustain all our hopes for a glorious life for all.

All this we owe both to ourselves and to the peoples of the world who are so well represented here today.

To my compatriots, I have no hesitation in saying that each one of us is as intimately attached to the soil of this beautiful country as are the famous jacaranda trees of Pretoria and the mimosa trees of the bushveld.

Each time one of us touches the soil of this land, we feel a sense of personal renewal. The national mood changes as the seasons change.

We are moved by a sense of joy and exhilaration when the grass turns green and the flowers bloom.

That spiritual and physical oneness we all share with this

common homeland explains the depth of the pain we all carried in our hearts as we saw our country tear itself apart in a terrible conflict, and as we saw it spurned, outlawed and isolated by the peoples of the world, precisely because it has become the universal base of the pernicious ideology and practice of racism and racial oppression.

We, the people of South Africa, feel fulfilled that humanity has taken us back into its bosom, that we, who were outlaws not so long ago, have today been given the rare privilege to be host to the nations of the world on our own soil.

We thank all our distinguished international guests for having come to take possession with the people of our country of what is, after all, a common victory for justice, for peace, for human dignity.

We trust that you will continue to stand by us as we tackle the challenges of building peace, prosperity, non-sexism, non-racialism and democracy.

We deeply appreciate the role that the masses of our people and their political mass democratic, religious, women, youth, business, traditional and other leaders have played to bring about this conclusion. Not least among them is my Second Deputy President, the Honourable F.W. de Klerk.

We would also like to pay tribute to our security forces, in all their ranks, for the distinguished role they have played in securing our first democratic elections and the transition to democracy, from blood-thirsty forces which still refuse to see the light.

The time for the healing of the wounds has come.

The moment to bridge the chasms that divide us has come.

The time to build is upon us.

We have, at last, achieved our political emancipation. We pledge ourselves to liberate all our people from the continuing bondage of poverty, deprivation, suffering, gender and other discrimination.

We succeeded to take our last steps to freedom in conditions of relative peace. We commit ourselves to the construction of a complete, just and lasting peace.

We have triumphed in the effort to implant hope in the breasts of the millions of our people. We enter into a covenant that we shall build the society in which all South Africans, both black and white, will be able to walk tall, without any fear in their hearts, assured of their inalienable right to human dignity – a rainbow nation at peace with itself and the world.

As a token of its commitment to the renewal of our country, the new Interim Government of National Unity will, as a matter of urgency, address the issue of amnesty for various categories of our people who are currently serving terms of imprisonment.

We dedicate this day to all the heroes and heroines in this country and the rest of the world who sacrificed in many ways and surrendered their lives so that we could be free.

Their dreams have become reality. Freedom is their reward.

We are both humbled and elevated by the honour and privilege that you, the people of South Africa, have bestowed on us, as the first President of a united, democratic, non-racial and non-sexist South Africa, to lead our country out of the valley of darkness.

We understand it still that there is no easy road to freedom.

We know it well that none of us acting alone can achieve success.

We must therefore act together as a united people, for national reconciliation, for nation building, for the birth of a new world.

Let there be justice for all.

Let there be peace for all.

Let there be work, bread, water and salt for all.

Let each know that for each the body, the mind and the soul have been freed to fulfill themselves.

Never, never and never again shall it be that this beautiful land will again experience the oppression of one by another and suffer the indignity of being the skunk of the world.

Let freedom reign.

The sun shall never set on so glorious a human achievement!

God bless Africa!

Thank you.

Gabriel García Márquez, *Acceptance Speech for the Nobel Prize in Literature*

[December 8, 1982, Oslo]

NOTE Gabriel García Márquez (1927-2014) was a Latin American writer. He worked many years as a journalist in Latin American and European cities and later also as a screenwriter and publicist, before settling in Mexico. His best-known work, the novel *One Hundred Years of Solitude* (1967), recounts the history of the fictional village of Macondo, the setting of much of his work; enormously admired and influential, it became the principal vehicle for the style known as magic realism. Later novels include *The Autumn of the Patriarch* (1975), *Love in the Time of Cholera* (1985), *The General in His Labyrinth* (1989), and *Memories of My Melancholy Whores* (2004). He received the Nobel Prize for Literature in 1982.

Antonio Pigafetta, a Florentine navigator who went with Magellan on the first voyage around the world, wrote, upon his passage through our southern lands of America, a strictly accurate account that nonetheless resembles a venture into fantasy. In it he recorded that he had seen hogs with navels on their haunches, clawless birds whose hens laid eggs on the backs of their mates, and others still, resembling tongueless pelicans, with beaks like spoons. He wrote of having seen a misbegotten creature with the head and ears of a mule, a camel's body, the legs of a deer and the whinny of a horse. He described how the first native encountered in Patagonia was confronted with a mirror, whereupon that impassioned giant lost his senses to the terror of his own image.

This short and fascinating book, which even then contained the seeds of our present-day novels, is by no means the most staggering account of our reality in that age. The

Chronicles of the Indies left us countless others. Eldorado, our so avidly sought and illusory land, appeared on numerous maps for many a long year, shifting its place and form to suit the fantasy of cartographers. In his search for the fountain of eternal youth, the mythical Alvar Núñez Cabeza de Vaca explored the north of Mexico for eight years, in a deluded expedition whose members devoured each other and only five of whom returned, of the six hundred who had undertaken it. One of the many unfathomed mysteries of that age is that of the eleven thousand mules, each loaded with one hundred pounds of gold, that left Cuzco one day to pay the ransom of Atahualpa and never reached their destination. Subsequently, in colonial times, hens were sold in Cartagena de Indias, that had been raised on alluvial land and whose gizzards contained tiny lumps of gold. One founder's lust for gold beset us until recently. As late as the last century, a German mission appointed to study the construction of an interoceanic railroad across the Isthmus of Panama concluded that the project was feasible on one condition: that the rails not be made of iron, which was scarce in the region, but of gold.

Our independence from Spanish domination did not put us beyond the reach of madness. General Antonio López de Santana, three times dictator of Mexico, held a magnificent funeral for the right leg he had lost in the so-called Pastry War. General Gabriel García Moreno ruled Ecuador for sixteen years as an absolute monarch; at his wake, the corpse was seated on the presidential chair, decked out in full-dress uniform and a protective layer of medals. General Maximiliano Hernández Martínez, the theosophical despot of El Salvador who had thirty thousand peasants slaughtered in a savage massacre, invented a pendulum to detect poison in his food, and had streetlamps draped in red paper to defeat an epidemic of scarlet fever. The statue to General Francisco Moraz'n erected in the main square of Tegucigalpa is actually one of Marshal Ney, purchased at a Paris warehouse of second-hand sculptures.

Eleven years ago, the Chilean Pablo Neruda, one of the outstanding poets of our time, enlightened this audience with his word. Since then, the Europeans of good will – and sometimes those of bad, as well – have been struck, with ever greater force, by the unearthly tidings of Latin America, that boundless realm of haunted men and historic women, whose unending obstinacy blurs into legend. We have not had a moment's rest. A promethean president, entrenched in his burning palace, died fighting an entire army, alone; and two suspicious airplane accidents, yet to be explained, cut short the life of another great-hearted president and that of a democratic soldier who had revived the dignity of his people. There have been five wars and seventeen military coups; there emerged a diabolic dictator who is carrying out, in God's name, the first Latin American ethnocide of our time. In the meantime, twenty million Latin American children died before the age of one – more than have been born in Europe since 1970. Those missing because of repression number nearly one hundred and twenty thousand, which is as if no one could account for all the inhabitants of Uppsala. Numerous women arrested while pregnant have given birth in Argentine prisons, yet nobody knows the whereabouts and identity of their children who were furtively adopted or sent to an orphanage by order of the military authorities. Because they tried to change this state of things, nearly two hundred thousand men and women have died throughout the continent, and over one hundred thousand have lost their lives in three small and ill-fated countries of Central America: Nicaragua, El Salvador and Guatemala. If this had happened in the United States, the corresponding figure would be that of one million six hundred thousand violent deaths in four years.

One million people have fled Chile, a country with a

tradition of hospitality – that is, ten per cent of its population. Uruguay, a tiny nation of two and a half million inhabitants which considered itself the continent's most civilized country, has lost to exile one out of every five citizens. Since 1979, the civil war in El Salvador has produced almost one refugee every twenty minutes. The country that could be formed of all the exiles and forced emigrants of Latin America would have a population larger than that of Norway.

I dare to think that it is this outsized reality, and not just its literary expression, that has deserved the attention of the Swedish Academy of Letters. A reality not of paper, but one that lives within us and determines each instant of our countless daily deaths, and that nourishes a source of insatiable creativity, full of sorrow and beauty, of which this roving and nostalgic Colombian is but one cipher more, singled out by fortune. Poets and beggars, musicians and prophets, warriors and scoundrels, all creatures of that unbridled reality, we have had to ask but little of imagination, for our crucial problem has been a lack of conventional means to render our lives believable. This, my friends, is the crux of our solitude.

And if these difficulties, whose essence we share, hinder us, it is understandable that the rational talents on this side of the world, exalted in the contemplation of their own cultures, should have found themselves without valid means to interpret us. It is only natural that they insist on measuring us with the yardstick that they use for themselves, forgetting that the ravages of life are not the same for all, and that the quest of our own identity is just as arduous and bloody for us as it was for them. The interpretation of our reality through patterns not our own, serves only to make us ever more unknown, ever less free, ever more solitary. Venerable Europe would perhaps be more perceptive if it tried to see us in its own past. If only it recalled that London took three hundred years to build its first city wall, and three hundred years more to acquire a bishop; that Rome labored in a gloom of uncertainty for twenty centuries, until an Etruscan King anchored it in history; and that the peaceful Swiss of today, who feast us with their mild cheeses and apathetic watches, bloodied Europe as soldiers of fortune, as late as the Sixteenth Century. Even at the height of the Renaissance, twelve thousand lansquenets in the pay of the imperial armies sacked and devastated Rome and put eight thousand of its inhabitants to the sword.

I do not mean to embody the illusions of Tonio Kröger, whose dreams of uniting a chaste north to a passionate south were exalted here, fifty-three years ago, by Thomas Mann. But I do believe that those clear-sighted Europeans who struggle, here as well, for a more just and humane homeland, could help us far better if they reconsidered their way of seeing us. Solidarity with our dreams will not make us feel less alone, as long as it is not translated into concrete acts of legitimate support for all the peoples that assume the illusion of having a life of their own in the distribution of the world.

Latin America neither wants, nor has any reason, to be a pawn without a will of its own; nor is it merely wishful thinking that its quest for independence and originality should become a Western aspiration. However, the navigational advances that have narrowed such distances between our Americas and Europe seem, conversely, to have accentuated our cultural remoteness. Why is the originality so readily granted us in literature so mistrustfully denied us in our difficult attempts at social change? Why think that the social justice sought by progressive Europeans for their own countries cannot also be a goal for Latin America, with different methods for dissimilar conditions? No: the immeasurable violence and pain of our history are the result of age-old inequities and untold bitterness, and not a conspiracy plotted three thousand leagues from our home. But many

European leaders and thinkers have thought so, with the childishness of old-timers who have forgotten the fruitful excess of their youth as if it were impossible to find another destiny than to live at the mercy of the two great masters of the world. This, my friends, is the very scale of our solitude.

In spite of this, to oppression, plundering and abandonment, we respond with life. Neither floods nor plagues, famines nor cataclysms, nor even the eternal wars of century upon century, have been able to subdue the persistent advantage of life over death. An advantage that grows and quickens: every year, there are seventy-four million more births than deaths, a sufficient number of new lives to multiply, each year, the population of New York sevenfold. Most of these births occur in the countries of least resources – including, of course, those of Latin America. Conversely, the most prosperous countries have succeeded in accumulating powers of destruction such as to annihilate, a hundred times over, not only all the human beings that have existed to this day, but also the totality of all living beings that have ever drawn breath on this planet of misfortune.

On a day like today, my master William Faulkner said, "I decline to accept the end of man." I would fall unworthy of standing in this place that was his, if I were not fully aware that the colossal tragedy he refused to recognize thirty-two years ago is now, for the first time since the beginning of humanity, nothing more than a simple scientific possiblity. Faced with this awesome reality that must have seemed a mere utopia through all of human time, we, the inventors of tales, who will believe anything, feel entitled to believe that it is not yet too late to engage in the creation of the opposite utopia. A new and sweeping utopia of life, where no one will be able to decide for others how they die, where love will prove true and happiness be possible, and where the races condemned to one hundred years of solitude will have, at last and forever, a second opportunity on earth.

José Mujica Cordano, *About Human Happiness*

[June 20, 2012, Rio de Janeiro]

NOTE José Alberto "Pepe" Mujica Cordano (1935) is a Uruguayan politician, who served as the 40th President of Uruguay from 2010 to 2015. He has been described as "the world's humblest head of state" due to his austere lifestyle and his donation of around 90 percent of his $12,000 monthly salary to charities that benefit poor people and small entrepreneurs.
This speech was delivered at the General Debate of the 2nd Plenary Meeting in Rio de Janeiro in Brazil (Rio+20 - United Nations Conference on Sustainable Development).

To all of the authorities present here, from every latitude and organization, thank you very much. I want to thank the people of Brazil and Mrs. President, Dilma Rousseff. Thank you all for the good faith undoubtedly expressed by all of the speakers that preceded me. We hereby express our innermost will as rulers, to adhere to all the agreements our wretched humanity, may chance to subscribe. Notwithstanding, let us take this opportunity to ask some questions out loud. All afternoon long, we have been talking about sustainable development, about rescuing the masses from the claws of poverty. What is it that flutters within our minds? Is it the model of development and consumption, which is shaped after that of affluent societies? I ask this question: what would happen to this planet if the people of India had the same number of cars per family as the Germans? How much oxygen would there be left for us to breathe? More clearly: Does the world today have the material elements to enable 7 or 8 billion people to enjoy the same level of consumption and squandering as the most affluent Western societies? WIll that ever be possible? Or will we have to start a different type of discussion one day? Because we have created this civilization in which we live: the progeny of the market, of the competition, which has begotten prodigious and explosive material progress. But the market economy has created market societies. And it has given us this globalization, which means being aware of the whole planet.

Are we ruling over globalization or is globalization ruling over us? Is it possible to speak of solidarity and of "being all together" in an economy based on ruthless competition? How far does our fraternity go? I am not saying any of to undermine the importance of this event. On the contrary, the challenge ahead of us is of a colossal magnitude and the great crisis is not an ecological crisis, but rather a political one. Today, man does not govern the forces he has un-leashed, but rather, it is these forces that govern man; and life. Because we do not come into this planet simply to de-velop, just like that, indiscriminately. We come into this planet to be happy. Because life is short and it slips away from us. And no material belonging is worth as much as life, and this is fundamental. But if life is going to slip through my fingers, working and over-working in order to be able to consume more, and the consumer society is the engine-be-cause ultimately, if consumption is paralyzed, the economy stops, and if you stop economy, the ghost of stagnation ap-pears for each one of us, but it is this hyper-consumption that is harming the planet. And this hyper-consumption needs to be generated, making things that have a short useful life, in order to sell a lot. Thus, a light bulb cannot last longer than 1000 hours. But there are light bulbs that last 100,000 hours! But these cannot be manufactured, because the problem is the market, because we have to work and we have to sustain a civilization of "use and discard", and so, we are trapped in a vicious cycle. These are problems of a political nature, which are showing us that it's time to start fighting for a different culture. I'm not talking about returning to the days of the caveman, or erecting a "monument to backwardness". But we cannot continue like this, indefinitely, being ruled by the market, on the contrary, we have to rule over the market. This is why I say, in my humble way of thinking, that the problem we are facing is political.

The old thinkers – Epicurus, Seneca and even the Aymaras (indios) – used to say: "A poor person is not someone who has little but one who needs infinitely more, and more and more". This is a cultural issue. So I salute the efforts and agreements being made. And I will adhere to them, as a ruler. I know some things I'm saying are not easy to digest. But we must realize that the water crisis and the aggression to the environment is not the cause. The cause is the model of civilization that we have created. And the thing we have to re-examine is our way of life. I belong to a small country well endowed with natural resources for life. In my country, there are a bit more than 3 million people. But there are about 13 million cows, some of the best in the world. And about 8 or 10 million excellent sheep. My country is an exporter of food, dairy, meat. It is a low-relief plain and almost 90% of the land is fertile. My fellow workers, fought hard for the 8 hour workday. And now they are making that 6 hours. But the person who works 6 hours, gets two jobs, therefore, he works longer than before. But why? Because he needs to make monthly payments for: the motorcycle, the car, more and more payments, and when he's done with that, he realizes he is a rheumatic old man, like me, and his life is already over.

And one asks this question: is this the fate of human life? These things I say are very basic: development cannot go against happiness. It has to work in favor of human happiness, of love on Earth, human relationships, caring for children, having friends, having our basic needs covered.

Precisely because this is the most precious treasure we have; happiness. When we fight for the environment, we must remember that the essential element of the environment is called human happiness.

Thanks.

Benito Mussolini, *Speech Declaring War*

[June 10, 1940, Rome]

NOTE On June 10, 1940, after withholding formal allegiance to either side in the battle between Germany and the Allies, Benito Mussolini (1883-1945), dictator of Italy, declares war on France and Great Britain.

Fighters of land, sea and air, Black shirts of the revolution and of the legions, men and women of Italy, of the empire and of the Kingdom of Albania, listen!

The hour destined by fate is sounding for us. The hour of irrevocable decision has come. A declaration of war already has been handed to the Ambassadors of Great Britain and France.

We take the field against the plutocratic and reactionary democracies who always have blocked the march and frequently plotted against the existence of the Italian people.

Several decades of recent history may be summarized in these words: Phrases, promises, threats of blackmail, and finally, crowning that ignoble edifice, the League of Nations of fifty-two nations.

Our conscience is absolutely clear.

With you, the entire world is witness that the Italy of fascism has done everything humanly possible to avoid the tempest that envelops Europe, but all in vain. It would have sufficed to revise treaties to adapt them to changing requirements vital to nations and not consider them untouchable for eternity.

It would have sufficed not to begin the stupid policy of guarantees, which proved particularly deadly for those who accepted them. It would have sufficed not to reject the proposal of the Fuehrer [Hitler] made last October 6 after the campaign in Poland ended.

Now all that belongs to the past.

If today we have decided to take the risks and sacrifices of war, it is because the honor, interests, and future firmly impose it since a great people is truly such if it considers its obligations sacred and does not avoid the supreme trails that determine the course of history.

We are taking up arms, after having solved the problem of our continental frontiers. We want to break the territorial and military chains that confine us in our sea because a country of 45,000,000 souls is not truly free if it has not free access to the ocean.

This gigantic conflict is only a phase of the logical development of our revolution. It is the conflict of poor, numerous peoples who labor against starvers who ferociously cling to a monopoly of all riches and all gold on earth.

It is a conflict of fruitful, useful peoples against peoples who are in a decline. It is a conflict between two ages, two ideas.

Now the die is cast and our will has burned our ships behind us.

I solemnly declare that Italy does not intend to drag other peoples bordering on her by sea or land into the conflict. Switzerland, Yugoslavia, Greece, Turkey, and Egypt, take note of these words of mine. It depends on them and only on them if these words are rigorously confirmed or not.

Italians, in a memorable mass meeting in Berlin, I said that according to the rules of Fascist morals when one has a friend one marches with him to the end. This we have done and will continue to do with Germany, her people and her victorious armed forces.

On this eve of an event of import for centuries, we turn our thoughts to His Majesty, the King and Emperor, who always has understood the thought of the country.

Lastly, we salute the new Fuehrer, the chief of great allied Germany.

Proletariat, Fascist Italy has arisen for the third time, strong, proud, compact as never before.

There is only one order. It is categorical and obligatory for every one. It already wings over and enflames hearts from the Alps to the Indian Ocean: Conquer!

And we will conquer in order, finally, to give a new world of peace with justice to Italy, to Europe and to the universe.

Italian people, rush to arms and show your tenacity, your courage, your valor.

Richard M. Nixon, *Resignation Address to the Nation*

[August 8, 1974, Washington]

NOTE President Richard Nixon (1913-1994) made an address to the American public from the Oval Office on August 8, 1974, to announce his resignation from the presidency (1969-1974) due to the Watergate scandal.

This is the 37th time I have spoken to you from this office, where so many decisions have been made that shape the history of this nation. Each time I have done so to discuss with you some matter that I believe affected the national interest. In all the decisions I have made in my public life I have always tried to do what was best for the nation.

Throughout the long and difficult period of Watergate, I have felt it was my duty to persevere – to make every possible effort to complete the term of office to which you elected me. In the past few days, however, it has become evident to me that I no longer have a strong enough political base in the Congress to justify continuing that effort. As long as there was such a base, I felt strongly that it was necessary to see the constitutional process through to its conclusion; that to do otherwise would be unfaithful to the spirit of that deliberately difficult process, and a dangerously destabilizing precedent for the future. But with the disappearance of that base, I now believe that the constitutional purpose has been served. And there is no longer a need for the process to be prolonged.

I would have preferred to carry through to the finish whatever the personal agony it would have involved, and my family unanimously urged me to do so. But the interests of the nation must always come before any personal considerations. From the discussions I have had with Congressional and other leaders I have concluded that because of the Watergate matter I might not have the support of the Congress that I would consider necessary to back the very difficult decisions and carry out the duties of this office in the way the interests of the nation will require.

I have never been a quitter.

To leave office before my term is completed is abhorrent to every instinct in my body. But as President, I must put the interests of America first.

America needs a full-time President and a full-time Congress, particularly at this time with problems we face at home and abroad. To continue to fight through the months ahead for my personal vindication would almost totally absorb the time and attention of both the President and the Congress in a period when our entire focus should be on the great issues of peace abroad and prosperity without inflation at home.

Therefore, I shall resign the Presidency effective at noon tomorrow.

Vice President Ford will be sworn in as President at that hour in this office.

As I recall the high hopes for America with which we began this second term, I feel a great sadness that I will not be here in this office working on your behalf to achieve those hopes in the next two and a half years. But in turning over direction of the Government to Vice President Ford I know, as I told the nation when I nominated him for that office ten months ago, that the leadership of America would be in good hands.

In passing this office to the Vice President, I also do so with the profound sense of the weight of responsibility that will fall on his shoulders tomorrow, and therefore of the understanding, the patience, the cooperation he will need from all Americans. As he assumes that responsibility he will deserve the help and the support of all of us. As we look to the future, the first essential is to begin healing the wounds of this nation. To put the bitterness and divisions of the recent past behind us and to rediscover those shared ideals that lie at the heart of our strength and unity as a great and as a free people.

By taking this action, I hope that I will have hastened the start of that process of healing which is so desperately needed in America. I regret deeply any injuries that may have been done in the course of the events that led to this decision. I would say only that if some of my judgments were wrong – and some were wrong – they were made in what I believed at the time to be the best interests of the nation.

To those who have stood with me during these past difficult months, to my family, my friends, the many others who joined in supporting my cause because they believed it was right, I will be eternally grateful for your support. And to those who have not felt able to give me your support, let me say I leave with no bitterness toward those who have opposed me, because all of us in the final analysis have been concerned with the good of the country, however our judgments might differ.

So let us all now join together in affirming that common commitment and in helping our new President succeed for the benefit of all Americans. I shall leave this office with regret at not completing my term but with gratitude for the privilege of serving as your President for the past five and a half years. These years have been a momentous time in the history of our nation and the world. They have been a time of achievement in which we can all be proud, achievements that represent the shared efforts of the administration, the Congress and the people. But the challenges ahead are equally great. And they, too, will require the support and the efforts of the Congress and the people, working in co-operation with the new Administration.

We have ended America's longest war. But in the work of securing a lasting peace in the world, the goals ahead are even more far-reaching and more difficult. We must complete a structure of peace, so that it will be said of this generation – our generation of Americans – by the people of all nations, not only that we ended one war but that we prevented future wars.

We have unlocked the doors that for a quarter of a century stood between the United States and the People's Republic of China. We must now insure that the one-quarter of the world's people who live in the People's Republic of China will be and remain, not our enemies, but our friends.

In the Middle East, 100 million people in the Arab countries, many of whom have considered us their enemy for nearly 20 years, now look on us as their friends. We must continue to build on that friendship so that peace can settle at last over the Middle East and so that the cradle of civilization will not become its grave. Together with the Soviet Union we have made the crucial breakthroughs that have begun the process of limiting nuclear arms. But, we must set as our goal, not just limiting, but reducing and finally destroying these terrible weapons, so that they cannot destroy civilization. And so that the threat of nuclear war will no longer hang over the world and the people. We have opened a new relation with the Soviet Union. We must continue to develop and expand that new relationship, so that the two strongest nations of the world will live together in cooperation rather than confrontation.

Around the world – in Asia, in Africa, in Latin America, in the Middle East – there are millions of people who live in terrible poverty, even starvation. We must keep as our goal turning away from production for war and expanding production for peace so that people everywhere on this earth can at last look forward, in their children's time, if not in our own time, to having the necessities for a decent life. Here, in America, we are fortunate that most of our people have not only the blessings of liberty but also the means to live full and good, and by the world's standards even abundant lives.

We must press on, however, toward a goal not only of more and better jobs but of full opportunity for every American, and of what we are striving so hard right now to achieve – prosperity without inflation.

For more than a quarter of a century in public life, I have shared in the turbulent history of this evening. I have fought for what I believe in. I have tried, to the best of my ability, to discharge those duties and meet those responsibilities that were entrusted to me. Sometimes I have succeeded. And sometimes I have failed. But always I have taken heart from what Theodore Roosevelt once said about the man in the arena, whose face is marred by dust and sweat and blood, who strives valiantly, who errs and comes short again and again because there is not effort without error and shortcoming, but who does actually strive to do the deed, who knows the great enthusiasms, the great devotions, who spends himself in a worthy cause, who at the best knows in the end the triumphs of high achievements and with the worst if he fails, at least fails while daring greatly.

I pledge to you tonight that as long as I have a breath of life in my body, I shall continue in that spirit. I shall continue to work for the great causes to which I have been dedicated throughout my years as a Congressman, a Senator, Vice President and President, the cause of peace – not just for America but among all nations – prosperity, justice and opportunity for all of our people.

There is one cause above all to which I have been devoted and to which I shall always be devoted for as long as I live.

When I first took the oath of office as President five and

a half years ago, I made this sacred commitment: to consecrate my office, my energies, and all the wisdom I can summon to the cause of peace among nations. I've done my very best in all the days since to be true to that pledge. As a result of these efforts, I am confident that the world is a safer place today, not only for the people of America but for the people of all nations, and that all of our children have a better chance than before of living in peace rather than dying in war.

This, more than anything, is what I hoped to achieve when I sought the Presidency.

This, more than anything, is what I hope will be my legacy to you, to our country, as I leave the Presidency.

To have served in this office is to have felt a very personal sense of kinship with each and every American.

In leaving it, I do so with this prayer: May God's grace be with you in all the days ahead.

Barack Obama, 2004 *Democratic National Convention Keynote Address*

[July 27, 2004, Boston]

NOTE Barack Obama (1961), was the 44th president of the United States (2009-17) and the first African American to hold the office. While campaigning for the U.S. Senate, Obama gained national recognition by delivering the keynote address at the Democratic National Convention in July 2004. The speech wove a personal narrative of Obama's biography with the theme that all Americans are connected in ways that transcend political, cultural, and geographical differences. The address lifted Obama's once obscure memoir onto best-seller lists, and, after taking office the following year, Obama quickly became a major figure in his party.

On behalf of the great state of Illinois, crossroads of a nation, Land of Lincoln, let me express my deepest gratitude for the privilege of addressing this convention.

Tonight is a particular honor for me because, let's face it, my presence on this stage is pretty unlikely. My father was a foreign student, born and raised in a small village in Kenya. He grew up herding goats, went to school in a tin-roof shack. His father – my grandfather – was a cook, a domestic servant to the British.

But my grandfather had larger dreams for his son. Through hard work and perseverance my father got a scholarship to study in a magical place, America, that shone as a beacon of freedom and opportunity to so many who had come before.

While studying here, my father met my mother. She was born in a town on the other side of the world, in Kansas. Her father worked on oil rigs and farms through most of the

Depression. The day after Pearl Harbor my grandfather signed up for duty; joined Patton's army, marched across Europe. Back home, my grandmother raised a baby and went to work on a bomber assembly line. After the war, they studied on the G.I. Bill, bought a house through F.H.A., and later moved west all the way to Hawaii in search of opportunity.

And they, too, had big dreams for their daughter. A common dream, born of two continents.

My parents shared not only an improbable love, they shared an abiding faith in the possibilities of this nation. They would give me an African name, Barack, or "blessed," believing that in a tolerant America your name is no barrier to success. They imagined – They imagined me going to the best schools in the land, even though they weren't rich, because in a generous America you don't have to be rich to achieve your potential.

They're both passed away now. And yet, I know that on this night they look down on me with great pride.

They stand here, and I stand here today, grateful for the diversity of my heritage, aware that my parents' dreams live on in my two precious daughters. I stand here knowing that my story is part of the larger American story, that I owe a debt to all of those who came before me, and that, in no other country on earth, is my story even possible.

Tonight, we gather to affirm the greatness of our Nation – not because of the height of our skyscrapers, or the power of our military, or the size of our economy. Our pride is based on a very simple premise, summed up in a declaration made over two hundred years ago:

We hold these truths to be self-evident, that all men are created equal, that they are endowed by their Creator with certain inalienable rights, that among these are Life, Liberty and the pursuit of Happiness.

That is the true genius of America, a faith – a faith in

simple dreams, an insistence on small miracles; that we can tuck in our children at night and know that they are fed and clothed and safe from harm; that we can say what we think, write what we think, without hearing a sudden knock on the door; that we can have an idea and start our own business without paying a bribe; that we can participate in the political process without fear of retribution, and that our votes will be counted – at least most of the time.

This year, in this election we are called to reaffirm our values and our commitments, to hold them against a hard reality and see how we're measuring up to the legacy of our forbearers and the promise of future generations.

And fellow Americans, Democrats, Republicans, Independents, I say to you tonight: We have more work to do – more work to do for the workers I met in Galesburg, Illinois, who are losing their union jobs at the Maytag plant that's moving to Mexico, and now are having to compete with their own children for jobs that pay seven bucks an hour; more to do for the father that I met who was losing his job and choking back the tears, wondering how he would pay 4500 dollars a month for the drugs his son needs without the health benefits that he counted on; more to do for the young woman in East St. Louis, and thousands more like her, who has the grades, has the drive, has the will, but doesn't have the money to go to college.

Now, don't get me wrong. The people I meet – in small towns and big cities, in diners and office parks – they don't expect government to solve all their problems. They know they have to work hard to get ahead, and they want to. Go into the collar counties around Chicago, and people will tell you they don't want their tax money wasted, by a welfare agency or by the Pentagon. Go in – Go into any inner city neighborhood, and folks will tell you that government alone can't teach our kids to learn; they know that parents have to teach, that children can't achieve unless we raise their expectations and turn off the television sets and eradicate the slander that says a black youth with a book is acting white. They know those things.

People don't expect – People don't expect government to solve all their problems. But they sense, deep in their bones, that with just a slight change in priorities, we can make sure that every child in America has a decent shot at life, and that the doors of opportunity remain open to all.

They know we can do better. And they want that choice.

In this election, we offer that choice. Our Party has chosen a man to lead us who embodies the best this country has to offer. And that man is John Kerry.

John Kerry understands the ideals of community, faith, and service because they've defined his life. From his heroic service to Vietnam, to his years as a prosecutor and lieutenant governor, through two decades in the United States Senate, he's devoted himself to this country. Again and again, we've seen him make tough choices when easier ones were available.

His values and his record affirm what is best in us. John Kerry believes in an America where hard work is rewarded; so instead of offering tax breaks to companies shipping jobs overseas, he offers them to companies creating jobs here at home.

John Kerry believes in an America where all Americans can afford the same health coverage our politicians in Washington have for themselves.

John Kerry believes in energy independence, so we aren't held hostage to the profits of oil companies, or the sabotage of foreign oil fields.

John Kerry believes in the Constitutional freedoms that have made our country the envy of the world, and he will never sacrifice our basic liberties, nor use faith as a wedge to divide us.

And John Kerry believes that in a dangerous world war

must be an option sometimes, but it should never be the first option.

You know, a while back – awhile back I met a young man named Shamus in a V.F.W. Hall in East Moline, Illinois. He was a good-looking kid – six two, six three, clear eyed, with an easy smile. He told me he'd joined the Marines and was heading to Iraq the following week. And as I listened to him explain why he'd enlisted, the absolute faith he had in our country and its leaders, his devotion to duty and service, I thought this young man was all that any of us might ever hope for in a child.

But then I asked myself, "Are we serving Shamus as well as he is serving us?"

I thought of the 900 men and women – sons and daughters, husbands and wives, friends and neighbors, who won't be returning to their own hometowns. I thought of the families I've met who were struggling to get by without a loved one's full income, or whose loved ones had returned with a limb missing or nerves shattered, but still lacked long-term health benefits because they were Reservists.

When we send our young men and women into harm's way, we have a solemn obligation not to fudge the numbers or shade the truth about why they're going, to care for their families while they're gone, to tend to the soldiers upon their return, and to never ever go to war without enough troops to win the war, secure the peace, and earn the respect of the world.

Now – Now let me be clear. Let me be clear. We have real enemies in the world. These enemies must be found. They must be pursued. And they must be defeated. John Kerry knows this. And just as Lieutenant Kerry did not hesitate to risk his life to protect the men who served with him in Vietnam, President Kerry will not hesitate one moment to use our military might to keep America safe and secure.

John Kerry believes in America. And he knows that it's

not enough for just some of us to prosper – for alongside our famous individualism, there's another ingredient in the American saga, a belief that we're all connected as one people. If there is a child on the south side of Chicago who can't read, that matters to me, even if it's not my child. If there is a senior citizen somewhere who can't pay for their prescription drugs, and having to choose between medicine and the rent, that makes my life poorer, even if it's not my grandparent. If there's an Arab American family being rounded up without benefit of an attorney or due process, that threatens my civil liberties.

It is that fundamental belief – It is that fundamental belief: I am my brother's keeper. I am my sister's keeper – that makes this country work. It's what allows us to pursue our individual dreams and yet still come together as one American family.

E pluribus unum: "Out of many, one."

Now even as we speak, there are those who are preparing to divide us – the spin masters, the negative ad peddlers who embrace the politics of "anything goes." Well, I say to them tonight, there is not a liberal America and a conservative America – there is the United States of America. There is not a Black America and a White America and Latino America and Asian America – there's the United States of America.

The pundits, the pundits like to slice-and-dice our country into red states and blue states; red states for Republicans, blue states for Democrats. But I've got news for them, too. We worship an awesome God in the blue states, and we don't like federal agents poking around in our libraries in the red states. We coach Little League in the blue states and yes, we've got some gay friends in the red states. There are patriots who opposed the war in Iraq and there are patriots who supported the war in Iraq. We are one people, all of us pledging allegiance to the stars and stripes, all of us defending the United States of America.

In the end – In the end – In the end, that's what this election is about. Do we participate in a politics of cynicism or do we participate in a politics of hope?

John Kerry calls on us to hope. John Edwards calls on us to hope.

I'm not talking about blind optimism here – the almost willful ignorance that thinks unemployment will go away if we just don't think about it, or the health care crisis will solve itself if we just ignore it. That's not what I'm talking about. I'm talking about something more substantial. It's the hope of slaves sitting around a fire singing freedom songs; the hope of immigrants setting out for distant shores; the hope of a young naval lieutenant bravely patrolling the Mekong Delta; the hope of a millworker's son who dares to defy the odds; the hope of a skinny kid with a funny name who believes that America has a place for him, too.

Hope – Hope in the face of difficulty. Hope in the face of uncertainty. The audacity of hope!

In the end, that is God's greatest gift to us, the bedrock of this nation. A belief in things not seen. A belief that there are better days ahead.

I believe that we can give our middle class relief and provide working families with a road to opportunity.

I believe we can provide jobs to the jobless, homes to the homeless, and reclaim young people in cities across America from violence and despair.

I believe that we have a righteous wind at our backs and that as we stand on the crossroads of history, we can make the right choices, and meet the challenges that face us.

America! Tonight, if you feel the same energy that I do, if you feel the same urgency that I do, if you feel the same passion that I do, if you feel the same hopefulness that I do – if we do what we must do, then I have no doubt that all across the country, from Florida to Oregon, from

Washington to Maine, the people will rise up in November, and John Kerry will be sworn in as President, and John Edwards will be sworn in as Vice President, and this country will reclaim its promise, and out of this long political darkness a brighter day will come.

Thank you very much everybody.

God bless you.

Thank you.

Barack Obama, *A More Perfect Union*

[March 18, 2008, Philadelphia)

NOTE "A More Perfect Union" is the title of a speech delivered by then-Senator Barack Obama on March 18, 2008, in the course of the contest for the 2008 Democratic Party presidential nomination.

Let me begin by thanking Harris Wofford for his contributions to this country. In so many different ways, he exemplifies what we mean by the word "citizen." And so we are very grateful to him for all the work he has done; and I'm thankful for the gracious and thoughtful introduction.

"We the people, in order to form a more perfect union." Two hundred and twenty one years ago, in a hall that still stands across the street, a group of men gathered and, with these simple words, launched America's improbable experiment in democracy. Farmers and scholars, statesmen and patriots who had traveled across the ocean to escape tyranny and persecution finally made real their Declaration of Independence at a Philadelphia convention that lasted through the spring of 1787.

The document they produced was eventually signed, but ultimately unfinished. It was stained by this nation's original sin of slavery, a question that divided the colonies and brought the convention to a stalemate until the founders chose to allow the slave trade to continue for at least 20 more years, and to leave any final resolution to future generations. Of course, the answer to the slavery question was already embedded within our Constitution – a Constitution that had at is very core the ideal of equal citizenship under the law; a Constitution that promised its people liberty and justice, and a union that could be and should be perfected over time.

And yet words on a parchment would not be enough to deliver slaves from bondage, or provide men and women of every color and creed their full rights and obligations as citizens of the United States. What would be needed were Americans in successive generations who were willing to do their part – through protests and struggles, on the streets and in the courts, through a civil war and civil disobedience, and always at great risk – to narrow that gap between the promise of our ideals and the reality of their time.

This was one of the tasks we set forth at the beginning of this presidential campaign: to continue the long march of those who came before us, a march for a more just, more equal, more free, more caring, and more prosperous America. I chose to run for President at this moment in history because I believe deeply that we cannot solve the challenges of our time unless we solve them together, unless we perfect our union by understanding that we may have different stories, but we hold common hopes; that we may not look the same and may not have come from the same place, but we all want to move in the same direction: towards a better future for our children and our grandchildren. And this belief comes from my unyielding faith in the decency and generosity of the American people. But it also comes from my own story.

I'm the son of a black man from Kenya and a white woman from Kansas. I was raised with the help of a white grandfather who survived a Depression to serve in Patton's army during World War II, and a white grandmother who worked on a bomber assembly line at Fort Leavenworth while he was overseas. I've gone to some of the best schools in America and I've lived in one of the world's poorest nations. I am married to a black American who carries within her the blood of slaves and slave owners, an inheritance we pass on to our two precious daughters. I have brothers, sisters, nieces, nephews, uncles, and cousins of every race and every hue scattered across three continents. And for as long as I live, I will never forget that in no other country on earth is my story even possible. It's a story that hasn't made me the most conventional of candidates. But it is a story that has seared into my genetic makeup the idea that this nation is more than the sum of its parts – that out of many, we are truly one.

Now throughout the first year of this campaign, against all predictions to the contrary, we saw how hungry the American people were for this message of unity. Despite the temptation to view my candidacy through a purely racial lens, we won commanding victories in states with some of the whitest populations in the country. In South Carolina, where the Confederate flag still flies, we built a powerful coalition of African Americans and white Americans. This is not to say that race has not been an issue in this campaign. At various stages in the campaign, some commentators have deemed me either "too black" or "not black enough." We saw racial tensions bubble to the surface during the week before the South Carolina primary. The press has scoured every single exit poll for the latest evidence of racial polarization, not just in terms of white and black, but black and brown as well.

And yet, it's only been in the last couple of weeks that the discussion of race in this campaign has taken a particularly divisive turn. On one end of the spectrum, we've heard the implication that my candidacy is somehow an exercise in affirmative action; that it's based solely on the desire of wild and wide-eyed liberals to purchase racial reconciliation on the cheap. On the other end, we've heard my former pastor, Jeremiah Wright, use incendiary language to express views that have the potential not only to widen the racial divide, but views that denigrate both the greatness and the goodness of our nation and that rightly offend white and black alike.

Now I've already condemned, in unequivocal terms, the statements of Reverend Wright that have caused such controversy, and in some cases, pain. For some, nagging questions remain: Did I know him to be an occasionally fierce critic of American domestic and foreign policy? Of course. Did I ever hear him make remarks that could be considered controversial while I sat in the church? Yes. Did I strongly disagree with many of his political views? Absolutely, just as I'm sure many of you have heard remarks from your pastors, priests, or rabbis with which you strongly disagree.

But the remarks that have caused this recent firestorm weren't simply controversial. They weren't simply a religious leader's efforts to speak out against perceived injustice. Instead, they expressed a profoundly distorted view of this country, a view that sees white racism as endemic and that elevates what is wrong with America above all that we know is right with America; a view that sees the conflicts in the Middle East as rooted primarily in the actions of stalwart allies like Israel instead of emanating from the perverse and hateful ideologies of radical Islam.

As such, Reverend Wright's comments were not only wrong but divisive, divisive at a time when we need unity; racially charged at a time when we need to come together to solve a set of monumental problems: two wars, a terrorist threat, a falling economy, a chronic health care crisis, and potentially devastating climate change – problems that are neither black or white or Latino or Asian, but rather problems that confront us all.

Given my background, my politics, and my professed values and ideals, there will no doubt be those for whom my statements of condemnation are not enough. Why associate myself with Reverend Wright in the first place, they may ask? Why not join another church? And I confess that if all that I knew of Reverend Wright were the snippets of those sermons that have run in an endless loop on the television sets and YouTube, if Trinity United Church of Christ conformed to the caricatures being peddled by some commentators, there is no doubt that I would react in much the same way.

But the truth is, that isn't all that I know of the man. The man I met more than twenty years ago is a man who helped introduce me to my Christian faith, a man who spoke to me about our obligations to love one another, to care for the sick and lift up the poor. He is a man who served his country as a United States Marine, and who has studied and lectured at some of the finest universities and seminaries in the country, and who over 30 years has led a church that serves the community by doing God's work here on Earth – by housing the homeless, ministering to the needy, providing day care services and scholarships and prison ministries, and reaching out to those suffering from HIV/AIDS.

In my first book, Dreams From My Father, I described the experience of my first service at Trinity, and it goes as follows:

People began to shout, to rise from their seats and clap and cry out, a forceful wind carrying the reverend's voice up to the rafters.

And in that single note – hope – I heard something else; at the foot of that cross, inside the thousands of churches across the city, I imagined the stories of ordinary black people merging with the stories of David and Goliath, Moses and Pharaoh, the Christians in the lion's den, Ezekiel's field of dry bones.

Those stories of survival and freedom and hope became our stories, my story. The blood that spilled was our blood; the tears our tears; until this black church, on this bright day, seemed once more a vessel carrying the story of a people into future generations and into a larger world. Our trials and triumphs became at once unique and universal, black and more than black. In chronicling our journey, the stories and songs gave us a meaning to reclaim memories that we didn't need to feel shame about – memories that all people might study and cherish and with which we could start to rebuild.

That has been my experience at Trinity. Like other predominantly black churches across the country, Trinity embodies the black community in its entirety – the doctor and the welfare mom, the model student and the former gangbanger. Like other black churches, Trinity's services are full of raucous laughter and sometimes bawdy humor. They are full of dancing and clapping and screaming and shouting that may seem jarring to the untrained ear. The church contains in full the kindness and cruelty, the fierce intelligence and the shocking ignorance, the struggles and successes, the love and, yes, the bitterness and biases that make up the black experience in America.

And this helps explain, perhaps, my relationship with Reverend Wright. As imperfect as he may be, he has been like family to me. He strengthens my faith, officiated my wedding, and baptized my children. Not once in my conversations with him have I heard him talk about any ethnic group in derogatory terms or treat whites with whom he interacted with anything but courtesy and respect. He contains within him the contradictions – the good and the bad – of the community that he has served diligently for so many years.

I can no more disown him than I can disown the black community. I can no more disown him than I can disown my white grandmother, a woman who helped raise me, a woman who sacrificed again and again for me, a woman who loves me as much as she loves anything in this world, but a woman who once confessed her fear of black men who passed her by on the street, and who on more than one occasion has uttered racial or ethnic stereotypes that made me cringe.

These people are part of me. And they are part of America, this country that I love.

Now, some will see this as an attempt to justify or excuse comments that are simply inexcusable. I can assure you it is not. And I suppose the politically safe thing to do would be to move on from this episode and just hope that it fades into the woodwork. We can dismiss Reverend Wright as a crank or a demagogue, just as some have dismissed Geraldine Ferraro in the aftermath of her recent statements as harboring some deep – deep-seated bias.

But race is an issue that I believe this nation cannot afford to ignore right now. We would be making the same mistake that Reverend Wright made in his offending sermons about America: to simplify and stereotype and amplify the negative to the point that it distorts reality. The fact is that the comments that have been made and the issues that have surfaced over the last few weeks reflect the complexities of race in this country that we've never really worked through, a part of our union that we have not yet made perfect. And if we walk away now, if we simply retreat into our respective corners, we will never be able to come together and solve challenges like health care or education or the need to find good jobs for every American.

Understanding – Understanding this reality requires a reminder of how we arrived at this point. As William Faulkner once wrote, "The past isn't dead and buried. In fact, it isn't even past." We do not need to recite here the history of racial injustice in this country. But we do need to remind ourselves that so many of the disparities that exist between the African-American community and the larger American community today can be traced directly to inequalities passed on from an earlier generation that suffered under the brutal legacy of slavery and Jim Crow. Segregated schools were, and are, inferior schools. We still haven't fixed them, 50 years after Brown versus Board of Education. And the inferior education they provided, then and now, helps explain the pervasive achievement gap between today's black and white students.

Legalized discrimination, where blacks were prevented, often through violence, from owning property, or loans were not granted to African-American business owners, or black homeowners could not access FHA mortgages, or blacks were excluded from unions, or the police force, or the fire department meant that black families could not amass any meaningful wealth to bequeath to future generations. That history helps explain the wealth and income gap between blacks and whites and the concentrated pockets of poverty that persist in so many of today's urban and rural communities. A lack of economic opportunity among black men and the shame and frustration that came from not being able to provide for one's family contributed to the erosion of black families, a problem that welfare policies for many years may have worsened. And the lack of basic services in so many urban black neighborhoods – parks for kids to play in, police walking the beat, regular garbage pick-up, building code enforcement – all helped create a cycle of violence, blight, and neglect that continues to haunt us.

This is the reality in which Reverend Wright and other African-Americans of his generation grew up. They came of age in the late '50s and early '60s, a time when segregation was still the law of the land and opportunity was systematically constricted. What's remarkable is not how many failed in the face of discrimination, but how many men and women overcame the odds, how many were able to make a way out of no way for those like me who would come after them.

But for all those who scratched and clawed their way to

get a piece of the American Dream, there were many who didn't make it — those who were ultimately defeated, in one way or another, by discrimination. That legacy of defeat was passed on to future generations — those young men and increasingly young women who we see standing on street corners or languishing in our prisons, without hope or prospects for the future. Even for those blacks who did make it, questions of race, and racism, continue to define their world view in fundamental ways. For the men and women of Reverend Wright's generation, the memories of humiliation and doubt and fear have not gone away, nor has the anger and the bitterness of those years.

That anger may not get expressed in public, in front of white co-workers or white friends, but it does find voice in the barbershop or the beauty shop or around the kitchen table. At times, that anger is exploited by politicians to gin up votes along racial lines or to make up for a politician's own failings. And occasionally it finds voice in the church on Sunday morning, in the pulpit and in the pews. The fact that so many people are surprised to hear that anger in some of Reverend Wright's sermons simply reminds us of that old truism that the most segregated hour of American life occurs on Sunday morning.

That — That anger is not always productive. Indeed, all too often it distracts attention from solving real problems. It keeps us from squarely facing our own complicity within the African-American community in our own condition. It prevents the African-American community from forging the alliances it needs to bring about real change. But the anger is real; it is powerful, and to simply wish it away, to condemn it without understanding its roots only serves to widen the chasm of misunderstanding that exists between the races.

In fact, a similar anger exists within segments of the white community. Most working and middle-class white Americans don't feel that they've been particularly privileged by their race. Their experience is the immigrant experience. As far as they're concerned, no one handed them anything; they built it from scratch. They've worked hard all their lives, many times only to see their jobs shipped overseas or their pensions dumped after a lifetime of labor. They are anxious about their futures, and they feel their dreams slipping away. And in an era of stagnant wages and global competition, opportunity comes to be seen as a zero sum game, in which your dreams come at my expense. So when they are told to bus their children to a school across town, when they hear that an African American is getting an advantage in landing a good job or a spot in a good college because of an injustice that they themselves never committed, when they're told that their fears about crime in urban neighborhoods are somehow prejudice, resentment builds over time.

Like the anger within the black community, these resentments aren't always expressed in polite company. But they have helped shape the political landscape for at least a generation. Anger over welfare and affirmative action helped forge the Reagan Coalition. Politicians routinely exploited fears of crime for their own electoral ends. Talk show hosts and conservative commentators built entire careers unmasking bogus claims of racism while dismissing legitimate discussions of racial injustice and inequality as mere political correctness or reverse racism. And just as black anger often proved counterproductive, so have these white resentments distracted attention from the real culprits of the middle class squeeze: a corporate culture rife with inside dealing, questionable accounting practices, and short-term greed; a Washington dominated by lobbyists and special interests; economic policies that favor the few over the many. And yet, to wish away the resentments of white Americans, to label them as misguided or even racist without recognizing they are grounded in legitimate concerns, this, too, widens the racial divide and blocks the path to understanding.

This is where we are right now.

It's a racial stalemate we've been stuck in for years. And contrary to the claims of some of my critics, black and white, I have never been so naive as to believe that we can get beyond our racial divisions in a single election cycle or with a single candidate, particularly – particularly a candidacy as imperfect as my own. But I have asserted a firm conviction, a conviction rooted in my faith in God and my faith in the American people, that, working together, we can move beyond some of our old racial wounds and that, in fact, we have no choice – we have no choice if we are to continue on the path of a more perfect union.

For the African-American community, that path means embracing the burdens of our past without becoming victims of our past. It means continuing to insist on a full measure of justice in every aspect of American life. But it also means binding our particular grievances, for better health care and better schools and better jobs, to the larger aspirations of all Americans – the white woman struggling to break the glass ceiling, the white man who's been laid off, the immigrant trying to feed his family. And it means also taking full responsibility for our own lives – by demanding more from our fathers, and spending more time with our children, and reading to them, and teaching them that while they may face challenges and discrimination in their own lives, they must never succumb to despair or cynicism. They must always believe – They must always believe that they can write their own destiny.

Ironically, this quintessentially American – and, yes, conservative – notion of self-help found frequent expression in Reverend Wright's sermons. But what my former pastor too often failed to understand is that embarking on a program of self-help also requires a belief that society can change. The profound mistake of Reverend Wright's sermons is not that he spoke about racism in our society. It's that he spoke as if our society was static, as if no progress had been made, as if this country – a country that has made it possible for one of his own members to run for the highest office in the land and build a coalition of white and black, Latino, Asian, rich, poor, young and old – is still irrevocably bound to a tragic past. What we know, what we have seen, is that America can change. That is true genius of this nation. What we have already achieved gives us hope – the audacity to hope – for what we can and must achieve tomorrow.

Now, in the white community, the path to a more perfect union means acknowledging that what ails the African-American community does not just exist in the minds of black people; that the legacy of discrimination – and current incidents of discrimination, while less overt than in the past – that these things are real and must be addressed. Not just with words, but with deeds – by investing in our schools and our communities; by enforcing our civil rights laws and ensuring fairness in our criminal justice system; by providing this generation with ladders of opportunity that were unavailable for previous generations. It requires all Americans to realize that your dreams do not have to come at the expense of my dreams, that investing in the health, welfare, and education of black and brown and white children will ultimately help all of America prosper.

In the end, then, what is called for is nothing more and nothing less than what all the world's great religions demand: that we do unto others as we would have them do unto us. Let us be our brother's keeper, Scripture tells us. Let us be our sister's keeper. Let us find that common stake we all have in one another, and let our politics reflect that spirit as well.

For we have a choice in this country. We can accept a politics that breeds division and conflict and cynicism. We can tackle race only as spectacle, as we did in the O.J. trial; or in the wake of tragedy, as we did in the aftermath of Katrina; or as fodder for the nightly news. We can play Reverend Wright's sermons on every channel every day and talk about them from now until the election, and make the only question in this campaign whether or not the American people think that I somehow believe or sympathize with his most offensive words. We can pounce on some gaffe by a Hillary supporter as evidence that she's playing the race card; or we can speculate on whether white men will all flock to John McCain in the general election regardless of his policies. We can do that. But if we do, I can tell you that in the next election, we'll be talking about some other distraction, and then another one, and then another one. And nothing will change.

That is one option.

Or, at this moment, in this election, we can come together and say, "Not this time." This time we want to talk about the crumbling schools that are stealing the future of black children and white children and Asian children and Hispanic children and Native-American children. This time we want to reject the cynicism that tells us that these kids can't learn; that those kids who don't look like us are somebody else's problem. The children of America are not "those kids," – they are our kids, and we will not let them fall behind in a 21st-century economy. Not this time. This time we want to talk about how the lines in the emergency room are filled with whites and blacks and Hispanics who do not have health care, who don't have the power on their own to overcome the special interests in Washington, but who can take them on if we do it together.

This time we want to talk about the shuttered mills that once provided a decent life for men and women of every race, and the homes for sale that once belonged to Americans from every religion, every region, every walk of life.

This time we want to talk about the fact that the real problem is not that someone who doesn't look like you might take your job; it's that the corporation you work for will ship it overseas for nothing more than a profit. This time – This time we want to talk about the men and women of every color and creed who serve together, and fight together, and bleed together under the same proud flag. We want to talk about how to bring them home from a war that should've never been authorized and should've never been waged. And we want to talk about how we'll show our patriotism by caring for them, and their families, and giving them the benefits that they have earned.

I would not be running for President if I didn't believe with all my heart that this is what the vast majority of Americans want for this country. This union may never be perfect, but generation after generation has shown that it can always be perfected. And today, whenever I find myself feeling doubtful or cynical about this possibility, what gives me the most hope is the next generation – the young people whose attitudes and beliefs and openness to change have already made history in this election.

There's one story in particular that I'd like to leave you with today, a story I told when I had the great honor of speaking on Dr. King's birthday at his home church, Ebenezer Baptist, in Atlanta. There's a young, 23-year-old woman, a white woman named Ashley Baia, who organized for our campaign in Florence, South Carolina. She'd been working to organize a mostly African-American community since the beginning of this campaign, and one day she was at a roundtable discussion where everyone went around telling their story and why they were there. And Ashley said that when she was 9 years old, her mother got cancer. And because she had to miss days of work, she was let go and lost her health care. They had to file for bankruptcy, and that's when Ashley decided that she had to do something to help her mom.

She knew that food was one of their most expensive costs, and so Ashley convinced her mother that what she really liked and really wanted to eat more than anything else was mustard and relish sandwiches – because that was the cheapest way to eat. That's the mind of a 9 year old. She did this for a year until her mom got better. And so Ashley told everyone at the roundtable that the reason she had joined our campaign was so that she could help the millions of other children in the country who want and need to help their parents too.

Now, Ashley might have made a different choice. Perhaps somebody told her along the way that the source of her mother's problems were blacks who were on welfare and too lazy to work, or Hispanics who were coming into the country illegally. But she didn't. She sought out allies in her fight against injustice.

Anyway, Ashley finishes her story and then goes around the room and asks everyone else why they're supporting the campaign. They all have different stories and different reasons. Many bring up a specific issue. And finally they come to this elderly black man who's been sitting there quietly the entire time. And Ashley asks him why he's there. And he doesn't bring up a specific issue. He does not say health care or the economy. He does not say education or the war. He does not say that he was there because of Barack Obama. He simply says to everyone in the room, "I am here because of Ashley." "I'm here because of Ashley."

Now, by itself, that single moment of recognition between that young white girl and that old black man is not enough. It is not enough to give health care to the sick, or jobs to the jobless, or education to our children. But it is where we start. It is where our union grows stronger. And as so many generations have come to realize over the course of the 221 years since a band of patriots signed that document right here in Philadelphia, that is where perfection begins. Thank you very much, everyone. Thank you.

Barack Obama, *What is Required:*
First Presidential Inaugural Address

[January 20, 2009, Washington]

I stand here today humbled by the task before us, grateful for the trust you've bestowed, mindful of the sacrifices borne by our ancestors. I thank President Bush for his service to our nation, as well as the generosity and cooperation he has shown throughout this transition.

Forty-four Americans have now taken the presidential Oath. The words have been spoken during rising tides of prosperity and the still waters of peace. Yet, every so often the Oath is taken amidst gathering clouds and raging storms. At these moments, America has carried on not simply because of the skill or vision of those in high office, but because We the People have remained faithful to the ideals of our forebearers [sic], and true to our founding documents.

So it has been. So it must be with this generation of Americans.

That we are in the midst of crisis is now well understood. Our nation is at war, against a far-reaching network of violence and hatred. Our economy is badly weakened, a consequence of greed and irresponsibility on the part of some, but also our collective failure to make hard choices and prepare the nation for a new age. Homes have been lost; jobs shed; businesses shuttered. Our health care is too costly; our schools fail too many; and each day brings further evidence that the ways we use energy strengthen our adversaries and threaten our planet.

These are the indicators of crisis, subject to data and statistics. Less measurable, but no less profound, is a sapping of confidence across our land – a nagging fear that America's decline is inevitable, that the next generation must lower its sights.

Today I say to you that the challenges we face are real. They are serious and they are many. They will not be met easily or in a short span of time. But know this, America: They will be met.

On this day, we gather because we have chosen hope over fear, unity of purpose over conflict and discord.

On this day, we come to proclaim an end to the petty grievances and false promises, the recriminations and worn out dogmas, that for far too long have strangled our politics.

We remain a young nation, but in the words of Scripture, the time has come to "set aside childish things."2 The time has come to reaffirm our enduring spirit; to choose our better history; to carry forward that precious gift, that noble idea, passed on from generation to generation: the God-given promise that all are equal, all are free, and all deserve a chance to pursue their full measure of happiness.

In reaffirming the greatness of our nation, we understand that greatness is never a given. It must be earned. Our journey has never been one of short-cuts or settling for less. It has not been the path for the faint-hearted – for those who prefer leisure over work, or seek only the pleasures of riches and fame. Rather, it has been the risk-takers, the doers, the makers of things – some celebrated but more often men and women obscure in their labor, who have carried us up the long, rugged path towards prosperity and freedom.

For us, they packed up their few worldly possessions and traveled across oceans in search of a new life.

For us, they toiled in sweatshops and settled the West; endured the lash of the whip and plowed the hard earth.

For us, they fought and died, in places like Concord and

Gettysburg; Normandy and Khe Sahn.

Time and again these men and women struggled and sacrificed and worked till their hands were raw so that we might live a better life. They saw America as bigger than the sum of our individual ambitions; greater than all the differences of birth or wealth or faction.

This is the journey we continue today. We remain the most prosperous, powerful nation on Earth. Our workers are no less productive than when this crisis began. Our minds are no less inventive, our goods and services no less needed than they were last week or last month or last year. Our capacity remains undiminished. But our time of standing pat, of protecting narrow interests and putting off unpleasant decisions – that time has surely passed. Starting today, we must pick ourselves up, dust ourselves off, and begin again the work of remaking America.

For everywhere we look, there is work to be done. The state of our economy calls for action, bold and swift, and we will act – not only to create new jobs, but to lay a new foundation for growth. We will build the roads and bridges, the electric grids and digital lines that feed our commerce and bind us together. We will restore science to its rightful place, and wield technology's wonders to raise health care's quality and lower its cost. We will harness the sun and the winds and the soil to fuel our cars and run our factories. And we will transform our schools and colleges and universities to meet the demands of a new age.

All this we can do.

All this we will do.

Now, there are some who question the scale of our ambitions – who suggest that our system cannot tolerate too many big plans. Their memories are short. For they have forgotten what this country has already done; what free men and women can achieve when imagination is joined to common purpose, and necessity to courage.

What the cynics fail to understand is that the ground has shifted beneath them – that the stale political arguments that have consumed us for so long no longer apply. The question we ask today is not whether our government is too big or too small, but whether it works – whether it helps families find jobs at a decent wage, care they can afford, a retirement that is dignified. Where the answer is yes, we intend to move forward. Where the answer is no, programs will end. And those of us who manage the public's dollars will be held to account – to spend wisely, reform bad habits, and do our business in the light of day – because only then can we restore the vital trust between a people and their government.

Nor is the question before us whether the market is a force for good or ill. Its power to generate wealth and expand freedom is unmatched, but this crisis has reminded us that without a watchful eye, the market can spin out of control. The nation cannot prosper long when it favors only the prosperous. The success of our economy has always depended not just on the size of our Gross Domestic Product, but on the reach of our prosperity; on the ability to extend opportunity to every willing heart – not out of charity, but because it is the surest route to our common good.

As for our common defense, we reject as false the choice between our safety and our ideals. Our Founding Fathers – Our Founding Fathers, faced with perils that we can scarcely imagine, drafted a charter to assure the rule of law and the rights of man, a charter expanded by the blood of generations. Those ideals still light the world, and we will not give them up for expedience'[s] sake. And so to all the other peoples and governments who are watching today, from the grandest capitals to the small village where my father was born: Know that America is a friend of each nation and every man, woman, and child who seeks a future of peace and dignity. And we are ready to lead once more.

Recall that earlier generations faced down fascism and communism not just with missiles and tanks, but with the sturdy alliances and enduring convictions. They understood that our power alone cannot protect us, nor does it entitle us to do as we please. Instead, they knew that our power grows through its prudent use; our security emanates from the justness of our cause, the force of our example, the tempering qualities of humility and restraint.

We are the keepers of this legacy. Guided by these principles once more, we can meet those new threats that demand even greater effort – even greater cooperation and understanding between nations. We will begin to responsibly leave Iraq to its people, and forge a hard-earned peace in Afghanistan. With old friends and former foes, we will work tirelessly to lessen the nuclear threat, and roll back the specter of a warming planet. We will not apologize for our way of life, nor will we waver in its defense, and for those who seek to advance their aims by inducing terror and slaughtering innocents, we say to you now that our spirit is stronger and cannot be broken. You cannot outlast us, and we will defeat you!

For we know that our patchwork heritage is a strength, not a weakness. We are a nation of Christians and Muslims, Jews and Hindus – and non-believers. We are shaped by every language and culture, drawn from every end of this Earth; and because we have tasted the bitter swill of civil war and segregation, and emerged from that dark chapter stronger and more united, we cannot help but believe that the old hatreds shall someday pass; that the lines of tribe shall soon dissolve; that as the world grows smaller, our common humanity shall reveal itself; and that America must play its role in ushering in a new era of peace.

To the Muslim world, we seek a new way forward, based on mutual interest and mutual respect. To those leaders around the globe who seek to sow conflict, or blame their society's ills on the West – know that your people will judge you on what you can build, not what you destroy. To those – To those who cling to power through corruption and deceit and the silencing of dissent, know that you are on the wrong side of history; but that we will extend a hand if you are willing to unclench your fist.

To the people of poor nations, we pledge to work alongside you to make your farms flourish and let clean waters flow; to nourish starved bodies and feed hungry minds. And to those nations like ours that enjoy relative plenty, we say we can no longer afford indifference to the suffering outside our borders; nor can we consume the world's resources without regard to effect. For the world has changed, and we must change with it.

As we consider the road that unfolds before us, we remember with humble gratitude those brave Americans who, at this very hour, patrol far-off deserts and distant mountains. They have something to tell us, just as the fallen heroes who lie in Arlington whisper through the ages. We honor them not only because they are the guardians of our liberty, but because they embody the spirit of service; a willingness to find meaning in something greater than themselves. And yet, at this moment – a moment that will define a generation – it is precisely this spirit that must inhabit us all.

For as much as government can do and must do, it is ultimately the faith and determination of the American people upon which this nation relies. It is the kindness to take in a stranger when the levees break, the selflessness of workers who would rather cut their hours than see a friend lose their job which sees us through our darkest hours. It is the firefighter's courage to storm a stairway filled with smoke, but also a parent's willingness to nurture a child, that finally decides our fate.

Our challenges may be new. The instruments with

which we meet them may be new. But those values upon which our success depends – honesty and hard work, courage and fair play, tolerance and curiosity, loyalty and patriotism – these things are old. These things are true. They have been the quiet force of progress throughout our history. What is demanded then is a return to these truths. What is required of us now is a new era of responsibility – a recognition, on the part of every American, that we have duties to ourselves, our nation, and the world, duties that we do not grudgingly accept but rather seize gladly, firm in the knowledge that there is nothing so satisfying to the spirit, so defining of our character, than giving our all to a difficult task.

This is the price and the promise of citizenship.

This is the source of our confidence – the knowledge that God calls on us to shape an uncertain destiny.

This is the meaning of our liberty and our creed – why men and women and children of every race and every faith can join in celebration across this magnificent mall, and why a man whose father less than sixty years ago might not have been served at a local restaurant can now stand before you to take a most sacred Oath.

So let us mark this day with remembrance, of who we are and how far we have traveled. In the year of America's birth, in the coldest of months, a small band of patriots huddled by dying campfires on the shores of an icy river. The Capitol was abandoned. The enemy was advancing. The snow was stained with blood. At a moment when the outcome of our revolution was most in doubt, the father of our nation ordered these words be read to the people:

Let it be told to the future world...that in the depth of winter, when nothing but hope and virtue could survive...that the city and the country, alarmed at one common danger, came forth to meet [it].

America: In the face of our common dangers, in this

winter of our hardship, let us remember these timeless words. With hope and virtue, let us brave once more the icy currents, and endure what storms may come. Let it be said by our children's children that when we were tested we refused to let this journey end, that we did not turn back nor did we falter; and with eyes fixed on the horizon and God's grace upon us, we carried forth that great gift of freedom and delivered it safely to future generations.

Thank you, God bless you, and God bless the United States of America.

Barack Obama, *Speech at the 'Together We Thrive: Tucson and America' Memorial*

[January 12, 2011, Tucson]

NOTE Barack Obama delivered a speech at the 'Together We Thrive: Tucson and America memorial' on January 12, 2011, held in the McKale Center on the University of Arizona campus. It honored the victims of the 2011 Tucson shooting and included themes of healing and national unity. Watched by more than 30 million Americans, it drew widespread praise from politicians and commentators across the political spectrum and from abroad.

To the families of those we've lost; to all who called them friends; to the students of this university, the public servants who are gathered here, the people of Tucson and the people of Arizona: I have come here tonight as an American who, like all Americans, kneels to pray with you today and will stand by you tomorrow.

There is nothing I can say that will fill the sudden hole torn in your hearts. But know this: The hopes of a nation are here tonight. We mourn with you for the fallen. We join you in your grief. And we add our faith to yours that Representative Gabrielle Giffords and the other living victims of this tragedy will pull through.

Scripture tells us:

> There is a river whose streams make glad the city of God,
> the holy place where the Most High dwells.
> God is within her, she will not fall;
> God will help her at break of day.

On Saturday morning, Gabby, her staff and many of her constituents gathered outside a supermarket to exercise their right to peaceful assembly and free speech. They were fulfilling a central tenet of the democracy envisioned by our founders — representatives of the people answering questions to their constituents, so as to carry their concerns back to our nation's capital. Gabby called it "Congress on Your Corner" -— just an updated version of government of and by and for the people.

And that quintessentially American scene, that was the scene that was shattered by a gunman's bullets. And the six people who lost their lives on Saturday — they, too, represented what is best in us, what is best in America.

Judge John Roll served our legal system for nearly 40 years. A graduate of this university and a graduate of this law school – Judge Roll was recommended for the federal bench by John McCain 20 years ago – appointed by President George H.W. Bush and rose to become Arizona's chief federal judge.

His colleagues described him as the hardest-working judge within the Ninth Circuit. He was on his way back from attending Mass, as he did every day, when he decided to stop by and say hi to his representative. John is survived by his loving wife, Maureen, his three sons and his five beautiful grandchildren.

George and Dorothy Morris -— "Dot" to her friends -— were high school sweethearts who got married and had two daughters. They did everything together – traveling the open road in their RV, enjoying what their friends called a 50-year honeymoon. Saturday morning, they went by the Safeway to hear what their congresswoman had to say. When gunfire rang out, George, a former Marine, instinctively tried to shield his wife. Both were shot. Dot passed away. A New Jersey native, Phyllis Schneck retired to Tucson to beat the snow. But in the summer, she would return

East, where her world revolved around her three children, her seven grandchildren and 2-year-old great-granddaughter. A gifted quilter, she'd often work under a favorite tree, or sometimes she'd sew aprons with the logos of the Jets and the Giants – to give out at the church where she volunteered. A Republican, she took a liking to Gabby, and wanted to get to know her better.

Dorwan and Mavy Stoddard grew up in Tucson together — about 70 years ago. They moved apart and started their own respective families. But after both were widowed they found their way back here, to, as one of Mavy's daughters put it, "be boyfriend and girlfriend again."

When they weren't out on the road in their motor home, you could find them just up the road, helping folks in need at the Mountain Avenue Church of Christ. A retired construction worker, Dorwan spent his spare time fixing up the church along with his dog, Tux. His final act of selflessness was to dive on top of his wife, sacrificing his life for hers.

Everything – everything – Gabe Zimmerman did, he did with passion. But his true passion was helping people. As Gabby's outreach director, he made the cares of thousands of her constituents his own, seeing to it that seniors got the Medicare benefits that they had earned, that veterans got the medals and the care that they deserved, that government was working for ordinary folks. He died doing what he loved — talking with people and seeing how he could help. And Gabe is survived by his parents, Ross and Emily, his brother, Ben, and his fiancée, Kelly, who he planned to marry next year.

And then there is nine-year-old Christina Taylor Green. Christina was an A student; she was a dancer; she was a gymnast; she was a swimmer. She decided that she wanted to be the first woman to play in the Major Leagues, and as the only girl on her Little League team, no one put it past her.

She showed an appreciation for life uncommon for a girl

her age. She'd remind her mother, "We are so blessed. We have the best life." And she'd pay those blessings back by participating in a charity that helped children who were less fortunate.

Our hearts are broken by their sudden passing. Our hearts are broken -- and yet, our hearts also have reason for fullness. Our hearts are full of hope and thanks for the 13 Americans who survived the shooting, including the congresswoman many of them went to see on Saturday.

I have just come from the University Medical Center, just a mile from here, where our friend Gabby courageously fights to recover even as we speak. And I want to tell you – her husband Mark is here and he allows me to share this with you – right after we went to visit, a few minutes after we left her room and some of her colleagues in Congress were in the room, Gabby opened her eyes for the first time. Gabby opened her eyes for the first time.

Gabby opened her eyes. Gabby opened her eyes, so I can tell you she knows we are here. She knows we love her. And she knows that we are rooting for her through what is undoubtedly going to be a difficult journey. We are there for her.

Our hearts are full of thanks for that good news, and our hearts are full of gratitude for those who saved others. We are grateful to Daniel Hernandez – a volunteer in Gabby's office.

And, Daniel, I'm sorry, you may deny it, but we've decided you are a hero because – you ran through the chaos to minister to your boss, and tended to her wounds and helped keep her alive.

We are grateful to the men who tackled the gunman as he stopped to reload. Right over there. We are grateful for petite Patricia Maisch, who wrestled away the killer's ammunition, and undoubtedly saved some lives. And we are grateful for the doctors and nurses and first responders who worked wonders to heal those who'd been hurt. We are grateful to them.

These men and women remind us that heroism is found not only on the fields of battle. They remind us that heroism does not require special training or physical strength. Heroism is here, in the hearts of so many of our fellow citizens, all around us, just waiting to be summoned — as it was on Saturday morning. Their actions, their selflessness poses a challenge to each of us. It raises a question of what, beyond prayers and expressions of concern, is required of us going forward. How can we honor the fallen? How can we be true to their memory?

You see, when a tragedy like this strikes, it is part of our nature to demand explanations — to try and pose some order on the chaos and make sense out of that which seems senseless. Already we've seen a national conversation commence, not only about the motivations behind these killings, but about everything from the merits of gun safety laws to the adequacy of our mental health system. And much of this process, of debating what might be done to prevent such tragedies in the future, is an essential ingredient in our exercise of self-government.

But at a time when our discourse has become so sharply polarized — at a time when we are far too eager to lay the blame for all that ails the world at the feet of those who happen to think differently than we do — it's important for us to pause for a moment and make sure that we're talking with each other in a way that heals, not in a way that wounds.

Scripture tells us that there is evil in the world, and that terrible things happen for reasons that defy human understanding. In the words of Job, "When I looked for light, then came darkness." Bad things happen, and we have to guard against simple explanations in the aftermath.

For the truth is none of us can know exactly what triggered this vicious attack. None of us can know with any certainty what might have stopped these shots from being fired, or what thoughts lurked in the inner recesses of a violent man's mind. Yes, we have to examine all the facts behind this tragedy. We cannot and will not be passive in the face of such violence. We should be willing to challenge old assumptions in order to lessen the prospects of such violence in the future. But what we cannot do is use this tragedy as one more occasion to turn on each other. That we cannot do. That we cannot do.

As we discuss these issues, let each of us do so with a good dose of humility. Rather than pointing fingers or assigning blame, let's use this occasion to expand our moral imaginations, to listen to each other more carefully, to sharpen our instincts for empathy and remind ourselves of all the ways that our hopes and dreams are bound together.

After all, that's what most of us do when we lose somebody in our family — especially if the loss is unexpected. We're shaken out of our routines. We're forced to look inward. We reflect on the past: Did we spend enough time with an aging parent, we wonder. Did we express our gratitude for all the sacrifices that they made for us? Did we tell a spouse just how desperately we loved them, not just once in a while but every single day?

So sudden loss causes us to look backward — but it also forces us to look forward; to reflect on the present and the future, on the manner in which we live our lives and nurture our relationships with those who are still with us.

We may ask ourselves if we've shown enough kindness and generosity and compassion to the people in our lives. Perhaps we question whether we're doing right by our children, or our community, whether our priorities are in order.

We recognize our own mortality, and we are reminded that in the fleeting time we have on this Earth, what matters is not wealth, or status, or power, or fame — but rather, how well we have loved – and what small part we have played in making the lives of other people better.

And that process – that process of reflection, of making sure we align our values with our actions — that, I believe, is what a tragedy like this requires.

For those who were harmed, those who were killed — they are part of our family, an American family 300 million strong. We may not have known them personally, but surely we see ourselves in them. In George and Dot, in Dorwan and Mavy, we sense the abiding love we have for our own husbands, our own wives, our own life partners. Phyllis — she's our mom or our grandma; Gabe our brother or son. In Judge Roll, we recognize not only a man who prized his family and doing his job well, but also a man who embodied America's fidelity to the law.

And in Gabby – in Gabby, we see a reflection of our public-spiritedness; that desire to participate in that sometimes frustrating, sometimes contentious, but always necessary and never-ending process to form a more perfect union.

And in Christina – in Christina we see all of our children. So curious, so trusting, so energetic, so full of magic. So deserving of our love. And so deserving of our good example.

If this tragedy prompts reflection and debate – as it should – let's make sure it's worthy of those we have lost. Let's make sure it's not on the usual plane of politics and point-scoring and pettiness that drifts away in the next news cycle.

The loss of these wonderful people should make every one of us strive to be better. To be better in our private lives, to be better friends and neighbors and coworkers and parents. And if, as has been discussed in recent days, their death helps usher in more civility in our public discourse, let us remember it is not because a simple lack of civility caused this tragedy – it did not – but rather because only a more civil and honest public discourse can help us face up to the challenges of our nation in a way that would make them proud.

We should be civil because we want to live up to the example of public servants like John Roll and Gabby Giffords, who knew first and foremost that we are all Americans, and that we can question each other's ideas without questioning each other's love of country and that our task, working together, is to constantly widen the circle of our concern so that we bequeath the American Dream to future generations.

They believed – they believed, and I believe that we can be better. Those who died here, those who saved life here – - they help me believe. We may not be able to stop all evil in the world, but I know that how we treat one another, that's entirely up to us.

And I believe that for all our imperfections, we are full of decency and goodness, and that the forces that divide us are not as strong as those that unite us.

That's what I believe, in part because that's what a child like Christina Taylor Green believed.

Imagine – imagine for a moment, here was a young girl who was just becoming aware of our democracy; just beginning to understand the obligations of citizenship; just starting to glimpse the fact that some day she, too, might play a part in shaping her nation's future. She had been elected to her student council. She saw public service as something exciting and hopeful. She was off to meet her congresswoman, someone she was sure was good and important and might be a role model. She saw all this through the eyes of a child, undimmed by the cynicism or vitriol that we adults all too often just take for granted.

I want to live up to her expectations. I want our democracy to be as good as Christina imagined it. I want America to be as good as she imagined it. All of us — we should do everything we can to make sure this country lives up to our children's expectations.

As has already been mentioned, Christina was given to us on September 11th, 2001, one of 50 babies born that day to be pictured in a book called "Faces of Hope." On either side of her photo in that book were simple wishes for a child's life. "I hope you help those in need," read one. "I hope you know all the words to the National Anthem and sing it with your hand over your heart." "I hope" – "I hope you jump in rain puddles."

If there are rain puddles in Heaven, Christina is jumping in them today. And here on this Earth – here on this Earth, we place our hands over our hearts, and we commit ourselves as Americans to forging a country that is forever worthy of her gentle, happy spirit.

May God bless and keep those we've lost in restful and eternal peace.

May He love and watch over the survivors.

And may He bless the United States of America.

Sidney Poitier, *Acceptance Speech for the Lifetime Achievement Award*

[March 24, 2002, Los Angeles]

NOTE In the 2002 Oscar edition, for the first time in the history of Hollywood, both the Best Actor and Best Actress awards went to two black artists, Halle Barry (for *Monster's Ball*) and Denzel Washington (for *Training Day*). And that is not all: the Lifetime Achievement Award is given to the progenitor of black actors, Sidney Poitier, until that day the only actor awarded with the Oscar as a protagonist (in 1963) in 74 editions. The intense and emotional speech of Sidney Poitier is probably one of the most beautiful speeches given by an actor during the night of the Oscars.

I arrived in Hollywood at the age of twenty-two in a time different than today's, a time in which the odds against my standing here tonight fifty-three years later would not have fallen in my favor. Back then, no route had been established for where I was hoping to go, no pathway left in evidence for me to trace, no custom for me to follow. Yet, here I am this evening at the end of a journey that in 1949 would have been considered almost impossible and in fact might never have been set in motion were there not an untold number of courageous, unselfish choices made by a handful of visionary American filmmakers, directors, writers and producers; each with a strong sense of citizenship responsibility to the times in which they lived; each unafraid to permit their art to reflect their views and values, ethical and moral, and moreover, acknowledge them as their own. They knew the odds that stood against them and their efforts were overwhelming and likely could have proven too high to overcome. Still those filmmakers persevered, speaking through their art to the best in all of us. And I've benefited from their effort. The industry benefited from their effort. America benefited from their effort. And in ways large and small the world has also benefited from their effort. Therefore, with respect, I share this great honor with the late Joe Mankiewicz, the late Richard Brooks, the late Ralph Nelson, the late Darryl Zanuck, the late Stanley Kramer, the Mirisch brothers, especially Walter whose friendship lies at the very heart of this moment, Guy Green, Norman Jewison, and all others who have had a hand in altering the odds for me and for others. Without them this most memorable moment would not have come to pass and the many excellent young actors who have followed in admirable fashion might not have as they have to enrich the tradition of American filmmaking as they have. I accept this award in memory of all the African American actors and actresses who went before me in the difficult years, on whose shoulders I was privileged to stand to see where I might go. My love and my thanks to my wonderful, wonderful wife, my children, my grandchildren, my agent and friend Martin Baum. And finally, to those audience members around the world who have placed their trust in my judgment as an actor and filmmaker, I thank each of you for your support through the years. Thank you.

Ronald Reagan, *The Space Shuttle "Challenger" Tragedy Address*

[January 28, 1986, Washington]

NOTE The Space Shuttle Challenger disaster was a fatal incident on January 28, 1986, in the United States space program where the Space Shuttle Challenger broke apart 73 seconds into its flight, killing all seven crew members aboard. It was the first fatal accident involving an American spacecraft in flight.

Ladies and Gentlemen, I'd planned to speak to you tonight to report on the state of the Union, but the events of earlier today have led me to change those plans. Today is a day for mourning and remembering. Nancy and I are pained to the core by the tragedy of the Shuttle Challenger. We know we share this pain with all of the people of our country. This is truly a national loss.

Nineteen years ago, almost to the day, we lost three astronauts in a terrible accident on the ground. But we've never lost an astronaut in flight. We've never had a tragedy like this.

And perhaps we've forgotten the courage it took for the crew of the shuttle. But they, the Challenger Seven, were aware of the dangers, but overcame them and did their jobs brilliantly. We mourn seven heroes: Michael Smith, Dick Scobee, Judith Resnik, Ronald McNair, Ellison Onizuka, Gregory Jarvis, and Christa McAuliffe.

We mourn their loss as a nation together.

For the families of the seven, we cannot bear, as you do, the full impact of this tragedy. But we feel the loss, and we're thinking about you so very much. Your loved ones were daring and brave, and they had that special grace, that special spirit that says, "Give me a challenge, and I'll meet it with joy." They had a hunger to explore the universe and discover its truths. They wished to serve, and they did. They served all of us.

We've grown used to wonders in this century. It's hard to dazzle us. But for twenty-five years the United States space program has been doing just that. We've grown used to the idea of space, and, perhaps we forget that we've only just begun. We're still pioneers. They, the members of the Challenger crew, were pioneers.

And I want to say something to the schoolchildren of America who were watching the live coverage of the shuttle's take-off. I know it's hard to understand, but sometimes painful things like this happen. It's all part of the process of exploration and discovery. It's all part of taking a chance and expanding man's horizons. The future doesn't belong to the fainthearted; it belongs to the brave. The Challenger crew was pulling us into the future, and we'll continue to follow them.

I've always had great faith in and respect for our space program. And what happened today does nothing to diminish it. We don't hide our space program. We don't keep secrets and cover things up. We do it all up front and in public. That's the way freedom is, and we wouldn't change it for a minute.

We'll continue our quest in space. There will be more shuttle flights and more shuttle crews and, yes, more volunteers, more civilians, more teachers in space. Nothing ends here; our hopes and our journeys continue.

I want to add that I wish I could talk to every man and woman who works for NASA, or who worked on this mission and tell them: "Your dedication and professionalism have moved and impressed us for decades. And we know of your anguish. We share it."

There's a coincidence today. On this day three hundred and ninety years ago, the great explorer Sir Francis Drake died aboard ship off the coast of Panama. In his lifetime the great frontiers were the oceans, and a historian later said, "He lived by the sea, died on it, and was buried in it." Well, today, we can say of the Challenger crew: Their dedication was, like Drake's, complete.

The crew of the Space Shuttle Challenger honored us by the manner in which they lived their lives. We will never forget them, nor the last time we saw them, this morning, as they prepared for their journey and waved goodbye and "slipped the surly bonds of earth" to "touch the face of God."

Thank you.

Franklin D. Roosevelt, *First Inaugural Address*

[March 4, 1933, Washington]

NOTE The first inauguration of Franklin D. Roosevelt (1882-1945) as the 32nd president of the United States was held on Saturday, March 4, 1933 rather than on Friday, January 20, 1933, at the East Portico of the United States Capitol in Washington, D.C. Roosevelt used his First Inaugural Speech to outline his plan for the Great Depression. He promised prompt, decisive action, and he conveyed some of his own unshakable self-confidence to millions of Americans listening on radios throughout the land. "This great nation will endure as it has endured, will revive and prosper," he asserted, adding, "the only thing we have to fear is fear itself."

This is a day of national consecration. And I am certain that on this day my fellow Americans expect that on my induction into the Presidency, I will address them with a candor and a decision which the present situation of our people impels.

This is preeminently the time to speak the truth, the whole truth, frankly and boldly. Nor need we shrink from honestly facing conditions in our country today. This great Nation will endure, as it has endured, will revive and will prosper.

So, first of all, let me assert my firm belief that the only thing we have to fear is fear itself – nameless, unreasoning, unjustified terror which paralyzes needed efforts to convert retreat into advance. In every dark hour of our national life, a leadership of frankness and of vigor has met with that understanding and support of the people themselves which is essential to victory. And I am convinced that you will again give that support to leadership in these critical days.

In such a spirit on my part and on yours we face our common difficulties. They concern, thank God, only material things. Values have shrunk to fantastic levels; taxes have risen; our ability to pay has fallen; government of all kinds is faced by serious curtailment of income; the means of exchange are frozen in the currents of trade; the withered leaves of industrial enterprise lie on every side; farmers find no markets for their produce; and the savings of many years in thousands of families are gone. More important, a host of unemployed citizens face the grim problem of existence, and an equally great number toil with little return. Only a foolish optimist can deny the dark realities of the moment.

And yet our distress comes from no failure of substance. We are stricken by no plague of locusts. Compared with the perils which our forefathers conquered, because they believed and were not afraid, we have still much to be thankful for. Nature still offers her bounty and human efforts have multiplied it. Plenty is at our doorstep, but a generous use of it languishes in the very sight of the supply.

Primarily, this is because the rulers of the exchange of mankind's goods have failed, through their own stubbornness and their own incompetence, have admitted their failure, and have abdicated. Practices of the unscrupulous money changers stand indicted in the court of public opinion, rejected by the hearts and minds of men.

True, they have tried. But their efforts have been cast in the pattern of an outworn tradition. Faced by failure of credit, they have proposed only the lending of more money. Stripped of the lure of profit by which to induce our people to follow their false leadership, they have resorted to exhortations, pleading tearfully for restored confidence. They only know the rules of a generation of self-seekers. They have no vision, and when there is no vision the people perish.

Yes, the money changers have fled from their high seats

in the temple of our civilization. We may now restore that temple to the ancient truths. The measure of that restoration lies in the extent to which we apply social values more noble than mere monetary profit.

Happiness lies not in the mere possession of money; it lies in the joy of achievement, in the thrill of creative effort. The joy, the moral stimulation of work no longer must be forgotten in the mad chase of evanescent profits. These dark days, my friends, will be worth all they cost us if they teach us that our true destiny is not to be ministered unto but to minister to ourselves, to our fellow men.

Recognition of that falsity of material wealth as the standard of success goes hand in hand with the abandonment of the false belief that public office and high political position are to be valued only by the standards of pride of place and personal profit; and there must be an end to a conduct in banking and in business which too often has given to a sacred trust the likeness of callous and selfish wrongdoing. Small wonder that confidence languishes, for it thrives only on honesty, on honor, on the sacredness of obligations, on faithful protection, and on unselfish performance; without them it cannot live.

Restoration calls, however, not for changes in ethics alone. This Nation is asking for action, and action now.

Our greatest primary task is to put people to work. This is no unsolvable problem if we face it wisely and courageously. It can be accomplished in part by direct recruiting by the Government itself, treating the task as we would treat the emergency of a war, but at the same time, through this employment, accomplishing great – greatly needed projects to stimulate and reorganize the use of our great natural resources.

Hand in hand with that we must frankly recognize the overbalance of population in our industrial centers and, by engaging on a national scale in a redistribution, endeavor to provide a better use of the land for those best fitted for the land.

Yes, the task can be helped by definite efforts to raise the values of agricultural products, and with this the power to purchase the output of our cities. It can be helped by preventing realistically the tragedy of the growing loss through foreclosure of our small homes and our farms. It can be helped by insistence that the Federal, the State, and the local governments act forthwith on the demand that their cost be drastically reduced. It can be helped by the unifying of relief activities which today are often scattered, uneconomical, unequal. It can be helped by national planning for and supervision of all forms of transportation and of communications and other utilities that have a definitely public character. There are many ways in which it can be helped, but it can never be helped by merely talking about it.

We must act. We must act quickly.

And finally, in our progress towards a resumption of work, we require two safeguards against a return of the evils of the old order. There must be a strict supervision of all banking and credits and investments. There must be an end to speculation with other people's money. And there must be provision for an adequate but sound currency.

These, my friends, are the lines of attack. I shall presently urge upon a new Congress in special session detailed measures for their fulfillment, and I shall seek the immediate assistance of the 48 States.

Through this program of action we address ourselves to putting our own national house in order and making income balance outgo. Our international trade relations, though vastly important, are in point of time, and necessity, secondary to the establishment of a sound national economy. I favor, as a practical policy, the putting of first things first. I shall spare no effort to restore world trade by international economic readjustment; but the emergency at home cannot wait on that accomplishment.

The basic thought that guides these specific means of national recovery is not nationally — narrowly nationalistic. It is the insistence, as a first consideration, upon the interdependence of the various elements in and parts of the United States of America — a recognition of the old and permanently important manifestation of the American spirit of the pioneer. It is the way to recovery. It is the immediate way. It is the strongest assurance that recovery will endure.

In the field of world policy, I would dedicate this Nation to the policy of the good neighbor: the neighbor who resolutely respects himself and, because he does so, respects the rights of others; the neighbor who respects his obligations and respects the sanctity of his agreements in and with a world of neighbors.

If I read the temper of our people correctly, we now realize, as we have never realized before, our interdependence on each other; that we can not merely take, but we must give as well; that if we are to go forward, we must move as a trained and loyal army willing to sacrifice for the good of a common discipline, because without such discipline no progress can be made, no leadership becomes effective.

We are, I know, ready and willing to submit our lives and our property to such discipline, because it makes possible a leadership which aims at the larger good. This, I propose to offer, pledging that the larger purposes will bind upon us, bind upon us all as a sacred obligation with a unity of duty hitherto evoked only in times of armed strife.

With this pledge taken, I assume unhesitatingly the leadership of this great army of our people dedicated to a disciplined attack upon our common problems.

Action in this image, action to this end is feasible under the form of government which we have inherited from our ancestors. Our Constitution is so simple, so practical that it is possible always to meet extraordinary needs by changes in emphasis and arrangement without loss of essential form. That is why our constitutional system has proved itself the most superbly enduring political mechanism the modern world has ever seen.

It has met every stress of vast expansion of territory, of foreign wars, of bitter internal strife, of world relations. And it is to be hoped that the normal balance of executive and legislative authority may be wholly equal, wholly adequate to meet the unprecedented task before us. But it may be that an unprecedented demand and need for undelayed action may call for temporary departure from that normal balance of public procedure.

I am prepared under my constitutional duty to recommend the measures that a stricken nation in the midst of a stricken world may require. These measures, or such other measures as the Congress may build out of its experience and wisdom, I shall seek, within my constitutional authority, to bring to speedy adoption.

But, in the event that the Congress shall fail to take one of these two courses, in the event that the national emergency is still critical, I shall not evade the clear course of duty that will then confront me. I shall ask the Congress for the one remaining instrument to meet the crisis – broad Executive power to wage a war against the emergency, as great as the power that would be given to me if we were in fact invaded by a foreign foe.

For the trust reposed in me, I will return the courage and the devotion that befit the time. I can do no less.

We face the arduous days that lie before us in the warm courage of national unity; with the clear consciousness of seeking old and precious moral values; with the clean satisfaction that comes from the stern performance of duty by old and young alike. We aim at the assurance of a rounded, a permanent national life.

We do not distrust the – the future of essential

democracy. The people of the United States have not failed. In their need they have registered a mandate that they want direct, vigorous action. They have asked for discipline and direction under leadership. They have made me the present instrument of their wishes. In the spirit of the gift I take it.

In this dedication – In this dedication of a Nation, we humbly ask the blessing of God.

May He protect each and every one of us.

May He guide me in the days to come."

Franklin D. Roosevelt, *The Arsenal of Democracy*

[December 29, 1940, Washington]

NOTE "Arsenal of Democracy" was the central phrase used by U.S. President Franklin D. Roosevelt in a radio broadcast on the threat to national security, delivered on December 29, 1940 - nearly a year before the United States entered the Second World War (1939-1945). For over 36 minutes and 53 seconds, Roosevelt spoke to his captive audience about the imperative of American engagement in the conflict. Staying true to his campaign pledge of several weeks earlier, that America would not declare war on the Axis powers unless it were attacked, the president still made a forceful case for American military support to Britain.

This is not a fireside chat on war. It is a talk on national security; because the nub of the whole purpose of your President is to keep you now, and your children later, and your grandchildren much later, out of a last-ditch war for the preservation of American independence, and all of the things that American independence means to you and to me and to ours.

Tonight, in the presence of a world crisis, my mind goes back eight years to a night in the midst of a domestic crisis. It was a time when the wheels of American industry were grinding to a full stop, when the whole banking system of our country had ceased to function. I well remember that while I sat in my study in the White House, preparing to talk with the people of the United States, I had before my eyes the picture of all those Americans with whom I was talking. I saw the workmen in the mills, the mines, the factories, the girl behind the counter, the small shopkeeper, the farmer doing his spring plowing, the widows and the old men wondering about their life's savings. I tried to convey to the great mass of American people what the banking crisis meant to them in their daily lives.

Tonight, I want to do the same thing, with the same people, in this new crisis which faces America. We met the issue of 1933 with courage and realism. We face this new crisis, this new threat to the security of our nation, with the same courage and realism. Never before since Jamestown and Plymouth Rock has our American civilization been in such danger as now. For on September 27th, 1940 – this year – by an agreement signed in Berlin, three powerful nations, two in Europe and one in Asia, joined themselves together in the threat that if the United States of America interfered with or blocked the expansion program of these three nations – a program aimed at world control – they would unite in ultimate action against the United States.

The Nazi masters of Germany have made it clear that they intend not only to dominate all life and thought in their own country, but also to enslave the whole of Europe, and then to use the resources of Europe to dominate the rest of the world. It was only three weeks ago that their leader stated this: "There are two worlds that stand opposed to each other." And then in defiant reply to his opponents he said this: "Others are correct when they say: 'With this world we cannot ever reconcile ourselves.'" I can beat any other power in the world." So said the leader of the Nazis.

In other words, the Axis not merely admits but the Axis proclaims that there can be no ultimate peace between their philosophy – their philosophy of government – and our philosophy of government. In view of the nature of this undeniable threat, it can be asserted, properly and categorically, that the United States has no right or reason to encourage talk of peace until the day shall come when there is a clear intention on the part of the aggressor nations to abandon all thought of dominating or conquering the world.

At this moment the forces of the States that are leagued against all peoples who live in freedom are being held away from our shores. The Germans and the Italians are being blocked on the other side of the Atlantic by the British and by the Greeks, and by thousands of soldiers and sailors who were able to escape from subjugated countries. In Asia the Japanese are being engaged by the Chinese nation in another great defense. In the Pacific Ocean is our fleet.

Some of our people like to believe that wars in Europe and in Asia are of no concern to us. But it is a matter of most vital concern to us that European and Asiatic war-makers should not gain control of the oceans which lead to this hemisphere. One hundred and seventeen years ago the Monroe Doctrine was conceived by our government as a measure of defense in the face of a threat against this hemisphere by an alliance in Continental Europe. Thereafter, we stood guard in the Atlantic, with the British as neighbors. There was no treaty. There was no "unwritten agreement." And yet there was the feeling, proven correct by history, that we as neighbors could settle any disputes in peaceful fashion. And the fact is that during the whole of this time the Western Hemisphere has remained free from aggression from Europe or from Asia.

Does anyone seriously believe that we need to fear attack anywhere in the Americas while a free Britain remains our most powerful naval neighbor in the Atlantic? And does anyone seriously believe, on the other hand, that we could rest easy if the Axis powers were our neighbors there? If Great Britain goes down, the Axis powers will control the Continents of Europe, Asia, Africa, Austral-Asia, and the high seas. And they will be in a position to bring enormous military and naval resources against this hemisphere. It is no exaggeration to say that all of us in all the Americas would be living at the point of a gun – a gun loaded with explosive bullets, economic as well as military. We should enter upon a new and terrible era in which the whole world, our hemisphere included, would be run by threats of brute force. And to survive in such a world, we would have to convert ourselves permanently into a militaristic power on the basis of war economy.

Some of us like to believe that even if Britain falls, we are still safe, because of the broad expanse of the Atlantic and of the Pacific. But the width of those oceans is not what it was in the days of clipper ships. At one point between Africa and Brazil the distance is less than it is from Washington to Denver, Colorado, five hours for the latest type of bomber. And at the north end of the Pacific Ocean, America and Asia almost touch each other. Why, even today we have planes that could fly from the British Isles to New England and back again without refueling. And remember that the range of the modern bomber is ever being increased.

During the past week many people in all parts of the nation have told me what they wanted me to say tonight. Almost all of them expressed a courageous desire to hear the plain truth about the gravity of the situation. One telegram, however, expressed the attitude of the small minority who want to see no evil and hear no evil, even though they know in their hearts that evil exists. That telegram begged me not to tell again of the ease with which our American cities could be bombed by any hostile power which had gained bases in this Western Hemisphere. The gist of that telegram was: "Please, Mr. President, don't frighten us by telling us the facts." Frankly and definitely there is danger ahead – danger against which we must prepare. But we well know that we cannot escape danger, or the fear of danger, by crawling into bed and pulling the covers over our heads.

Some nations of Europe were bound by solemn nonintervention pacts with Germany. Other nations were assured by Germany that they need never fear invasion.

Nonintervention pact or not, the fact remains that they

were attacked, overrun, thrown into modern slavery at an hour's notice – or even without any notice at all. As an exiled leader of one of these nations said to me the other day, "The notice was a minus quantity. It was given to my government two hours after German troops had poured into my country in a hundred places." The fate of these nations tells us what it means to live at the point of a Nazi gun.

The Nazis have justified such actions by various pious frauds. One of these frauds is the claim that they are occupying a nation for the purpose of "restoring order." Another is that they are occupying or controlling a nation on the excuse that they are "protecting it" against the aggression of somebody else. For example, Germany has said that she was occupying Belgium to save the Belgians from the British. Would she then hesitate to say to any South American country: "We are occupying you to protect you from aggression by the United States"? Belgium today is being used as an invasion base against Britain, now fighting for its life. And any South American country, in Nazi hands, would always constitute a jumping off place for German attack on any one of the other republics of this hemisphere.

Analyze for yourselves the future of two other places even nearer to Germany if the Nazis won. Could Ireland hold out? Would Irish freedom be permitted as an amazing pet exception in an unfree world? Or the islands of the Azores, which still fly the flag of Portugal after five centuries? You and I think of Hawaii as an outpost of defense in the Pacific. And yet the Azores are closer to our shores in the Atlantic than Hawaii is on the other side.

There are those who say that the Axis powers would never have any desire to attack the Western Hemisphere. That is the same dangerous form of wishful thinking which has destroyed the powers of resistance of so many conquered peoples. The plain facts are that the Nazis have proclaimed, time and again, that all other races are their inferiors and therefore subject to their orders. And most important of all, the vast resources and wealth of this American hemisphere constitute the most tempting loot in all of the round world.

Let us no longer blind ourselves to the undeniable fact that the evil forces which have crushed and undermined and corrupted so many others are already within our own gates. Your government knows much about them and every day is ferreting them out. Their secret emissaries are active in our own and in neighboring countries. They seek to stir up suspicion and dissension, to cause internal strife. They try to turn capital against labor, and vice versa. They try to reawaken long slumbering racial and religious enmities which should have no place in this country. They are active in every group that promotes intolerance. They exploit for their own ends our own natural bhorrence of war. These trouble-breeders have but one purpose. It is to divide our people, to divide them into hostile groups and to destroy our unity and shatter our will to defend ourselves.

There are also American citizens, many of them in high places, who, unwittingly in most cases, are aiding and abetting the work of these agents. I do not charge these American citizens with being foreign agents. But I do charge them with doing exactly the kind of work that the dictators want done in the United States. These people not only believe that we can save our own skins by shutting our eyes to the fate of other nations. Some of them go much further than that. They say that we can and should become the friends and even the partners of the Axis powers. Some of them even suggest that we should imitate the methods of the dictatorships. But Americans never can and never will do that.

The experience of the past two years has proven beyond doubt that no nation can appease the Nazis. No man can tame a tiger into a kitten by stroking it. There can be no appeasement with ruthlessness. There can be no reasoning with an incendiary bomb. We know now that a nation can have peace with the Nazis only at the price of total surrender. Even the people of Italy have been forced to become accomplices of the Nazis; but at this moment they do not know how soon they will be embraced to death by their allies.

The American appeasers ignore the warning to be found in the fate of Austria, Czechoslovakia, Poland, Norway, Belgium, the Netherlands, Denmark, and France. They tell you that the Axis powers are going to win anyway; that all of this bloodshed in the world could be saved, that the United States might just as well throw its influence into the scale of a dictated peace and get the best out of it that we can. They call it a "negotiated peace." Nonsense! Is it a negotiated peace if a gang of outlaws surrounds your community and on threat of extermination makes you pay tribute to save your own skins? For such a dictated peace would be no peace at all. It would be only another armistice, leading to the most gigantic armament race and the most devastating trade wars in all history. And in these contests the Americas would offer the only real resistance to the Axis power. With all their vaunted efficiency, with all their parade of pious purpose in this war, there are still in their background the concentration camp and the servants of God in chains.

The history of recent years proves that the shootings and the chains and the concentration camps are not simply the transient tools but the very altars of modern dictatorships. They may talk of a "new order" in the world, but what they have in mind is only a revival of the oldest and the worst tyranny. In that there is no liberty, no religion, no hope. The proposed "new order" is the very opposite of a United States of Europe or a United States of Asia. It is not a government based upon the consent of the governed. It is not a union of ordinary, self-respecting men and women to protect themselves and their freedom and their dignity from oppression. It is an unholy alliance of power and pelf to dominate and to enslave the human race.

The British people and their allies today are conducting an active war against this unholy alliance. Our own future security is greatly dependent on the outcome of that fight. Our ability to "keep out of war" is going to be affected by that outcome. Thinking in terms of today and tomorrow, I make the direct statement to the American people that there is far less chance of the United States getting into war if we do all we can now to support the nations defending themselves against attack by the Axis than if we acquiesce in their defeat, submit tamely to an Axis victory, and wait our turn to be the object of attack in another war later on.

If we are to be completely honest with ourselves, we must admit that there is risk in any course we may take. But I deeply believe that the great majority of our people agree that the course that I advocate involves the least risk now and the greatest hope for world peace in the future.

The people of Europe who are defending themselves do not ask us to do their fighting. They ask us for the implements of war, the planes, the tanks, the guns, the freighters which will enable them to fight for their liberty and for our security. Emphatically, we must get these weapons to them, get them to them in sufficient volume and quickly enough so that we and our children will be saved the agony and suffering of war which others have had to endure.

Let not the defeatists tell us that it is too late. It will never be earlier. Tomorrow will be later than today.

Certain facts are self-evident.

In a military sense Great Britain and the British Empire are today the spearhead of resistance to world conquest. And they are putting up a fight which will live forever in the story of human gallantry. There is no demand for sending an American expeditionary force outside our own borders. There is no intention by any member of your government to send such a force. You can therefore, nail, nail any talk about sending armies to Europe as deliberate untruth. Our national policy is not directed toward war. Its sole purpose is to keep war away from our country and away from our people.

Democracy's fight against world conquest is being greatly aided, and must be more greatly aided, by the rearmament of the United States and by sending every ounce and every ton of munitions and supplies that we can possibly spare to help the defenders who are in the front lines. And it is no more un-neutral for us to do that than it is for Sweden, Russia, and other nations near Germany to send steel and ore and oil and other war materials into Germany every day in the week.

We are planning our own defense with the utmost urgency, and in its vast scale we must integrate the war needs of Britain and the other free nations which are resisting aggression. This is not a matter of sentiment or of controversial personal opinion. It is a matter of realistic, practical military policy, based on the advice of our military experts who are in close touch with existing warfare. These military and naval experts and the members of the Congress and the Administration have a single-minded purpose: the defense of the United States.

This nation is making a great effort to produce everything that is necessary in this emergency, and with all possible speed. And this great effort requires great sacrifice. I would ask no one to defend a democracy which in turn would not defend every one in the nation against want and privation. The strength of this nation shall not be diluted by the failure of the government to protect the economic well-being of its citizens. If our capacity to produce is limited by machines, it must ever be remembered that these machines are operated by the skill and the stamina of the workers.

As the government is determined to protect the rights of the workers, so the nation has a right to expect that the men who man the machines will discharge their full responsibilities to the urgent needs of defense. The worker possesses the same human dignity and is entitled to the same security of position as the engineer or the manager or the owner. For the workers provide the human power that turns out the destroyers, and the planes, and the tanks. The nation expects our defense industries to continue operation without interruption by strikes or lockouts. It expects and insists that management and workers will reconcile their differences by voluntary or legal means, to continue to produce the supplies that are so sorely needed. And on the economic side of our great defense program, we are, as you know, bending every effort to maintain stability of prices and with that the stability of the cost of living.

Nine days ago I announced the setting up of a more effective organization to direct our gigantic efforts to increase the production of munitions. The appropriation of vast sums of money and a well-coordinated executive direction of our defense efforts are not in themselves enough. Guns, planes, ships and many other things have to be built in the factories and the arsenals of America. They have to be produced by workers and managers and engineers with the aid of machines which in turn have to be built by hundreds of thousands of workers throughout the land. In this great work there has been splendid cooperation between the government and industry and labor. And I am very thankful.

American industrial genius, unmatched throughout all the world in the solution of production problems, has been called upon to bring its resources and its talents into action. Manufacturers of watches, of farm implements, of Linotypes and cash registers and automobiles, and sewing machines and lawn mowers and locomotives, are now making fuses and bomb packing crates and telescope mounts and shells and pistols and tanks.

But all of our present efforts are not enough. We must

have more ships, more guns, more planes – more of everything. And this can be accomplished only if we discard the notion of "business as usual." This job cannot be done merely by superimposing on the existing productive facilities the added requirements of the nation for defense. Our defense efforts must not be blocked by those who fear the future consequences of surplus plant capacity. The possible consequences of failure of our defense efforts now are much more to be feared. And after the present needs of our defense are past, a proper handling of the country's peacetime needs will require all of the new productive capacity, if not still more. No pessimistic policy about the future of America shall delay the immediate expansion of those industries essential to defense. We need them.

I want to make it clear that it is the purpose of the nation to build now with all possible speed every machine, every arsenal, every factory that we need to manufacture our defense material. We have the men, the skill, the wealth, and above all, the will. I am confident that if and when production of consumer or luxury goods in certain industries requires the use of machines and raw materials that are essential for defense purposes, then such production must yield, and will gladly yield, to our primary and compelling purpose.

So I appeal to the owners of plants, to the managers, to the workers, to our own government employees to put every ounce of effort into producing these munitions swiftly and without stint. With this appeal I give you the pledge that all of us who are officers of your government will devote ourselves to the same whole-hearted extent to the great task that lies ahead.

As planes and ships and guns and shells are produced, your government, with its defense experts, can then determine how best to use them to defend this hemisphere. The decision as to how much shall be sent abroad and how much shall remain at home must be made on the basis of our over-all military necessities.

We must be the great arsenal of democracy.

For us this is an emergency as serious as war itself. We must apply ourselves to our task with the same resolution, the same sense of urgency, the same spirit of patriotism and sacrifice as we would show were we at war.

We have furnished the British great material support and we will furnish far more in the future. There will be no "bottlenecks" in our determination to aid Great Britain. No dictator, no combination of dictators, will weaken that determination by threats of how they will construe that determination. The British have received invaluable military support from the heroic Greek Army and from the forces of all the governments in exile. Their strength is growing. It is the strength of men and women who value their freedom more highly than they value their lives.

I believe that the Axis powers are not going to win this war. I base that belief on the latest and best of information.

We have no excuse for defeatism. We have every good reason for hope – hope for peace, yes, and hope for the defense of our civilization and for the building of a better civilization in the future. I have the profound conviction that the American people are now determined to put forth a mightier effort than they have ever yet made to increase our production of all the implements of defense, to meet the threat to our democratic faith.

As President of the United States, I call for that national effort. I call for it in the name of this nation which we love and honor and which we are privileged and proud to serve. I call upon our people with absolute confidence that our common cause will greatly succeed."

Franklin D. Roosevelt, *Four Freedoms Speech: The 1941 State of the Union address*

[January 6, 1941, Washington]

NOTE "The Four Freedom"s were goals articulated by U.S. President Franklin D. Roosevelt on Monday, January 6, 1941. In an address known as the Four 'Freedoms speech' (technically the 1941 State of the Union address), he proposed four fundamental freedoms that people "everywhere in the world" ought to enjoy.

I address you, the members of this new Congress, at a moment unprecedented in the history of the union. I use the word "unprecedented" because at no previous time has American security been as seriously threatened from without as it is today.

Since the permanent formation of our government under the Constitution in 1789, most of the periods of crisis in our history have related to our domestic affairs. And, fortunately, only one of these – the four-year war between the States – ever threatened our national unity. Today, thank God, 130,000,000 Americans in 48 States have forgotten points of the compass in our national unity.

It is true that prior to 1914 the United States often has been disturbed by events in other continents. We have even engaged in two wars with European nations and in a number of undeclared wars in the West Indies, in the Mediterranean and in the Pacific, for the maintenance of American rights and for the principles of peaceful commerce. But in no case had a serious threat been raised against our national safety or our continued independence.

What I seek to convey is the historic truth that the

United States as a nation has at all times maintained opposition – clear, definite opposition – to any attempt to lock us in behind an ancient Chinese wall while the procession of civilization went past. Today, thinking of our children and of their children, we oppose enforced isolation for ourselves or for any other part of the Americas.

That determination of ours, extending over all these years, was proved, for example, in the early days during the quarter century of wars following the French Revolution. While the Napoleonic struggles did threaten interests of the United States because of the French foothold in the West Indies and in Louisiana, and while we engaged in the War of 1812 to vindicate our right to peaceful trade, it is nevertheless clear that neither France nor Great Britain nor any other nation was aiming at domination of the whole world.

And in like fashion, from 1815 to 1914 – ninety-nine years – no single war in Europe or in Asia constituted a real threat against our future or against the future of any other American nation.

Except in the Maximilian interlude in Mexico, no foreign power sought to establish itself in this hemisphere. And the strength of the British fleet in the Atlantic has been a friendly strength; it is still a friendly strength.

Even when the World War broke out in 1914, it seemed to contain only small threat of danger to our own American future. But as time went on, as we remember, the American people began to visualize what the downfall of democratic nations might mean to our own democracy.

We need not overemphasize imperfections in the peace of Versailles. We need not harp on failure of the democracies to deal with problems of world reconstruction. We should remember that the peace of 1919 was far less unjust than the kind of pacification which began even before Munich, and which is being carried on under the new order of tyranny that seeks to spread over every continent today. The

American people have unalterably set their faces against that tyranny.

I suppose that every realist knows that the democratic way of life is at this moment being directly assailed in every part of the world – assailed either by arms or by secret spreading of poisonous propaganda by those who seek to destroy unity and promote discord in nations that are still at peace. During 16 long months this assault has blotted out the whole pattern of democratic life in an appalling number of independent nations, great and small. And the assailants are still on the march, threatening other nations, great and small.

Therefore, as your President, performing my constitutional duty to "give to the Congress information of the state of the union," I find it unhappily necessary to report that the future and the safety of our country and of our democracy are overwhelmingly involved in events far beyond our borders.

Armed defense of democratic existence is now being gallantly waged in four continents. If that defense fails, all the population and all the resources of Europe and Asia, and Africa and Austral-Asia will be dominated by conquerors. And let us remember that the total of those populations in those four continents, the total of those populations and their resources greatly exceed the sum total of the population and the resources of the whole of the Western Hemisphere – yes, many times over.

In times like these it is immature – and, incidentally, untrue – for anybody to brag that an unprepared America, single-handed and with one hand tied behind its back, can hold off the whole world.

No realistic American can expect from a dictator's peace international generosity, or return of true independence, or world disarmament, or freedom of expression, or freedom of religion – or even good business. Such a peace would bring no security for us or for our neighbors. Those who would give up essential liberty to purchase a little temporary safety deserve neither liberty nor safety.

As a nation we may take pride in the fact that we are soft-hearted; but we cannot afford to be soft-headed. We must always be wary of those who with sounding brass and a tinkling cymbal preach the "ism" of appeasement. We must especially beware of that small group of selfish men who would clip the wings of the American eagle in order to feather their own nests.

I have recently pointed out how quickly the tempo of modern warfare could bring into our very midst the physical attack which we must eventually expect if the dictator nations win this war.

There is much loose talk of our immunity from immediate and direct invasion from across the seas. Obviously, as long as the British Navy retains its power, no such danger exists. Even if there were no British Navy, it is not probable that any enemy would be stupid enough to attack us by landing troops in the United States from across thousands of miles of ocean, until it had acquired strategic bases from which to operate.

But we learn much from the lessons of the past years in Europe – particularly the lesson of Norway, whose essential seaports were captured by treachery and surprise built up over a series of years. The first phase of the invasion of this hemisphere would not be the landing of regular troops. The necessary strategic points would be occupied by secret agents and by their dupes – and great numbers of them are already here and in Latin America. As long as the aggressor nations maintain the offensive they, not we, will choose the time and the place and the method of their attack.

And that is why the future of all the American Republics is today in serious danger. That is why this annual message to the Congress is unique in our history. That is why every member of the executive branch of the government and every member of the Congress face great responsibility, great accountability. The need of the moment is that our actions and our policy should be devoted primarily – almost exclusively – to meeting this foreign peril. For all our domestic problems are now a part of the great emergency.

Just as our national policy in internal affairs has been based upon a decent respect for the rights and the dignity of all our fellow men within our gates, so our national policy in foreign affairs has been based on a decent respect for the rights and the dignity of all nations, large and small. And the justice of morality must and will win in the end.

Our national policy is this:

First, by an impressive expression of the public will and without regard to partisanship, we are committed to all-inclusive national defense.

Secondly, by an impressive expression of the public will and without regard to partisanship, we are committed to full support of all those resolute people everywhere who are resisting aggression and are thereby keeping war away from our hemisphere. By this support we express our determination that the democratic cause shall prevail, and we strengthen the defense and the security of our own nation.

Third, by an impressive expression of the public will and without regard to partisanship, we are committed to the proposition that principles of morality and considerations for our own security will never permit us to acquiesce in a peace dictated by aggressors and sponsored by appeasers. We know that enduring peace cannot be bought at the cost of other people's freedom.

In the recent national election there was no substantial difference between the two great parties in respect to that national policy. No issue was fought out on this line before the American electorate. And today it is abundantly evident that American citizens everywhere are demanding and supporting speedy and complete action in recognition of obvious danger.

Therefore, the immediate need is a swift and driving increase in our armament production. Leaders of industry and labor have responded to our summons. Goals of speed have been set. In some cases these goals are being reached ahead of time. In some cases we are on schedule; in other cases there are slight but not serious delays. And in some cases – and, I am sorry to say, very important cases – we are all concerned by the slowness of the accomplishment of our plans.

The Army and Navy, however, have made substantial progress during the past year. Actual experience is improving and speeding up our methods of production with every passing day. And today's best is not good enough for tomorrow.

I am not satisfied with the progress thus far made. The men in charge of the program represent the best in training, in ability, and in patriotism. They are not satisfied with the progress thus far made. None of us will be satisfied until the job is done.

No matter whether the original goal was set too high or too low, our objective is quicker and better results.

To give you two illustrations:

We are behind schedule in turning out finished airplanes. We are working day and night to solve the innumerable problems and to catch up.

We are ahead of schedule in building warships, but we are working to get even further ahead of that schedule.

To change a whole nation from a basis of peacetime production of implements of peace to a basis of wartime production of implements of war is no small task. And the greatest difficulty comes at the beginning of the program, when new tools, new plant facilities, new assembly lines, new shipways must first be constructed before the actual material begins to flow steadily and speedily from them.

The Congress of course, must rightly keep itself informed at all times of the progress of the program. However, there is certain information, as the Congress itself will readily recognize, which, in the interests of our own security and those of the nations that we are supporting, must of needs be kept in confidence.

New circumstances are constantly begetting new needs for our safety. I shall ask this Congress for greatly increased new appropriations and authorizations to carry on what we have begun.

I also ask this Congress for authority and for funds sufficient to manufacture additional munitions and war supplies of many kinds, to be turned over to those nations which are now in actual war with aggressor nations. Our most useful and immediate role is to act as an arsenal for them as well as for ourselves. They do not need manpower, but they do need billions of dollars' worth of the weapons of defense.

The time is near when they will not be able to pay for them all in ready cash. We cannot, and we will not, tell them that they must surrender merely because of present inability to pay for the weapons which we know they must have.

I do not recommend that we make them a loan of dollars with which to pay for these weapons – a loan to be repaid in dollars. I recommend that we make it possible for those nations to continue to obtain war materials in the United States, fitting their orders into our own program. And nearly all of their material would, if the time ever came, be useful in our own defense.

Taking counsel of expert military and naval authorities, considering what is best for our own security, we are free to decide how much should be kept here and how much should be sent abroad to our friends who, by their determined and heroic resistance, are giving us time in which to make ready our own defense.

For what we send abroad we shall be repaid, repaid

within a reasonable time following the close of hostilities, repaid in similar materials, or at our option in other goods of many kinds which they can produce and which we need.

Let us say to the democracies: "We Americans are vitally concerned in your defense of freedom. We are putting forth our energies, our resources, and our organizing powers to give you the strength to regain and maintain a free world. We shall send you in ever-increasing numbers, ships, planes, tanks, guns. That is our purpose and our pledge."

In fulfillment of this purpose we will not be intimidated by the threats of dictators that they will regard as a breach of international law or as an act of war our aid to the democracies which dare to resist their aggression. Such aid — Such aid is not an act of war, even if a dictator should unilaterally proclaim it so to be.

And when the dictators — if the dictators — are ready to make war upon us, they will not wait for an act of war on our part.

They did not wait for Norway or Belgium or the Netherlands to commit an act of war. Their only interest is in a new one-way international law, which lacks mutuality in its observance and therefore becomes an instrument of oppression. The happiness of future generations of Americans may well depend on how effective and how immediate we can make our aid felt. No one can tell the exact character of the emergency situations that we may be called upon to meet. The nation's hands must not be tied when the nation's life is in danger.

Yes, and we must prepare, all of us prepare, to make the sacrifices that the emergency — almost as serious as war itself — demands. Whatever stands in the way of speed and efficiency in defense, in defense preparations of any kind, must give way to the national need.

A free nation has the right to expect full cooperation from all groups. A free nation has the right to look to the leaders of business, of labor, and of agriculture to take the lead in stimulating effort, not among other groups but within their own group.

The best way of dealing with the few slackers or troublemakers in our midst is, first, to shame them by patriotic example, and if that fails, to use the sovereignty of government to save government.

As men do not live by bread alone, they do not fight by armaments alone. Those who man our defenses and those behind them who build our defenses must have the stamina and the courage which come from unshakable belief in the manner of life which they are defending. The mighty action that we are calling for cannot be based on a disregard of all the things worth fighting for.

The nation takes great satisfaction and much strength from the things which have been done to make its people conscious of their individual stake in the preservation of democratic life in America. Those things have toughened the fiber of our people, have renewed their faith and strengthened their devotion to the institutions we make ready to protect.

Certainly this is no time for any of us to stop thinking about the social and economic problems which are the root cause of the social revolution which is today a supreme factor in the world. For there is nothing mysterious about the foundations of a healthy and strong democracy.

The basic things expected by our people of their political and economic systems are simple. They are:

> Equality of opportunity for youth and for others.
> Jobs for those who can work.
> Security for those who need it.
> The ending of special privilege for the few.
> The preservation of civil liberties for all.
> The enjoyment – The enjoyment of the fruits of scientific progress in a wider and constantly rising standard of living.

These are the simple, the basic things that must never be lost sight of in the turmoil and unbelievable complexity of our modern world. The inner and abiding strength of our economic and political systems is dependent upon the degree to which they fulfill these expectations.

Many subjects connected with our social economy call for immediate improvement. As examples:

We should bring more citizens under the coverage of old-age pensions and unemployment insurance.

We should widen the opportunities for adequate medical care.

We should plan a better system by which persons deserving or needing gainful employment may obtain it.

I have called for personal sacrifice, and I am assured of the willingness of almost all Americans to respond to that call. A part of the sacrifice means the payment of more money in taxes. In my budget message I will recommend that a greater portion of this great defense program be paid for from taxation than we are paying for today. No person should try, or be allowed to get rich out of the program, and the principle of tax payments in accordance with ability to pay should be constantly before our eyes to guide our legislation.

If the Congress maintains these principles the voters, putting patriotism ahead pocketbooks, will give you their applause.

In the future days, which we seek to make secure, we look forward to a world founded upon four essential human freedoms.

The first is freedom of speech and expression – everywhere in the world.

The second is freedom of every person to worship God in his own way – everywhere in the world.

The third is freedom from want, which, translated into world terms, means economic understandings which will secure to every nation a healthy peacetime life for its inhabitants – everywhere in the world.

The fourth is freedom from fear, which, translated into world terms, means a world-wide reduction of armaments to such a point and in such a thorough fashion that no nation will be in a position to commit an act of physical aggression against any neighbor – anywhere in the world.

That is no vision of a distant millennium. It is a definite basis for a kind of world attainable in our own time and generation. That kind of world is the very antithesis of the so-called "new order" of tyranny which the dictators seek to create with the crash of a bomb.

To that new order we oppose the greater conception – the moral order. A good society is able to face schemes of world domination and foreign revolutions alike without fear.

Since the beginning of our American history we have been engaged in change, in a perpetual, peaceful revolution, a revolution which goes on steadily, quietly, adjusting itself to changing conditions without the concentration camp or the quicklime in the ditch. The world order which we seek is the cooperation of free countries, working together in a friendly, civilized society.

This nation has placed its destiny in the hands and heads and hearts of its millions of free men and women, and its faith in freedom under the guidance of God. Freedom means the supremacy of human rights everywhere. Our support goes to those who struggle to gain those rights and keep them. Our strength is our unity of purpose.

To that high concept there can be no end save victory."

Franklin D. Roosevelt, *Pearl Harbor Address to the Nation*

[December 8, 1941, Washington]

NOTE President Roosevelt called the unprovoked attack on Pearl Harbor a "date which will live in infamy," in a famous address to the nation delivered after Japan's deadly strike against U.S. naval and military forces in Hawaii. He also asked Congress to declare war.

Yesterday, December 7th, 1941 – a date which will live in infamy – the United States of America was suddenly and deliberately attacked by naval and air forces of the Empire of Japan.

The United States was at peace with that nation and, at the solicitation of Japan, was still in conversation with its government and its emperor looking toward the maintenance of peace in the Pacific.

Indeed, one hour after Japanese air squadrons had commenced bombing in the American island of Oahu, the Japanese ambassador to the United States and his colleague delivered to our Secretary of State a formal reply to a recent American message. And while this reply stated that it seemed useless to continue the existing diplomatic negotiations, it contained no threat or hint of war or of armed attack.[1]

It will be recorded that the distance of Hawaii from Japan makes it obvious that the attack was deliberately planned many days or even weeks ago. During the intervening time, the Japanese government has deliberately sought to deceive the United States by false statements and expressions of hope for continued peace.

The attack yesterday on the Hawaiian islands has caused severe damage to American naval and military forces. I regret to tell you that very many American lives have been lost. In addition, American ships have been reported torpedoed on the high seas between San Francisco and Honolulu.

Yesterday, the Japanese government also launched an attack against Malaya.

Last night, Japanese forces attacked Hong Kong.

Last night, Japanese forces attacked Guam.

Last night, Japanese forces attacked the Philippine Islands.

Last night, the Japanese attacked Wake Island.

And this morning, the Japanese attacked Midway Island.

Japan has, therefore, undertaken a surprise offensive extending throughout the Pacific area. The facts of yesterday and today speak for themselves. The people of the United States have already formed their opinions and well understand the implications to the very life and safety of our nation.

As Commander in Chief of the Army and Navy, I have directed that all measures be taken for our defense. But always will our whole nation remember the character of the onslaught against us.

No matter how long it may take us to overcome this premeditated invasion, the American people in their righteous might will win through to absolute victory.

I believe that I interpret the will of the Congress and of the people when I assert that we will not only defend ourselves to the uttermost, but will make it very certain that this form of treachery shall never again endanger us.

Hostilities exist. There is no blinking at the fact that our people, our territory, and our interests are in grave danger.

With confidence in our armed forces, with the unbounding determination of our people, we will gain the inevitable triumph – so help us God.

I ask that the Congress declare that since the unprovoked and dastardly attack by Japan on Sunday, December 7th, 1941, a state of war has existed between the United States and the Japanese empire.

John Steinbeck, *Banquet Speech for the Nobel Prize in Literature*

[December 10, 1962, Stockholm]

NOTE John Steinbeck (1902-1968) was one of the best-known of the 20th century. He wrote the Pulitzer Prize-winning novel *The Grapes of Wrath* (1939) and a total of twenty-five books, novels, non-fiction and short stories. In 1962 Steinbeck received the Nobel Prize for Literature.

I thank the Swedish Academy for finding my work worthy of this highest honor.

In my heart there may be doubt that I deserve the Nobel award over other men of letters whom I hold in respect and reverence – but there is no question of my pleasure and pride in having it for myself.

It is customary for the recipient of this award to offer personal or scholarly comment on the nature and the direction of literature. At this particular time, however, I think it would be well to consider the high duties and the responsibilities of the makers of literature.

Such is the prestige of the Nobel award and of this place where I stand that I am impelled, not to squeak like a grateful and apologetic mouse, but to roar like a lion out of pride in my profession and in the great and good men who have practiced it through the ages.

Literature was not promulgated by a pale and emasculated critical priesthood singing their litanies in empty churches – nor is it a game for the cloistered elect, the tinhorn mendicants of low calorie despair.

Literature is as old as speech. It grew out of human need

for it, and it has not changed except to become more needed.

The skalds, the bards, the writers are not separate and exclusive. From the beginning, their functions, their duties, their responsibilities have been decreed by our species.

Humanity has been passing through a gray and desolate time of confusion. My great predecessor, William Faulkner, speaking here, referred to it as a tragedy of universal fear so long sustained that there were no longer problems of the spirit, so that only the human heart in conflict with itself seemed worth writing about.

Faulkner, more than most men, was aware of human strength as well as of human weakness. He knew that the understanding and the resolution of fear are a large part of the writer's reason for being.

This is not new. The ancient commission of the writer has not changed. He is charged with exposing our many grievous faults and failures, with dredging up to the light our dark and dangerous dreams for the purpose of improvement.

Furthermore, the writer is delegated to declare and to celebrate man's proven capacity for greatness of heart and spirit – for gallantry in defeat – for courage, compassion and love.

In the endless war against weakness and despair, these are the bright rally-flags of hope and of emulation.

I hold that a writer who does not passionately believe in the perfectibility of man, has no dedication nor any membership in literature.

The present universal fear has been the result of a forward surge in our knowledge and manipulation of certain dangerous factors in the physical world.

It is true that other phases of understanding have not yet caught up with this great step, but there is no reason to presume that they cannot or will not draw abreast. Indeed it is a part of the writer's responsibility to make sure that they do.

With humanity's long proud history of standing firm against natural enemies, sometimes in the face of almost certain defeat and extinction, we would be cowardly and stupid to leave the field on the eve of our greatest potential victory.

Understandably, I have been reading the life of Alfred Nobel – a solitary man, the books say, a thoughtful man. He perfected the release of explosive forces, capable of creative good or of destructive evil, but lacking choice, ungoverned by conscience or judgment.

Nobel saw some of the cruel and bloody misuses of his inventions. He may even have foreseen the end result of his probing – access to ultimate violence – to final destruction. Some say that he became cynical, but I do not believe this. I think he strove to invent a control, a safety valve. I think he found it finally only in the human mind and the human spirit. To me, his thinking is clearly indicated in the categories of these awards.

They are offered for increased and continuing knowledge of man and of his world – for understanding and communication, which are the functions of literature. And they are offered for demonstrations of the capacity for peace – the culmination of all the others.

Less than fifty years after his death, the door of nature was unlocked and we were offered the dreadful burden of choice.

We have usurped many of the powers we once ascribed to God.

Fearful and unprepared, we have assumed lordship over the life or death of the whole world – of all living things.

The danger and the glory and the choice rest finally in man. The test of his perfectibility is at hand.

Having taken Godlike power, we must seek in ourselves for the responsibility and the wisdom we once prayed some deity might have.

Man himself has become our greatest hazard and our only hope.

So that today, St. John the apostle may well be paraphrased ...

In the end is the Word, and the Word is Man – and the Word is with Men.

Greta Thunberg, *This is All Wrong*

[September 23, 2019, New York]

NOTE On Monday New York time, Swedish climate activist Greta Thunberg, 16, was asked at the UN's Climate Action Summit if she had a message for the world's leaders. Her speech was impassioned, emotional and divisive.

My message is that we'll be watching you.

This is all wrong. I shouldn't be up here. I should be back in school on the other side of the ocean. Yet you all come to us young people for hope. How dare you!

You have stolen my dreams and my childhood with your empty words. And yet I'm one of the lucky ones. People are suffering. People are dying. Entire ecosystems are collapsing. We are in the beginning of a mass extinction, and all you can talk about is money and fairy tales of eternal economic growth. How dare you!

For more than 30 years, the science has been crystal clear. How dare you continue to look away and come here saying that you're doing enough, when the politics and solutions needed are still nowhere in sight.

You say you hear us and that you understand the urgency. But no matter how sad and angry I am, I do not want to believe that. Because if you really understood the situation and still kept on failing to act, then you would be evil. And that I refuse to believe.

The popular idea of cutting our emissions in half in 10 years only gives us a 50% chance of staying below 1.5 degrees [Celsius], and the risk of setting off irreversible chain reactions beyond human control.

Fifty percent may be acceptable to you. But those numbers do not include tipping points, most feedback loops, additional warming hidden by toxic air pollution or the aspects of equity and climate justice. They also rely on my generation sucking hundreds of billions of tons of your CO_2 out of the air with technologies that barely exist.

So a 50% risk is simply not acceptable to us – we who have to live with the consequences.

To have a 67% chance of staying below a 1.5 degrees global temperature rise – the best odds given by the [Intergovernmental Panel on Climate Change] – the world had 420 gigatons of CO_2 left to emit back on Jan. 1st, 2018. Today that figure is already down to less than 350 gigatons.

How dare you pretend that this can be solved with just 'business as usual' and some technical solutions? With today's emissions levels, that remaining CO_2 budget will be entirely gone within less than 8 1/2 years.

There will not be any solutions or plans presented in line with these figures here today, because these numbers are too uncomfortable. And you are still not mature enough to tell it like it is.

You are failing us. But the young people are starting to understand your betrayal. The eyes of all future generations are upon you. And if you choose to fail us, I say: We will never forgive you.

We will not let you get away with this. Right here, right now is where we draw the line. The world is waking up. And change is coming, whether you like it or not.

Thank you.

Elie Wiesel, *Acceptance Speech for the Nobel Peace Prize*

[December 10, 1986, Oslo]

NOTE In 1986, at the age of fifty-eight, Romanian-born Jewish-American writer and political activist Elie Wiesel (1928-2016) was awarded the Nobel Peace Prize. He made it his life's work to bear witness to the genocide committed by the Nazis during World War II. He was the world's leading spokesman on the Holocaust. After Hitler's forces had moved into Hungary in 1944, the Wiesel family was deported to the Auschwitz extermination camp in Poland. Elie Wiesel's mother and younger sister perished in the gas chamber there. In 1945 Elie and his father were sent on to Buchenwald, where his father died of starvation and dysentery. Seventeen-year-old Elie was still alive when American soldiers opened the camp. For the world to remember and learn from the Holocaust was not Elie Wiesel's only goal. He thought it equally important to fight indifference and the attitude that "it's no concern of mine". Elie Wiesel saw the struggle against indifference as a struggle for peace. In his words, "The opposite of love is not hate, but indifference".

Words of gratitude. First to our common Creator. This is what the Jewish tradition commands us to do. At special occasions, one is duty-bound to recite the following prayer: "Barukh shehekhyanu vekiymanu vehigianu lazman haze" – "Blessed be Thou for having sustained us until this day."

Then – thank you, Chairman Aarvik, for the depth of your eloquence. And for the generosity of your gesture. Thank you for building bridges between people and generations. Thank you, above all, for helping humankind make peace its most urgent and noble aspiration.

I am moved, deeply moved by your words, Chairman Aarvik. And it is with a profound sense of humility that I accept the honor – the highest there is – that you have chosen to bestow upon me. I know your choice transcends my person.

Do I have the right to represent the multitudes who have perished? Do I have the right to accept this great honor on their behalf? I do not. No one may speak for the dead, no one may interpret their mutilated dreams and visions. And yet, I sense their presence. I always do – and at this moment more than ever. The presence of my parents, that of my little sister. The presence of my teachers, my friends, my companions…

This honor belongs to all the survivors and their children and, through us to the Jewish people with whose destiny I have always identified.

I remember: it happened yesterday, or eternities ago. A young Jewish boy discovered the Kingdom of Night. I remember his bewilderment, I remember his anguish. It all happened so fast. The ghetto. The deportation. The sealed cattle car. The fiery altar upon which the history of our people and the future of mankind were meant to be sacrificed.

I remember he asked his father: "Can this be true? This is the twentieth century, not the Middle Ages. Who would allow such crimes to be committed? How could the world remain silent?"

And now the boy is turning to me. "Tell me," he asks, "what have you done with my future, what have you done with your life?" And I tell him that I have tried. That I have tried to keep memory alive, that I have tried to fight those who would forget. Because if we forget, we are guilty, we are accomplices.

And then I explain to him how naïve we were, that the world did know and remained silent. And that is why I swore never to be silent whenever wherever human beings endure suffering and humiliation. We must take sides. Neutrality helps the oppressor, never the victim. Silence encourages the tormentor, never the tormented. Sometimes we must interfere. When human lives are endangered, when human dignity is in jeopardy, national borders and sensitivities become irrelevant. Wherever men and women are persecuted because of their race, religion, or political views, that place must – at that moment – become the center of the universe.

Of course, since I am a Jew profoundly rooted in my people's memory and tradition, my first response is to Jewish fears, Jewish needs, Jewish crises. For I belong to a traumatized generation, one that experienced the abandonment and solitude of our people. It would be unnatural for me not to make Jewish priorities my own: Israel, Soviet Jewry, Jews in Arab land... But others are important to me. Apartheid is, in my view, as abhorrent as anti-Semitism. To me, Andrei Sakharov's isolation is as much a disgrace as Joseph Begun's imprisonment and Ida Nudel's exile. As is the denial of solidarity and it's leader Lech Walesa's right to dissent. And Nelson Mandela's interminable imprisonment.

There is so much injustice and suffering crying out for our attention: victims of hunger, of racism and political persecution – in Chile, for instance, or in Ethiopia – writers and poets, prisoners in so many lands governed by the Left and by the Right.

Human rights are being violated on every continent. More people are oppressed than free. How can one not be sensitive to their plight? Human suffering anywhere concerns men and women everywhere. That applies also to Palestinians to whose plight I am sensitive but whose methods I deplore when they lead to violence. Violence is not the answer. Terrorism is the most dangerous of answers. They are frustrated, that is understandable, something must be done. The refugees and their misery. The children and their fear. The uprooted and their hopelessness. Something must be done about their situation. Both the Jewish people and the Palestinian people have lost too many sons and daughters and have shed too much blood. This must stop, and all attempts to stop it must be encouraged. Israel will cooperate, I am sure of that. I trust Israel for I have faith in the Jewish people. Let Israel be given a chance, let hatred and danger be removed from their horizons, and there will be peace in and around the Holy Land. Please understand my deep and total commitment to Israel: if you could remember what I remember, you would understand. Israel is the only nation in the world whose existence is threatened. Should Israel lose but one war, it would mean her end and ours as well. But I have faith. Faith in the God of Abraham, Isaac, and Jacob, and even in His creation. Without it no action would be possible. And action is the only remedy to indifference, the most insidious danger of all. Isn't that the meaning of Alfred Nobel's legacy? Wasn't his fear of war a shield against war?

There is so much to be done, there is so much that can be done. One person – a Raoul Wallenberg, an Albert Schweitzer, Martin Luther King, Jr. – one person of integrity, can make a difference, a difference of life and death. As long as one dissident is in prison, our freedom will not be true. As long as one child is hungry, our life will be filled with anguish and shame. What all these victims need above all is to know that they are not alone; that we are not forgetting them, that when their voices are stifled we shall lend them ours, that while their freedom depends on ours, the quality of our freedom depends on theirs.

This is what I say to the young Jewish boy wondering what I have done with his years. It is in his name that I speak to you and that I express to you my deepest gratitude as one who has emerged from the Kingdom of Night. We know that every moment is a moment of grace, every hour an offering; not to share them would mean to betray them.

Our lives no longer belong to us alone; they belong to all those who need us desperately.

Thank you, Chairman Aarvik. Thank you, members of the Nobel Committee. Thank you, people of Norway, for declaring on this singular occasion that our survival has meaning for mankind.

Malala Yousafzai, *The Right of Education*

[July 12, 2013, New York]

NOTE Malala Yousafzai was born in 1997 in the Swat district of Pakistan. In 2007, the Taliban began fighting the Pakistani government for control of Swat. Among their restrictive laws, the Taliban declared girls would no longer be allowed to go to school. Malala, who was only 11, was willing to risk speaking out. Originally posting online under a pseudonym, she shared stories about life under the Taliban. Inspired by her father's pro-education activism, she eventually revealed her real name and began advocating for education as a human right for girls.

Her international renown came with increased danger. On October 9, 2012, a gunman shot her on a bus full of girls. Malala was rushed to the hospital, treated by the best doctors, and survived to continue her fight. With her father, she established the Malala Fund, a charity dedicated to giving every girl access to free, safe, quality education. Malala has also held world leaders accountable for their promises to girls. In recognition of her work, she received the Nobel Peace Prize in 2014, becoming the youngest-ever Nobel laureate. Malala, who graduated from the University of Oxford in 2020, remains dedicated to education, equality, and her message of peace.

Yousafzai gave this speech to the United Nations on July 12, 2013, her 16th birthday and "Malala Day" at the United Nations.

Today is it an honor for me to be speaking again after a long time. Being here with such honorable people is a great moment in my life and it is an honor for me that today I am wearing a shawl of the late Benazir Bhutto. I don't know where to begin my speech. I don't know what people would be expecting me to say, but first of all thank you to God for whom we all are equal and thank you to every person who has prayed for my fast recovery and new life. I cannot believe how much love people have shown me. I have received thousands of good wish cards and gifts from all over the world. Thank you to all of them. Thank you to the children whose innocent words encouraged me. Thank you to my elders whose prayers strengthened me. I would like to thank my nurses, doctors and the staff of the hospitals in Pakistan and the UK and the UAE government who have helped me to get better and recover my strength.

I fully support UN Secretary General Ban Ki-moon in his Global Education First Initiative and the work of UN Special Envoy for Global Education Gordon Brown and the respectful president of the UN General Assembly Vuk Jeremic. I thank them for the leadership they continue to give. They continue to inspire all of us to action. Dear brothers and sisters, do remember one thing: Malala Day is not my day. Today is the day of every woman, every boy and every girl who have raised their voice for their rights.

There are hundreds of human rights activists and social workers who are not only speaking for their rights, but who are struggling to achieve their goal of peace, education and equality. Thousands of people have been killed by the terrorists and millions have been injured. I am just one of them. So here I stand. So here I stand, one girl, among many. I speak not for myself, but so those without a voice can be heard. Those who have fought for their rights. Their right to live in peace. Their right to be treated with dignity. Their right to equality of opportunity. Their right to be educated.

Dear friends, on 9 October 2012, the Taliban shot me on the left side of my forehead. They shot my friends, too. They thought that the bullets would silence us, but they failed. And out of that silence came thousands of voices. The terrorists thought they would change my aims and stop my ambitions. But nothing changed in my life except this:

weakness, fear and hopelessness died. Strength, power and courage was born.

I am the same Malala. My ambitions are the same. My hopes are the same. And my dreams are the same. Dear sisters and brothers, I am not against anyone. Neither am I here to speak in terms of personal revenge against the Taliban or any other terrorist group. I am here to speak for the right of education for every child. I want education for the sons and daughters of the Taliban and all the terrorists and extremists. I do not even hate the Talib who shot me. Even if there was a gun in my hand and he was standing in front of me, I would not shoot him. This is the compassion I have learned from Mohammed, the prophet of mercy, Jesus Christ and Lord Buddha. This the legacy of change I have inherited from Martin Luther King, Nelson Mandela and Mohammed Ali Jinnah.

This is the philosophy of nonviolence that I have learned from Gandhi, Bacha Khan and Mother Teresa. And this is the forgiveness that I have learned from my father and from my mother. This is what my soul is telling me: be peaceful and love everyone.

Dear sisters and brothers, we realize the importance of light when we see darkness. We realize the importance of our voice when we are silenced. In the same way, when we were in Swat, the north of Pakistan, we realized the importance of pens and books when we saw the guns. The wise saying, "The pen is mightier than the sword." It is true. The extremists are afraid of books and pens. The power of education frightens them. They are afraid of women. The power of the voice of women frightens them. This is why they killed 14 innocent students in the recent attack in Quetta. And that is why they kill female teachers. That is why they are blasting schools every day because they were and they are afraid of change and equality that we will bring to our society. And I remember that there was a boy in our school who was asked by a journalist why are the Taliban against education? He answered very simply by pointing to his book, he said, "a Talib doesn't know what is written inside this book."

They think that God is a tiny, little conservative being who would point guns at people's heads just for going to school. These terrorists are misusing the name of Islam for their own personal benefit. Pakistan is a peace loving, democratic country. Pashtuns want education for their daughters and sons. Islam is a religion of peace, humanity and brotherhood. It is the duty and responsibility to get education for each child, that is what it says. Peace is a necessity for education. In many parts of the world, especially Pakistan and Afghanistan, terrorism, war and conflicts stop children from going to schools. We are really tired of these wars. Women and children are suffering in many ways in many parts of the world.

In India, innocent and poor children are victims of child labor. Many schools have been destroyed in Nigeria. People in Afghanistan have been affected by extremism. Young girls have to do domestic child labor and are forced to get married at an early age. Poverty, ignorance, injustice, racism and the deprivation of basic rights are the main problems, faced by both men and women.

Today I am focusing on women's rights and girls' education because they are suffering the most. There was a time when women activists asked men to stand up for their rights. But this time we will do it by ourselves. I am not telling men to step away from speaking for women's rights, but I am focusing on women to be independent and fight for themselves. So dear sisters and brothers, now it's time to speak up. So today, we call upon the world leaders to change their strategic policies in favor of peace and prosperity. We call upon the world leaders that all of these deals must protect women and children's rights. A deal that goes against the rights of women is unacceptable.

We call upon all governments to ensure free, compulsory education all over the world for every child. We call upon all the governments to fight against terrorism and violence. To protect children from brutality and harm. We call upon the developed nations to support the expansion of education opportunities for girls in the developing world. We call upon all communities to be tolerant, to reject prejudice based on caste, creed, sect, color, religion or agenda to ensure freedom and equality for women so they can flourish. We cannot all succeed when half of us are held back. We call upon our sisters around the world to be brave, to embrace the strength within themselves and realize their full potential.

Dear brothers and sisters, we want schools and education for every child's bright future. We will continue our journey to our destination of peace and education. No one can stop us. We will speak up for our rights and we will bring change to our voice. We believe in the power and the strength of our words. Our words can change the whole world because we ware all together, united for the cause of education. And if we want to achieve our goal, then let us empower ourselves with the weapon of knowledge and let us shield ourselves with unity and togetherness.

Dear brothers and sisters, we must not forget that millions of people are suffering from poverty and injustice and ignorance. We must not forget that millions of children are out of their schools. We must not forget that our sisters and brothers are waiting for a bright, peaceful future.

So let us wage, so let us wage a glorious struggle against illiteracy, poverty and terrorism, let us pick up our books and our pens, they are the most powerful weapons. One child, one teacher, one book and one pen can change the world. Education is the only solution. Education first. Thank you.

Malala Yousafzai, *Acceptance Speech for the Nobel Peace Prize*

[December 10, 2014, Oslo, Norway]

NOTE The Pakistani activist for female education, and human rights gives her Nobel Peace Prize acceptance speech as the youngest recipient ever.

In the name of God the most beneficent, the most merciful who is the God of all mankind. Wherever I go and speak, the only problem I face is that the podium is usually taller than me. So I hope it will be good this time.

I'm feeling honored that I am being chosen as a Nobel laureate and I have been honored with this – this precious award, the Nobel Peace Prize. And I'm proud that I'm the first Pakistani and the first young woman or the first young person who is getting this award. It's a great honor for me. And I'm also really happy that I'm sharing this award with a person – with a person from India whose name is Kailash Satyarthi and his great work for child's right, his great work against – against child slavery.

Totally inspires me and I am really happy that there are so many people who are working for children's right and I'm not alone. And he totally deserved this award.

So I am feeling honored that I'm sharing this award with him.

He recieved this award and we both are the two Nobel award receivers, one is from Pakistan, one is from India, one believes in Hinduism, one strongly believes in Islam. And it gives a message to people – it gives a message to people of love between Pakistan and India and between – between different religions and we both support each other.

It does not matter what's the color of your skin, what language do you speak, what religion you believe in. It is that we should all consider each other as human beings and we should respect each other and we should all fight for our rights, for the rights of children, for the rights of women and for the rights of every human being.

First of all, I would like to thank my family, my dear father, my dear mother for their love, for their support. As my father always say, he did not give me something extra, but what he did Dad, he did not clip my wings. So I'm thankful to my father for not clipping my wings, for – for letting me to fly and achieve my goals, for showing to the world that a girl is not supposed to be the – a slave.

A girl has the power to go forward in her life. And she's not only a mother, she's not only a sister, she's not only a wife. But a girl has the – she should have an identity. She should be recognized and she has equal rights as a boy. Even though my brother thinks that they are treated um…um… – that I am treated very well and they are not treated very well. But that's fine. If it comes – if it's that – that's fine.

I would like to share with you how I found out about the Nobel Peace Prize and it's quite exciting because I was in my chemistry class and we were studying about electrolysis and [inaudible] and the time was, I think 10:15. So the time of the announcement of the Nobel Peace Prize was gone and before that I was not expecting that I would get this award and when it went to, like, 10:15, I was totally sure that I haven't won it. But then suddenly one of my teachers came to the class and she called me and she said, "I have something important to tell you." And I was totally surprised when she told me congratulations, you have won the Nobel Peace Prize and you are sharing it with a – with a great person who is also working for children's rights. And I – it's sometimes quite difficult to express your feelings, but I felt really honored.

I felt more powerful and more courageous because this award is not just a piece of metal or a medal that you would wear, or an award that you would keep in your room, but this is really an encouragement for me to go forward and to believe in myself. To know that there are people who are supporting me in this campaign. And we are standing together. We all want to make sure that every child gets quality education. So this is really – this is really something – something great for me.

However, when I found that I have won the Nobel Peace Prize, I decided that I would not leave my school, rather I would finish my school time, I would – I went to physics lesson, I learned, I went to English lessons and it was totally like … I considered it as a normal day and I was really happy by the response of my teachers and my fellow students. They were all saying that we are proud of you and I'm really thankful to my school, to my teachers, to my school fellows for their love, for their support and really encouraged me and they're supporting me. So I'm happy. Even though it's not going to help me in my tests and exams because it totally depends on my hard work. But, still, I'm really happy that they are supporting me.

I have got – I have received this award, but this is not the end. This is not the end. This is not the end of this campaign which I have started. I think this is really the beginning and I want to see every child going to school. There are still 57 million children who have not received education, who are still out of the primary schools and I want to see every child going to school and getting – getting education because I have – I have myself suffered through the same situation when I was in swat valley and you all may know that in swat there was Talibanization and because of that no girl was allowed to go to school.

At that time I stood up for my rights and I said I would

speak up. I do not wait for someone else. I do not wait for someone else. I had really two options. One was not to speak and wait to be killed. And the second was – and the second was to speak up and then be killed and I chose the second one because at that time there was terrorism, women were not allowed to go outside of their houses because education was totally banned, people were killed. At that time I needed to raise my voice because I wanted to go back to school. I was also one of those girls who could not get education.

I wanted to learn I wanted to learn and be who – who I can be in my future. And I also had dreams. I also had dreams like a normal child has.

I wanted to become a doctor at that time. Now I want to become a politician, a good politician. And when I heard that I can not go to school, I just for a second thought that I would never able become a doctor or I would never be able to be who I want to be in the future and my life would be just getting married at the age of 13 or 14, not going to school, not becoming who I really can be so I decided that – that I will speak up.

So through my story I want to tell other children all around the world that they should stand up for their rights. They should not wait for someone else and their voices are more powerful. Their voices – it would seem that they are weak, but at the time when no one speak, your voice gets so loud that everyone has to listen to it. Everyone has to hear it. So it's my message to children all around the world that they should stand up for their rights.

And the award that I have received uh…Nobel Peace Prize. I believe that the Nobel Committee, they – they haven't given this just to me. But this award is for all those children who are voiceless, whose voices need to be heard. And I speak for them and I stand up with them and I join them in their campaign, that their voices should be heard and they should be listened and they have rights. They have rights. They have the right to receive quality education. They have the right not to suffer from child labor, not to suffer from child trafficking. They have the right to live a happy life. So I stand up with – with all those children and this award is especially for them. It gives them courage.

At the end, I would like to share with you that I had a phone call with honorable Kailash. I cannot pronounce his surname accurately so please I just ask for forgiveness for that. I will just call him Kailash if he wouldn't mind. So I had a phone call with him right now and we both talked about how important it is that every child goes to school and every child gets quality education and how many issues are there that the children are suffering, but I'm not yet highlighted. So we both decide – we both decided that we will work together for the cause that every child gets quality education and do not suffer from these issues.

Other than that, we also decided that as he's from India and I'm from Pakistan we will try to build strong relationships between India and Pakistan. And nowadays you know that there is tension on the border and the situation is getting … it's not like as we are expecting, we want Pakistan and India to have good relationships and the tension that is going on is disappointing and I'm really sad because I want both the countries to have dialogue, to have talks about peace, and to – to think about progress, to think about development, rather than fighting with each other. It's important that both countries focus more on education, focus more on development and progress, which is good for both of them.

So we both decided that … I requested him that would it be possible that he request His Honorable Prime Minister Narendra Modi to join us when we receive the Nobel Peace Prize in December. And I promised him that I would also request the honorable prime minister of Pakistan, Nawaz Sharif, to join us when I get and he gets the Nobel Peace

Prize. So, and I myself request the honorable Prime Minister Narendra Modi and honorable Prime Minister Nawaz Sharif, that they both join us when we receive the Nobel Peace Prize.

I really believe in peace. I really believe in tolerance and patience and it is very important for the progress of both countries that they have peace and they have good relationships. This is how they are going to achieve success and this is how they're going to – they are going to progress.

So it is my humble request and I hope it will be – hope it will be listened.

At the end, I want to say that I'm really happy for your support.

I used to say that I think I do not deserve the Nobel Peace Prize. I still believe that. But I believe that it is not only an award for what I have done but also an encouragement for giving me hope, for giving me the courage to go and continue this campaign, to believe in myself and to know that I'm not alone, there are hundreds and thousands and millions who are supporting me.

So once again, thank you so much to all of you. Thank you.

Volodymyr Zelenskyy, *Address to the Nation Before Russian Invasion*

[February 24, 2022, Kiev]

NOTE On 24 February, as Russia prepared to attack Ukraine, President Volodymyr Zelenskyy made an emotional address to his nation.

Today I initiated a phone call with the president of the Russian federation. The result was silence. Though the silence should be in Donbass. That's why I want to address today the people of Russia. I am addressing you not as a president, I am addressing you as a citizen of Ukraine. More than 2,000 km of the common border is dividing us. Along this border your troops are stationed, almost 200,000 soldiers, thousands of military vehicles. Your leaders approved them to make a step forward, to the territory of another country. And this step can be the beginning of a big war on European continent.

We know for sure that we don't need the war. Not a Cold War, not a hot war. Not a hybrid one. But if we'll be attacked by the [enemy] troops, if they try to take our country away from us, our freedom, our lives, the lives of our children, we will defend ourselves. Not attack, but defend ourselves. And when you will be attacking us, you will see our faces, not our backs, but our faces.

The war is a big disaster, and this disaster has a high price. With every meaning of this word. People lose money, reputation, quality of life, they lose freedom. But the main thing is that people lose their loved ones, they lose themselves.

They told you that Ukraine is posing a threat to Russia. It was not the case in the past, not in the present, it's not going to be in the future. You are demanding security guarantees from NATO, but we also demand security guarantees. Security for Ukraine from you, from Russia and other guarantees of the Budapest memorandum.

But our main goal is peace in Ukraine and the safety of our people, Ukrainians. For that we are ready to have talks with anybody, including you, in any format, on any platform. The war will deprive [security] guarantees from everybody – nobody will have guarantees of security anymore. Who will suffer the most from it? The people. Who doesn't want it the most? The people! Who can stop it? The people. But are there those people among you? I am sure.

I know that they [the Russian state] won't show my address on Russian TV, but Russian people have to see it. They need to know the truth, and the truth is that it is time to stop now, before it is too late. And if the Russian leaders don't want to sit with us behind the table for the sake of peace, maybe they will sit behind the table with you. Do Russians want the war? I would like to know the answer. But the answer depends only on you, citizens of the Russian Federation.

edizioni intra

SERIES

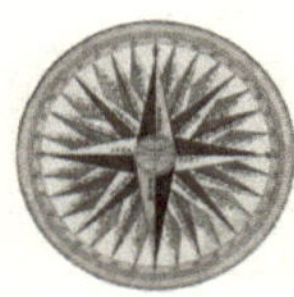

Il Disoriente
Great Classic Novels
Pirandello Short Stories for a Year
Thriller & Noir
Science-Fiction, Fantasy & Adventure

Mysteria
Mystery Stories & Essays

Astra
Stories and tales. Beyond the Earth

Saggiamente
Essays on human and social sciences

Retoricamente
Essays and handbooks on rhetoric,
language and public speaking

 **Politicamente**
Political essays and writings

 **Brĕvitĕr**
Legal handbooks

 **Visio**
Graphic and visual arts

 **Teatro da leggere**
Plays

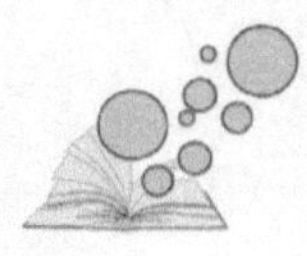 **Mille bolle blu**
Books for children

www.intrapublishing.com

www.ingramcontent.com/pod-product-compliance
Lightning Source LLC
Chambersburg PA
CBHW031441160726
47994CB00005B/1821